BARRON'S

W9-BTB-463

Pass Key to the
ASVAB

With Intensive Review of:
- Arithmetic Reasoning
- Math Knowledge
- Word Knowledge
- Paragraph Comprehension

SEVENTH EDITION

Terry L. Duran, Major, U.S. Army

DISCARD
MESSENGER PUBLIC LIBRARY
NORTH AURORA, ILLINOIS

BIBLIOGRAPHY

Anderson, John D., Jr. *Introduction to Flight.* McGraw-Hill, Inc., New York, 1978.

Bartlett, John, author; Beck, Emily Morison, editor. *Familiar Quotations (14th Edition),* Little, Brown and Company, Boston, 1968.

Duran, Terry L. *Barron's Military Flight Aptitude Tests, 2nd Edition.* Barron's Educational Series, Hauppauge, NY, 2010.

Edwards, Gabrielle I. *Biology the Easy Way.* Barron's Educational Series, Hauppauge, NY, 2000.

Gilroy, Curtis L. "Defending the All-Volunteer Force," *Armed Forces Journal,* April 2010.

Hawking, Stephen W. *A Brief History of Time.* New York: Bantam Books, 1988.

Headquarters, Department of the Army. *Field Manual 6-22: Army Leadership.* Department of the Army, Washington, D.C., 2006.

Headquarters, Department of the Army. *Field Manual 7-0: Training for Full Spectrum Operations.* Department of the Army, Washington, D.C., 2008.

Hibbeler, R.C. *Statics and Dynamics, 12th Ed.* Pearson Prentice Hall, Upper Saddle River, NJ, 2010.

http://www.101science.com/
http://www.familycar.com/
http://www.official-asvab.com/
http://www.physics.about.com/
http://www.sciencedaily.com/

Keegan, John. *A History of Warfare.* Alfred A. Knopf, Inc., New York, 1993.

Kleiner, Fred S., and Mamiya, Christin J. *Gardner's Art Through the Ages: The Western Perspectives, Volume II,* 12th Edition, Thomson/Wadsworth, Mason, OH, 2006.

Lehrman, Robert L. *Physics the Easy Way.* Barron's Educational Series, Hauppauge, NY, 1998.

Miller, Rex. *Electronics the Easy Way.* Barron's Educational Series, Hauppauge, NY, 2002.

Matloff, Maurice (editor). *American Military History, Vol. 1: 1775–1902.* Combined Books, Conshohocken, PA, 1996.

Nevins, Allan, and Commager, Henry Steele, with Morris, Jeffrey. *A Pocket History of the United States (9th revised edition).* Simon & Schuster, New York, 1992.

Nickels, William G., McHugh, James M., and McHugh, Susan M. *Understanding Business,* 7th edition. McGraw-Hill, New York, 2005.

The New York Public Library Desk Reference. Simon & Schuster, New York, 1989.

Powers, Rod. *Barron's Officer Candidate School Tests.* Barron's Educational Series, Hauppauge, NY, 2006.

U.S. Military Entrance Processing Command. *ASVAB Counselor Manual.* North Chicago, IL, 2005.

U.S. Military Entrance Processing Command. *ASVAB: Your Future Is Now.* North Chicago, IL.

U.S. Military Entrance Processing Command. *How to Use Your ASVAB Results.* North Chicago, IL.

Young, Hugh D.; Freedman, Roger A.; and Ford, A. Lewis. *University Physics,* 12th Ed. Pearson Addison-Wesley, San Francisco, 2008.

Williams, Mary H. *The U.S. Army in World War II: Chronology 1941–1945.* Center of Military History, Washington, D.C., 1958.

Material in this book was adapted from Barron's *ASVAB,* 10th edition.

© Copyright 2012, 2009, 2006, 2003, 2001, 1997, 1992 by Barron's Educational Series, Inc.

All rights reserved.

No part of this book may be reproduced or distributed in any form or by any means without the written permission of the copyright owner.

All inquiries should be addressed to:
Barron's Educational Series, Inc.
250 Wireless Boulevard
Hauppauge, New York 11788
www.barronseduc.com

ISBN: 978-0-7641-4799-9
Library of Congress Control Number: 2012931380

PRINTED IN THE UNITED STATES OF AMERICA
9 8 7 6 5 4 3 2 1

Contents

PART FOUR
TEST YOURSELF—AFQT

PART FIVE
COMPLETE ASVAB PRACTICE EXAMINATION

PART ONE
INTRODUCTION

About the ASVAB and the AFQT

1

WHAT IS THE ASVAB?

The Armed Services Vocational Aptitude Battery, the ASVAB, is a group of 10 subtests that measures your ability in separate career areas and provides an indication of your academic ability.

Only **four** of these subtests—Arithmetic Reasoning, Word Knowledge, Paragraph Comprehension, and Mathematics Knowledge—count toward your Armed Forces Qualifying Test (AFQT) score. The AFQT score determines whether or not you can enlist in the Armed Forces.

ASVAB HISTORY

During World War I, the Army developed the Army Alpha Test to classify draftees. It consisted of 212 multiple-choice and true/false questions about vocabulary, sentence structure, arithmetic problems, number series, general knowledge, and "common sense."

When it became apparent that many draftees couldn't read or write—and therefore couldn't be properly classified using the Army Alpha Test—the Army developed the Army Beta Test, which minimized verbal knowledge and used only pictures and diagrams. The current ASVAB, originally developed by the Department of Defense in the 1960s, is an outgrowth of these initial classification tests.

ASVAB COMPOSITION AND VERSIONS

Currently, the ASVAB consists of 9 individual subtests on the following subjects: General Science (GS), Arithmetic Reasoning (AR), Word Knowledge (WK), Paragraph Comprehension (PC), Mathematics Knowledge (MK), Mechanical Comprehension (MC), Electronics Information (EI), Automotive and Shop Information (SI), and Assembling Objects (AO).

There are currently three versions of the ASVAB. Results from any one of them can be used for military recruiting purposes.

Paper ASVAB for High School

The high school version is a paper-based test usually given to juniors and seniors in high school through a cooperative program between the Department of Defense and the Department of Education. The test is offered at more than 14,000 high schools and postsecondary schools in the United States. The primary purpose of this test is not for enlistment in the military—although the test scores can be used for military enlistment—but rather to help school counselors and students discover where a student's basic aptitudes lie. Almost one million students take the high school version of the ASVAB each year.

Paper ASVAB for Recruiting

This version is given by the Armed Forces for enlistment purposes only. While the questions on the high school version and the recruiting version are different, they are of equal difficulty. Fewer people take the paper recruiting version of the ASVAB because more people interested in joining the military take the computerized version at a Military Entrance Processing Station (MEPS), but both are equally valid.

Computer-Administered Test (CAT)-ASVAB

The third version of the test is the CAT-ASVAB. The CAT-ASVAB is adaptive, which means that it tailors questions to the ability level of each test taker (in the paper version, all test takers answer the same questions, regardless of their ability). For example, on the computer version, your first test question is given in the middle ability range, not too difficult and not too easy. If you answer it correctly, the next question is more difficult. If, however, you don't answer the first item correctly, the next item is less difficult. The test continues in this manner until your proficiency level is determined. You answer questions that are appropriate for your ability level, so you won't waste time answering questions that are too easy or too difficult—therefore, there are fewer questions and less time available in each section.

The CAT-ASVAB is advantageous in that you can finish it in less time, it can be scored immediately, and you don't need to wait for the next administered test. However, you can't skip around or go back to change an answer, and you can't go back and review your answers at the end of the test.

Unlike the paper ASVAB subtest raw scores, CAT-ASVAB subtest raw scores are not equal to the total number of correct answers. CAT-ASVAB subtest scores are computed using formulas that take into account the difficulty of the test item and the correctness of the answer. By equating CAT-ASVAB raw scores with paper-and-pencil ASVAB raw scores, both scores become equivalent.

ASVAB SCORING

Many people find that they score higher on the CAT-ASVAB than they do on the paper version. On overall ASVAB score calculation (not individual subtest scores, known as "line scores"), the mathematics knowledge (MK) and arithmetic reasoning (AR) questions on the ASVAB are "weighted," with harder questions worth more points than easier questions. However, the ASVAB is not an IQ or intelligence test. It was designed specifically to measure an individual's aptitude (i.e., probability of success) to be trained in a range of specific jobs.

Although there are minimum scores necessary for enlistment, there is no "failing grade" on the ASVAB. If you want to enlist in the military, you must achieve a minimum AFQT (Armed Forces Qualification Test) score—and then you may have to score at a certain level on particular subtests to qualify for certain specialties. The AFQT score is calculated from your scores on the WK, PC, AR, and MK subtests. Various combinations of all 10 scores are used to determine qualification for particular specialties. For example, to qualify for a technical communications specialty, you might have to have sufficiently high scores on the math, electronics, and general science subtests.

THE TEST FORMAT

Subtest	Paper test minutes	CAT minutes	Paper questions	CAT questions	Emphasis
1. General Science	11	8	25	16	Knowledge of physical and biological sciences
2. Arithmetic Reasoning	36	39	30	16	Ability to solve arithmetic word problems
3. Word Knowledge	11	8	35	16	Ability to select correct meaning of words in context and to identify the best synonym for a given word
4. Paragraph Comprehension	13	22	15	11	Ability to interpret and obtain information from written passages
5. Mathematics Knowledge	24	18	25	16	Knowledge of high school mathematics principles
6. Electronics Information	9	8	20	16	Knowledge of electricity and electronics
7. Automotive Information	N/A	6	N/A	11	Knowledge of automobiles
8. Shop Information	N/A	5	N/A	11	Knowledge of tools and shop terminology and practices
9. Automotive and Shop Information	11	N/A	25	N/A	Knowledge of automobiles and of tools and shop terminology and practices
10. Mechanical Comprehension	19	19	25	20	Knowledge of mechanical and physical principles and ability to visualize how illustrated objects work
11. Assembling Objects	20	9	20	16	How an object will look when its parts are mentally assembled

*Note that Subtests 7 and 8 have been combined in the current paper version of the test.

The overall minimum enlistment score, as well as the scores needed to qualify for particular jobs, vary from time to time based on the needs of the individual services.

If you've taken the ASVAB in high school, those scores (if they aren't over two years old) should be acceptable for enlistment. If you'd like a chance to increase your scores, you may want the recruiter to arrange for you to take the version of the ASVAB given to people who didn't take the high school version.

If you did well on the SAT or ACT, or if you get good grades in school, you should have no problem with the ASVAB math and verbal subtests; having a mechanical or electronics background will help you in the other ASVAB subtests.

The ASVAB is offered at many high schools across the country; if your high school isn't one of them, ask your guidance counselor for alternatives. If you are already out of high school, call a local military recruiter.

The information collected when someone takes the ASVAB is used by the Department of Defense for recruiting and research purposes. Scores and personal information obtained during the test are also released to the United States armed forces, the United States Coast Guard, and your local school.

WHY SHOULD I TAKE THE ASVAB?

An aptitude battery helps you measure your potential. It can give you a good indication of where your talents lie. By looking at your composite scores and your own personal interests, you can make more intelligent career decisions. The higher your score, the more choices you'll have when it comes to job specialties.

The ASVAB will also help predict your success in secondary and postsecondary courses and selected civilian career fields. If you're a high school senior trying to decide what to do after high school, your test scores can help you identify fields that you might explore. No matter what your age or inclination, the ASVAB can be valuable to you because it can tell you more about yourself.

If your score on a particular subtest is not as high as you would like, this book can help you raise your scores.

WHERE CAN I TAKE THE ASVAB?

The ASVAB is administered year-round at Military Entrance Processing Station (MEPS) locations throughout the United States, as well as by mobile teams. Officials of the Military Entrance Processing Command proctor the tests.

HOW DO I APPLY?

Ask your guidance counselor to make arrangements for you, or contact the nearest recruiter of the service of your choice. There is no cost for this examination, since the Department of Defense wants to tell you about military service opportunities and assist you in career exploration.

AM I OBLIGATED TO JOIN THE MILITARY?

No. Taking the ASVAB does not obligate you to the military in any way. You are free to use your test results in whatever manner you wish. Additionally, ASVAB results will *not* be used to enter your name in any draft registration system.

You will, however, be required to sign a statement authorizing the release of your test scores to representatives of all the military services, and (like the majority of high school students), if you are an upperclassman, you will probably be contacted by a recruiter sometime before you graduate. You should expect this whether or not you ever take the ASVAB.

Nevertheless, be sure to find out about the many job opportunities with the military services (Air Force, Army, Marine Corps, and Navy) and the U.S. Coast Guard.

Hundreds of thousands of students enter one of the military services each year. Your ASVAB test scores are good for enlistment purposes for two years after you take the test. Phone or visit a service recruiter to determine whether you would qualify to enter that service (assuming that you meet other qualifications such as age, physical requirements, etc.).

WHO SEES MY TEST SCORES?

The ASVAB is used by the Armed Services for recruiting purposes and by your counselor for guidance counseling. Therefore, your test scores will be provided to your counselor and to the recruiting services and the Coast Guard.

The personal information you will provide at the time of testing will be maintained in a computer file and on microfiche records. After two years, individual test scores, identified by student name and social security number, are retained by the Department of Defense only for research purposes to assist in evaluating and updating test materials.

Your personal identity information and related test information will not be released to any agency outside the Department of Defense and your school system. This information will not be used for any purpose other than recruiting by the Armed Services, counseling in your school, and research on test development and personnel measurement. Information on your test scores provided to your school will be handled and disposed of in accordance with the policies of the governing state or local school system.

WHAT EFFECT DO MY ASVAB SCORES HAVE?

If you plan to enter the military, your scores are very important. Your scores on the four subject tests that make up the AFQT determine whether or not you can enter the military at all. Once you have enlisted, your scores on the other subtests determine which military specialties you are eligible to be trained for.

HOW CAN I USE MY TEST SCORES?

Since the ASVAB is a vocational aptitude test, its primary value is in relating your test scores to jobs in the vocational-technical career fields. Whether or not you plan on going on to college, you should be aware of the range of jobs in the trades, what skills and training they require, and how much they can pay. (Some technical careers pay surprisingly well.)

COMPUTERIZED ASVAB CAREER EXPLORATION SYSTEM (ACES)

For use on school computers, the software automatically matches a student's attributes to occupations. Each student is able to see which occupations have characteristics consistent with his or her own and which may not be such good matches. This system is currently available to schools for use with those students who participate in the ASVAB program. Call your local ASVAB representative for more information.

WHAT SHOULD I EXPECT ON THE DAY OF THE TEST?

When you go to the examining station to take the ASVAB, if you are taking the paper version, you will be given a booklet with eight subtests, each consisting of *practice questions* and *actual test questions*. You will also be given a separate answer sheet on which to mark your answers, a special pencil to use, and some scratch paper for doing any figuring you may want to do.

If you are taking the computerized version, you will be seated at a table with a computer keyboard and monitor. The computer keyboard that you'll use for the CAT-ASVAB is modified so that only the keys you need to answer the test questions are labeled—the letters on the rest of the keys have been covered. You will have "A," "B," "C," and "D" keys (different than what you're used to) and the 0–9 numbers on the keypad; the spacebar becomes the ENTER key, and the F1 key will be your HELP key.

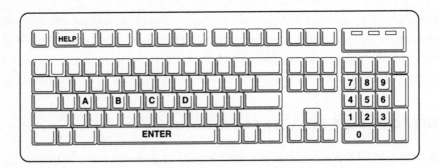

You'll get an on-screen orientation that describes the modified keyboard and explains how to use the keys that are available to answer test questions, change answers if desired, and move from one question to the next.

You will be instructed to press the red HELP key only if a problem comes up that requires the attention of a monitor or the test administrator. If you do press the HELP key, the time stops for the test you are on and does not resume until you return to the test questions. Time spent reading instructions won't count against you, either.

At the examining station, you will be given complete instructions as to what to do in taking the tests and how much time you have to work on each test. After you have been given the instructions, you will be allowed to practice by answering some sample questions. Finally, you will be given plenty of opportunity to ask questions before you start, so that you will understand exactly what you are supposed to do on the tests.

WHAT IS THE AFQT?

These initials stand for the Armed Forces Qualification Test. As mentioned previously, the scores of certain of the subtests are combined into various composites. One of these composite scores is derived from combining the results of the Arithmetic Reasoning, Mathematics Knowledge, Word Knowledge, and

Paragraph Comprehension tests—essentially, the mathematics and verbal sections of the ASVAB.

While the ASVAB is basically a vocational and aptitude battery, designed to assist in vocational placement, the AFQT is also used as an entrance examination for the armed forces, and is a major tool for the recruiting services in determining eligibility for admittance to one of the services. Thus, it is one of the more important composite scores.

This book includes some information and practice for the non-AFQT sections of the ASVAB, but **the primary focus of the *Pass Key to the ASVAB* is on the AFQT sections**—verbal and mathematical abilities and knowledge.

HOW TO TAKE THE TEST

In each of the 9 ASVAB subtests, there are four possible answers, labeled A, B, C, and D, for each question. Only one answer in each question is correct. Your job is to read each question carefully and decide which of the answers given is the best choice. Then you record your choice on the separate answer sheet by blackening out the space that has the same number and letter as your choice.

In all cases, you are to choose the best answer and mark your answer sheet in the space for it. You must not make any stray marks on the answer sheet because the scoring machine might record those marks as wrong answers. You also should not make any marks in the ASVAB test booklet.

In most of the tests, you will have enough time to try every question, and you should try every one. Be sure to work as quickly and accurately as you can. Do not go on to the next page until the examiner tells you to.

Some tests will be easier for you than others, but do the best you can on each. All are important. Your score on each test of the ASVAB will be based on the number of answers you mark correctly. *Wrong answers will not count against you.*

SAMPLE QUESTIONS

General Science—Subtest 1

Directions: This test has questions about general science, including biology, chemistry, earth science, and physics, as usually covered in high school courses.

1. Water is an example of a

    (A) solid.
    (B) gas.
    (C) liquid.
    (D) crystal.

2. Which of the following foods contains the most iron?

    (A) liver
    (B) cucumbers
    (C) eggs
    (D) candy

3. An eclipse of the sun throws the shadow of the

    (A) earth on the moon.
    (B) moon on the earth.
    (C) moon on the sun.
    (D) earth on the sun.

4. Lack of iodine is often related to which of the following diseases?

    (A) beriberi
    (B) scurvy
    (C) rickets
    (D) goiter

Arithmetic Reasoning—Subtest 2 (AFQT)

> *Directions:* This is a test of your ability to solve arithmetic problems. Use your scratch paper for any figuring you wish to do.

5. A person buys a sandwich for $3.50, soda for 50¢, and pie for 90¢. What is the total cost?

   (A) $3.75
   (B) $4.90
   (C) $5.00
   (D) $6.10

6. If 12 workers are needed to run 4 machines, how many workers are needed to run 20 machines?

   (A) 24
   (B) 48
   (C) 60
   (D) 80

7. It cost a couple $13.50 to go out for the evening. Sixty percent of this was for the theater tickets. What was the cost for each ticket?

   (A) $3.95
   (B) $4.05
   (C) $5.40
   (D) $8.10

8. A pole 24 feet high has a shadow 8 feet long. A nearby pole is 72 feet high. How long is its shadow?

   (A) 16 feet
   (B) 24 feet
   (C) 32 feet
   (D) 56 feet

Word Knowledge—Subtest 3 (AFQT)

> _Directions:_ This test has questions about the meaning of words. Each question has an underlined boldface word. You are to decide which of the four possible answers most nearly means the same as the underlined word, then blacken the appropriate space on your answer sheet.

9. **Small** most nearly means

   (A) sturdy
   (B) round
   (C) cheap
   (D) little

10. The accountant **discovered** an error.

    (A) searched
    (B) found
    (C) enlarged
    (D) entered

11. The wind is **variable** today.

    (A) shifting
    (B) chilling
    (C) steady
    (D) mild

12. **Cease** most nearly means

    (A) start
    (B) change
    (C) continue
    (D) stop

Paragraph Comprehension—Subtest 4 (AFQT)

Directions: This is a test of your ability to understand what you read. In this section you will find one or more paragraphs of reading material followed by incomplete statements or questions. You are to read the paragraph and select one of four lettered choices that best completes the statement or answers the question. When you have selected your answer, blacken in the correct numbered letter on your answer sheet.

13. The duty of the lighthouse keeper is to keep the light burning no matter what happens, so that ships will be warned of the presence of dangerous rocks. If a shipwreck should occur near the lighthouse, even though he would like to aid in the rescue of its crew and passengers, the lighthouse keeper must

    (A) stay at his light.
    (B) rush to their aid.
    (C) turn out the light.
    (D) quickly sound the siren.

14. From a building designer's standpoint, three things that make a home livable are the client, the building site, and the amount of money the client has to spend.

    According to the passage, to make a home livable

    (A) the prospective piece of land makes little difference.
    (B) it can be built on any piece of land.
    (C) the design must fit the owner's income and site.
    (D) the design must fit the designer's income.

Mathematics Knowledge—Subtest 5 (AFQT)

Directions: This is a test of your ability to solve problems using high school mathematics. Use your scratch paper for any figuring you wish to do.

15. If $a + 6 = 7$ then a is equal to

    (A) 0
    (B) 1
    (C) −1
    (D) $\dfrac{7}{6}$

16. What is the area of this square?

    (A) 1 square foot
    (B) 5 square feet
    (C) 10 square feet
    (D) 25 square feet

17. Angle B is 90 degrees. Which line in the triangle is the longest?

    (A) AB
    (B) AC
    (C) neither
    (D) can't be determined from the information given

18. If $3x = -5$, then $x =$

    (A) $\dfrac{3}{5}$

    (B) $-\dfrac{5}{3}$

    (C) $-\dfrac{3}{5}$

    (D) −2

Electronics Information—Subtest 6

Directions: This is a test of your knowledge of electrical, radio, and electronics information. This information can be learned through working on radios, electrical equipment, reading books, or taking courses.

19. The safest way to run an extension cord to a lamp is

    (A) under a rug.
    (B) along a baseboard.
    (C) under a sofa.
    (D) behind a sofa.

20. Which of the following has the least resistance?

    (A) rubber
    (B) silver
    (C) wood
    (D) iron

A. 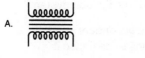 B.

C.   D.

21. Which of the above is the symbol for a transformer?

    (A) A
    (B) B
    (C) C
    (D) D

Automotive & Shop Information—Subtest 7

Directions: This test has questions about automobiles and shop practices and the use of tools. Try to acquaint yourself with the parts of an automobile, the operation of the drive and braking systems, and the function of the engine.

22. A clutch pedal must have free play so that

    (A) the clutch grabs early.
    (B) the clutch grabs late.
    (C) there is clearance between the disc and the flywheel.
    (D) there is clearance between the clutch fingers and the throwout bearing.

23. A limited slip differential is used to

    (A) allow a car to climb hills faster.
    (B) give better traction on ice.
    (C) keep the rear end cooler.
    (D) give a softer ride.

24. What are the two main functions of the ignition system?

    (A) to provide a primary arc and a secondary spark
    (B) to provide a spark and a means to decrease it
    (C) to provide a high-voltage spark and the means to time the engine
    (D) to provide a path for the wires and the spark plugs

25. Which of these tools breaks easily when twisted?

    (A) folding rule.
    (B) ruler.
    (C) yardstick.
    (D) handsaw.

26. A tool used for marking wood is called a

    (A) file.
    (B) chisel.
    (C) hammer.
    (D) scratch awl.

27. A chisel is used for

    (A) cutting.
    (B) prying.
    (C) twisting.
    (D) grinding.

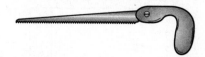

28. The saw shown above is used mainly to cut

    (A) across the grain of the wood.
    (B) along the grain of the wood.
    (C) plywood.
    (D) odd-shaped holes in wood.

Mechanical Comprehension—Subtest 8

Directions: This test has questions about general mechanical and physical principles. An understanding of these principles comes from observing the physical world, working with or operating mechanical devices, or reading and studying.

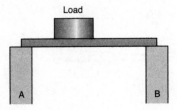

29. Which post holds up the greater part of the load?

(A) Post A
(B) Post B
(C) Both equal
(D) Not clear

30. If all of these are the same temperature, which will feel coldest?

(A) A
(B) B
(C) C
(D) D

Assembling Objects—Subtest 9

Directions: This test measures your ability to picture how an object will look when its parts are put together mentally. Pick the best answer for each question.

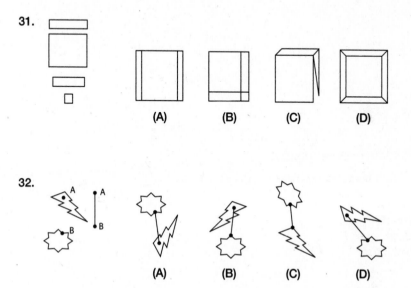

31.

(A)   (B)   (C)   (D)

32.

(A)   (B)   (C)   (D)

Answer Key

1. C	5. B	9. D	13. A	17. B	21. A	25. D	29. A
2. A	6. C	10. B	14. C	18. B	22. D	26. D	30. B
3. B	7. B	11. A	15. B	19. B	23. B	27. A	31. B
4. D	8. B	12. D	16. D	20. B	24. C	28. D	32. A

Test-Taking Techniques

2

Many people incorrectly believe that the amount of time spent studying is the most important factor in test preparation. Efficient study habits are part of the key to successful test preparation. Of course, all else being equal, the amount of time you devote to your studies is a critical factor. But spending time reading is not necessarily studying. If you want to retain what you read, you must develop a system. For example, a person who devotes 60 minutes a day to uninterrupted study in a quiet, private area will generally retain more than someone who puts in twice that time by studying five or six times a day for 15 to 20 minutes at a time.

RULES FOR STUDYING MORE EFFECTIVELY

We have listed a number of rules for you to follow to increase study time efficiency. If you abide by these rules, you will get the most out of this book.

- **MAKE SURE YOU UNDERSTAND THE MEANING OF EVERY WORD YOU READ.** Your ability to understand what you read is the most important skill needed to pass any test. Therefore, starting now, every time you see a word that you don't fully understand, make certain that you write it down and make note of where you saw it. Then, when you have a chance, look up the meaning of the word in the dictionary. When you think you know what the word means, go back to the reading material that contained the word, and make certain that you fully understand the meaning of the word.

  Keep a list of all words you don't know, and periodically review them. Also, try to use these words whenever you can in conversation. If you do this faithfully, you will quickly build an extensive vocabulary, which will be helpful to you not only when you take this examination, but for the rest of your life.

- **STUDY FOR AT LEAST 30 MINUTES UNINTERRUPTED.** Unless you can study for at least an uninterrupted period of 30 minutes, you should not bother to study at all. It is essential that you concentrate for extended periods of time. When you take the practice examinations, do a complete examination in one sitting, just as you must do at the actual examination.

- **SIMULATE EXAMINATION CONDITIONS WHEN STUDYING.** As much as possible, study under the same conditions as those of the examination. Eliminate as many outside interferences as you can.
- **ALWAYS FOLLOW THE RECOMMENDED TECHNIQUE FOR ANSWERING MULTIPLE-CHOICE QUESTIONS.** In this chapter we provide an invaluable technique for answering multiple-choice questions.
- **ALWAYS TIME YOURSELF WHEN DOING PRACTICE QUESTIONS.** Running out of time on a multiple-choice examination is a tragic error that is easily avoided. Learn, through practice, to move to the next question after a reasonable period of time has been spent on any one question. When you are doing practice questions, always time yourself so that you will stay within the recommended time limits.
- **CONCENTRATE YOUR STUDY TIME IN YOUR WEAKEST AREAS.** The model examinations will give you an idea of the most difficult question types for you. Though you should spend most of your time improving yourself in these areas, do not ignore the other types of questions.
- **EXERCISE REGULARLY AND STAY IN GOOD PHYSICAL CONDITION.** Students who are in good physical condition have an advantage over those who are not. It is a well-established principle that good physical health improves the ability of the mind to function smoothly and efficiently.
- **ESTABLISH A SCHEDULE FOR STUDYING, AND STICK TO IT.** Do not put off studying to those times when you have nothing else to do. Schedule your study time, and try not to let anything else interfere with that schedule.

STRATEGIES FOR HANDLING MULTIPLE-CHOICE QUESTIONS

The remainder of this chapter outlines a very specific test-taking strategy valuable for a multiple-choice examination. Study the technique, practice it, then study it again until you have mastered it.

1. **READ THE DIRECTIONS.** Do *not* assume that you know what the directions are without reading them. Make sure you read and understand them. Note particularly whether there are differing directions from one section of the examination to another.

2. **TAKE A CLOSE LOOK AT THE ANSWER SHEET.** The answer sheets on your practice examinations are typical of the one you will see on your exam. However, do *not* take anything for granted. Review the directions on the answer sheet carefully, and familiarize yourself with its format.

3. **BE CAREFUL WHEN MARKING YOUR ANSWERS.** Be sure to mark your answers in accordance with the directions on the answer sheet.

Be extremely careful that:
- you mark only one answer for each question,
- you do not make extraneous markings on your answer sheet,
- you completely darken the allotted space for the answer you choose,
- you erase completely any answer that you wish to change.

4. **MAKE ABSOLUTELY CERTAIN YOU ARE MARKING THE ANSWER TO THE RIGHT QUESTION.** Many multiple-choice tests have been failed because of carelessness in this area. All it takes is one mistake. If you put down one answer in the wrong space, you will probably continue the mistake for a number of questions until you realize your error. We recommend that you use the following procedure when marking your answer sheet:

- Select your answer, blacken that choice on the answer form, and ask yourself what question number you are working on.
- If you select "C" as the answer for question eleven, blacken choice "C" on the answer form, and say to yourself, "C is the answer to question eleven."
- Then find the space on your answer sheet for question eleven, and again say "C is the answer to question eleven" as you mark the answer.

While this might seem rather elementary and repetitive, after a while it becomes automatic. If followed properly, it guarantees that you will not fail the examination because of a careless mistake.

5. **MAKE CERTAIN THAT YOU UNDERSTAND WHAT THE QUESTION IS ASKING.** Read the stem of the question (the part before the choices) very carefully to make certain that you know what the examiner is asking. In fact, it's a good idea to read it twice.

6. **ALWAYS READ ALL THE CHOICES BEFORE YOU SELECT AN ANSWER.** Don't make the mistake of falling into the trap that the best distractor, or wrong answer, comes before the correct choice! Read all choices.

7. **BE AWARE OF KEY WORDS THAT OFTEN TIP OFF CORRECT AND INCORRECT ANSWERS.**

Absolute Words—*Usually a Wrong Choice*
(They are generally too broad and difficult to defend)

never	nothing	always	everyone	only
none	nobody	all	everybody	any

Limiting Words—*Usually a Correct Choice*

usually	few	some	many	often
generally	sometimes	possible	occasionally	

---

8. **NEVER MAKE A CHOICE BASED ON THE FREQUENCY OF PREVIOUS ANSWERS.** Some students pay attention to the pattern of answers when taking the exam. Always answer the question, without regard to what the previous choices have been.

9. **ELIMINATE CHOICES YOU KNOW ARE WRONG.** As you read through the choices, eliminate any choice you know is wrong. If you eliminate all but one of the choices, the remaining choice should be the answer. Read the choice one more time to satisfy yourself, and blacken its letter designation (if you still feel it is the best answer) on the answer sheet. If you were not able to narrow the choices to one, many times, the second time you read the remaining choices, the answer is clear.

10. **SKIP OVER QUESTIONS THAT GIVE YOU TROUBLE.** The first time through the examination be certain not to dwell too long on any one question. Simply skip the question after blackening any answer on the answer sheet (to keep your answers from getting out of sequence), and go to the next question. Circle the question number in your test booklet so that you can go back to it if you have time.

11. **RETURN TO THE QUESTIONS YOU SKIPPED IN A SUBTEST AFTER YOU FINISH THAT PORTION OF THE EXAMINATION.** Once you have answered all of the questions you were sure of in a subtest of the examination, check the time remaining. If time permits, return to each question you did not answer and reread the stem and the choices. If the answer is still not clear and you are running out of time, then make an "educated guess" among those choices. When making an "educated guess," follow the guidelines that are presented in Strategy 13.

12. **NEVER LEAVE QUESTIONS UNANSWERED SINCE THERE IS NO PENALTY FOR WRONG ANSWERS.**

13. **RULES FOR MAKING AN "EDUCATED GUESS."** Your chances of picking the correct answer to questions you are not sure of will be significantly increased if you use the following rules:

   - Never consider answer choices that you have already eliminated. (See Strategy 9.)
   - Be aware of key words that give you clues as to which answer might be right or wrong. (See Strategy 7.)
   - If two choices have a conflicting meaning, one of them is probably the correct answer. And, if two choices are too close in meaning, probably neither is correct.
   - If all else fails and you have to make an outright guess at more than one question, guess the same lettered choice for each question. The odds are that you will pick up some valuable points.

14. **BE VERY RELUCTANT TO CHANGE ANSWERS.** Unless you have a very good reason, do not change an answer once you have chosen it. Studies have shown that all too often people change their answer from the right one to the wrong one.

PART TWO
ARMED FORCES QUALIFICATION TEST (AFQT)

Diagnostic Test

3

The purpose of this Diagnostic Test is to introduce you to the format and content of the sections of the ASVAB Test (Arithmetic Reasoning, Word Knowledge, Paragraph Comprehension, and Mathematics Knowledge) that are used to determine your AFQT score. This test will also identify your strengths and weaknesses, and help you devise the most effective study plan for the actual test.

To get the most useful results, take the examination under simulated testing conditions: find a quiet room where you will not be interrupted while taking the test; detach the answer sheet provided and mark your answers directly on it; follow the directions given for each of the four sections of the test; do not exceed the amount of time allotted for each section.

After you finish the entire examination, check your answers against the answer key provided. Study the "Answer Explanations" sections, paying close attention to the solutions to questions you answered incorrectly. You may need to devote more study time to those areas. You should study the review sections in this book as well as other texts if necessary.

ANSWER SHEET—DIAGNOSTIC TEST

Arithmetic Reasoning	Word Knowledge	Paragraph Comprehension	Mathematics Knowledge
1. Ⓐ Ⓑ Ⓒ Ⓓ	1. Ⓐ Ⓑ Ⓒ Ⓓ	1. Ⓐ Ⓑ Ⓒ Ⓓ	1. Ⓐ Ⓑ Ⓒ Ⓓ
2. Ⓐ Ⓑ Ⓒ Ⓓ	2. Ⓐ Ⓑ Ⓒ Ⓓ	2. Ⓐ Ⓑ Ⓒ Ⓓ	2. Ⓐ Ⓑ Ⓒ Ⓓ
3. Ⓐ Ⓑ Ⓒ Ⓓ	3. Ⓐ Ⓑ Ⓒ Ⓓ	3. Ⓐ Ⓑ Ⓒ Ⓓ	3. Ⓐ Ⓑ Ⓒ Ⓓ
4. Ⓐ Ⓑ Ⓒ Ⓓ	4. Ⓐ Ⓑ Ⓒ Ⓓ	4. Ⓐ Ⓑ Ⓒ Ⓓ	4. Ⓐ Ⓑ Ⓒ Ⓓ
5. Ⓐ Ⓑ Ⓒ Ⓓ	5. Ⓐ Ⓑ Ⓒ Ⓓ	5. Ⓐ Ⓑ Ⓒ Ⓓ	5. Ⓐ Ⓑ Ⓒ Ⓓ
6. Ⓐ Ⓑ Ⓒ Ⓓ	6. Ⓐ Ⓑ Ⓒ Ⓓ	6. Ⓐ Ⓑ Ⓒ Ⓓ	6. Ⓐ Ⓑ Ⓒ Ⓓ
7. Ⓐ Ⓑ Ⓒ Ⓓ	7. Ⓐ Ⓑ Ⓒ Ⓓ	7. Ⓐ Ⓑ Ⓒ Ⓓ	7. Ⓐ Ⓑ Ⓒ Ⓓ
8. Ⓐ Ⓑ Ⓒ Ⓓ	8. Ⓐ Ⓑ Ⓒ Ⓓ	8. Ⓐ Ⓑ Ⓒ Ⓓ	8. Ⓐ Ⓑ Ⓒ Ⓓ
9. Ⓐ Ⓑ Ⓒ Ⓓ	9. Ⓐ Ⓑ Ⓒ Ⓓ	9. Ⓐ Ⓑ Ⓒ Ⓓ	9. Ⓐ Ⓑ Ⓒ Ⓓ
10. Ⓐ Ⓑ Ⓒ Ⓓ	10. Ⓐ Ⓑ Ⓒ Ⓓ	10. Ⓐ Ⓑ Ⓒ Ⓓ	10. Ⓐ Ⓑ Ⓒ Ⓓ
11. Ⓐ Ⓑ Ⓒ Ⓓ	11. Ⓐ Ⓑ Ⓒ Ⓓ	11. Ⓐ Ⓑ Ⓒ Ⓓ	11. Ⓐ Ⓑ Ⓒ Ⓓ
12. Ⓐ Ⓑ Ⓒ Ⓓ	12. Ⓐ Ⓑ Ⓒ Ⓓ	12. Ⓐ Ⓑ Ⓒ Ⓓ	12. Ⓐ Ⓑ Ⓒ Ⓓ
13. Ⓐ Ⓑ Ⓒ Ⓓ	13. Ⓐ Ⓑ Ⓒ Ⓓ	13. Ⓐ Ⓑ Ⓒ Ⓓ	13. Ⓐ Ⓑ Ⓒ Ⓓ
14. Ⓐ Ⓑ Ⓒ Ⓓ	14. Ⓐ Ⓑ Ⓒ Ⓓ	14. Ⓐ Ⓑ Ⓒ Ⓓ	14. Ⓐ Ⓑ Ⓒ Ⓓ
15. Ⓐ Ⓑ Ⓒ Ⓓ	15. Ⓐ Ⓑ Ⓒ Ⓓ	15. Ⓐ Ⓑ Ⓒ Ⓓ	15. Ⓐ Ⓑ Ⓒ Ⓓ
16. Ⓐ Ⓑ Ⓒ Ⓓ	16. Ⓐ Ⓑ Ⓒ Ⓓ		16. Ⓐ Ⓑ Ⓒ Ⓓ
17. Ⓐ Ⓑ Ⓒ Ⓓ	17. Ⓐ Ⓑ Ⓒ Ⓓ		17. Ⓐ Ⓑ Ⓒ Ⓓ
18. Ⓐ Ⓑ Ⓒ Ⓓ	18. Ⓐ Ⓑ Ⓒ Ⓓ		18. Ⓐ Ⓑ Ⓒ Ⓓ
19. Ⓐ Ⓑ Ⓒ Ⓓ	19. Ⓐ Ⓑ Ⓒ Ⓓ		19. Ⓐ Ⓑ Ⓒ Ⓓ
20. Ⓐ Ⓑ Ⓒ Ⓓ	20. Ⓐ Ⓑ Ⓒ Ⓓ		20. Ⓐ Ⓑ Ⓒ Ⓓ
21. Ⓐ Ⓑ Ⓒ Ⓓ	21. Ⓐ Ⓑ Ⓒ Ⓓ		21. Ⓐ Ⓑ Ⓒ Ⓓ
22. Ⓐ Ⓑ Ⓒ Ⓓ	22. Ⓐ Ⓑ Ⓒ Ⓓ		22. Ⓐ Ⓑ Ⓒ Ⓓ
23. Ⓐ Ⓑ Ⓒ Ⓓ	23. Ⓐ Ⓑ Ⓒ Ⓓ		23. Ⓐ Ⓑ Ⓒ Ⓓ
24. Ⓐ Ⓑ Ⓒ Ⓓ	24. Ⓐ Ⓑ Ⓒ Ⓓ		24. Ⓐ Ⓑ Ⓒ Ⓓ
25. Ⓐ Ⓑ Ⓒ Ⓓ	25. Ⓐ Ⓑ Ⓒ Ⓓ		25. Ⓐ Ⓑ Ⓒ Ⓓ
26. Ⓐ Ⓑ Ⓒ Ⓓ	26. Ⓐ Ⓑ Ⓒ Ⓓ		
27. Ⓐ Ⓑ Ⓒ Ⓓ	27. Ⓐ Ⓑ Ⓒ Ⓓ		
28. Ⓐ Ⓑ Ⓒ Ⓓ	28. Ⓐ Ⓑ Ⓒ Ⓓ		
29. Ⓐ Ⓑ Ⓒ Ⓓ	29. Ⓐ Ⓑ Ⓒ Ⓓ		
30. Ⓐ Ⓑ Ⓒ Ⓓ	30. Ⓐ Ⓑ Ⓒ Ⓓ		
	31. Ⓐ Ⓑ Ⓒ Ⓓ		
	32. Ⓐ Ⓑ Ⓒ Ⓓ		
	33. Ⓐ Ⓑ Ⓒ Ⓓ		
	34. Ⓐ Ⓑ Ⓒ Ⓓ		
	35. Ⓐ Ⓑ Ⓒ Ⓓ		

ARITHMETIC REASONING

> *Directions:* This test has questions about arithmetic. Each question is followed by four possible answers. Decide which answer is correct. Then, on your answer form, blacken the space that has the same number and letter as your choice. Use your scratch paper for any figuring you wish to do.

SAMPLE QUESTION

1. If 10 pounds of sugar cost $2.00, what is the cost of one pound?

   (A) 90 cents
   (B) 80 cents
   (C) 50 cents
   (D) 20 cents

The cost of one pound is 20 cents; therefore, answer D is correct.

Your score on this test will be based on the number of questions you answer correctly. You should try to answer every question. Do not spend too much time on any one question.

**The actual test will say:
Do not turn this page until told to do so.**

Arithmetic Reasoning

Time —36 minutes
30 Questions

1. A platoon is composed of 11 enlisted men and one noncommissioned officer. A company of 132 enlisted men is to be divided into platoons. How many noncommissioned officers will be needed?

   (A) 11
   (B) 12
   (C) 13
   (D) 10

2. A man earns $350 per week. A total of $27.75 is withheld for federal income taxes, $5.65 for F.I.C.A., $9.29 for state income taxes, and $3.58 for union dues and welfare fund. How much will his net pay for the week be?

   (A) $314.73
   (B) $304.73
   (C) $303.73
   (D) $313.73

3. Temperature readings on a certain day ranged from a low of –4°F to a high of 16°F. What was the average temperature for the day?

   (A) 10°
   (B) 6°
   (C) 12°
   (D) 8°

4. On the scale drawing $\frac{1}{4}$ inch represents 1 foot. How long would a line on the drawing have to be to represent a length of $3\frac{1}{2}$ feet?

   (A) $\frac{3}{4}$ inch

   (B) $\frac{7}{8}$ inch

   (C) $1\frac{7}{8}$ inch

   (D) $1\frac{1}{4}$ inch

5. An automobile manufacturer offers a 15% rebate on the list price of a new car. What would be the rebate on a car that lists for $13,620?

   (A) $900
   (B) $11,577
   (C) $204.30
   (D) $2,043

6. The price of gasoline rose from $1.90 to $2.08 per gallon. What was the percent of increase?

   (A) 4.2%
   (B) 8.7%
   (C) 9.5%
   (D) 19.0%

7. A team won 70% of the 40 games it played. How many games did it lose?

   (A) 28
   (B) 30
   (C) 22
   (D) 12

8. A flight is scheduled for departure at 3:50 P.M. If the flight takes 2 hours and 55 minutes, at what time is it scheduled to arrive at its destination?

   (A) 5:05 P.M.
   (B) 6:05 P.M.
   (C) 6:15 P.M.
   (D) 6:45 P.M.

9. How many 4-ounce candy bars are there in a 3-pound package of candy?

   (A) 12
   (B) 16
   (C) 48
   (D) 9

10. What is the fifth term of the series $2\frac{5}{6}$, $3\frac{1}{2}$, $4\frac{1}{6}$, $4\frac{5}{6}$,...?

   (A) $5\frac{1}{6}$

   (B) $5\frac{1}{2}$

   (C) $5\frac{5}{6}$

   (D) $6\frac{1}{6}$

11. In a restaurant, a diner orders an entree with vegetables for $10.50, dessert for $1.50, and coffee for $.50. If the tax on meals is 6%, what tax should be added to his check?

   (A) $.06
   (B) $.63
   (C) $.72
   (D) $.75

12. A 55-gallon drum of oil is to be used to fill cans that hold 2 quarts each. How many cans can be filled from the drum?

   (A) 55
   (B) $27\frac{1}{2}$
   (C) 110
   (D) 220

13. In a factory that makes wooden spindles, a lathe operator takes 45 minutes to do the finish work on 9 spindles. How many hours will it take him to finish 96 spindles at the same rate?

   (A) 8
   (B) 14.4
   (C) 80
   (D) 96

14. A triangle has two equal sides. The third side has a length of 13 feet, 2 inches. If the perimeter of the triangle is 40 feet, what is the length of one of the equal sides?

   (A) 13 feet, 4 inches
   (B) 26 feet, 10 inches
   (C) 13 feet, 11 inches
   (D) 13 feet, 5 inches

15. A lawn is 21 feet wide and 39 feet long. How much will it cost to weed and feed it if a gardening service charges $.40 per square yard for such treatment?

   (A) $109.20
   (B) $36.40
   (C) $327.60
   (D) $24.00

16. A motorist drove for 7 hours at a rate of 48 miles per hour. Her car gets 21 miles per gallon of gas. How many gallons of gas did she use?

    (A) 24
    (B) 14
    (C) 18
    (D) 16

17. Two partners operate a business that shows a profit for the year of $63,000. Their partnership agreement calls for them to share the profits in the ratio 5:4. How much of the profit should go to the partner who gets the larger share?

    (A) $35,000
    (B) $28,000
    (C) $32,000
    (D) $36,000

18. A purchaser paid $17.16 for an article that had recently been increased in price by 4%. What was the price of the article before the increase?

    (A) $17.00
    (B) $17.12
    (C) $16.50
    (D) $16.47

19. In a clothing factory, 5 workers finish production of 6 garments each per day, 3 others turn out 4 garments each per day, and one worker turns out 12 per day. What is the average number of garments produced per worker per day?

    (A) $2\frac{2}{9}$
    (B) 6
    (C) 4
    (D) $7\frac{1}{3}$

20. A man makes a 255-mile trip by car. He drives the first 2 hours at 45 miles per hour. At what speed must he travel for the remainder of the trip in order to arrive at his destination 5 hours after he started the trip?

    (A) 31 miles per hour
    (B) 50 miles per hour
    (C) 51 miles per hour
    (D) 55 miles per hour

21. A contractor bids $300,000 as his price for erecting a building. He estimates that $\frac{1}{10}$ of this amount will be spent for masonry materials and labor, $\frac{1}{3}$ for lumber and carpentry, $\frac{1}{5}$ for plumbing and heating, and $\frac{1}{6}$ for electrical and lighting work.

The balance will be his profit. How much profit does he expect to make?
(A) $24,000
(B) $80,000
(C) $60,000
(D) $50,000

22. The list price of a TV set is $325, but the retailer offers successive discounts of 20% and 30%. What price does a customer actually pay?

(A) $182
(B) $270
(C) $162.50
(D) $176.67

23. A certain brand of motor oil is regularly sold at a price of 2 quart cans for $1.99. On a special sale, a carton containing 6 of the quart cans is sold for $5.43. What is the saving per quart if the oil is bought at the special sale?

(A) $.27
(B) $.09
(C) $.54
(D) $.54$\frac{1}{4}$

24. A worker earns $7.20 an hour. She is paid time and a half for overtime beyond a 40-hour week. How much will she earn in a week in which she works 43 hours?

(A) $295.20
(B) $320.40
(C) $432.00
(D) $464.40

25. A tree 36 feet high casts a shadow 8 feet long. At the same time, another tree casts a shadow 6 feet long. How tall is the second tree?

(A) 30 feet
(B) 27 feet
(C) 24 feet
(D) 32 feet

26. A company spends $\frac{3}{5}$ of its advertising budget on newspaper ads and $\frac{1}{3}$ on radio commercials. What portion of the advertising budget is left for TV commercials?

   (A) $\frac{1}{2}$

   (B) $\frac{7}{30}$

   (C) $\frac{1}{15}$

   (D) $\frac{1}{8}$

27. A VCR is programmed to record a TV show that lasts for a half-hour. If the cassette tape that is used can accommodate 180 minutes of programming, what percent of the tape is used for this recording?

   (A) $16\frac{2}{3}\%$
   (B) 30%
   (C) 60%
   (D) $33\frac{1}{3}\%$

28. We bought 5 pounds of cashew nuts worth $1.80 per pound, mixed with 4 pounds of peanuts worth $1.62 per pound. What is the value per pound of the mixture?

   (A) $1.72
   (B) $1.71
   (C) $3.42
   (D) $1.82

29. A wall is 7 feet 8 inches in height; four vertical pieces of wallpaper are needed to cover the wall. Assuming there is no waste, what is the minimum length that a roll of wallpaper must be to cover the wall?

   (A) 29 feet, 2 inches
   (B) 31 feet, 2 inches
   (C) 31 feet
   (D) 30 feet, 8 inches

30. A night watchman is required to check in every 40 minutes while making his rounds. His tour of duty extends from 9:00 P.M. to 5:00 A.M. If he checks in at the start of his rounds and also when he finishes, how many times does he check in during the night?

   (A) 12
   (B) 13
   (C) 8
   (D) 20

WORD KNOWLEDGE

**Directions:** This test has questions about the meanings of words. Each question has an underlined boldface word. You are to decide which one of the four words in the choices most nearly means the same as the underlined boldface word; then, mark the space on your answer form that has the same number and letter as your choice.

SAMPLE QUESTION

1. It was a **small** table.

    (A) sturdy
    (B) round
    (C) cheap
    (D) little

The question asks which of the four words means the same as the boldface word, **small**. Little means the same as **small**. Answer D is the best one.

Your score on this test will be based on the number of questions you answer correctly. You should try to answer every question. Do not spend too much time on any one question.

The actual test will say:
Do not turn this page until told to do so.

Word Knowledge

1. He reached the **pinnacle** of his career.

   (A) lowest point
   (B) final days
   (C) smallest salary
   (D) summit

2. **Brawl** most nearly means

   (A) trap
   (B) fight
   (C) speak
   (D) provide

3. She acted like a **pauper**.

   (A) poor person
   (B) slenderer
   (C) patriot
   (D) peculiar person

4. She has always been **punctual**.

   (A) a jokester
   (B) prompt
   (C) correct
   (D) prepared

5. **Segment** most nearly means

   (A) secret
   (B) hermit
   (C) part
   (D) seep

6. **Revere** most nearly means

   (A) esteem
   (B) regulate
   (C) reverse
   (D) hold

7. The speaker's audience appreciated **brevity**.

   (A) brilliance
   (B) illustrations
   (C) activity
   (D) conciseness

8. **Illogical** most nearly means

   (A) coherent
   (B) illusive
   (C) fallacious
   (D) real

9. **Excerpt** most nearly means

   (A) exam
   (B) extract
   (C) eventual
   (D) superfluous

10. The surface had a **sheen**.

    (A) color
    (B) luster
    (C) scratch
    (D) cover

11. **Divulge** most nearly means

    (A) divide
    (B) fatten
    (C) dissolve
    (D) tell

12. The attorney could **cite** examples.

    (A) cultivate
    (B) change
    (C) specify
    (D) grasp

13. I cannot **allay** your concerns.

    (A) ease
    (B) confirm
    (C) reverse
    (D) tempt

14. The animal had **vitality**.

    (A) liveliness
    (B) viciousness
    (C) cunning
    (D) understanding

15. **Defer** most nearly means

    (A) ascertain
    (B) define
    (C) abase
    (D) delay

16. I **deplore** your actions.

    (A) approve
    (B) applaud
    (C) regret
    (D) deprive

17. **Concur** most nearly means

    (A) defeat
    (B) agree
    (C) confine
    (D) truth

18. **Refute** most nearly means

    (A) refer
    (B) disapprove
    (C) disprove
    (D) regard

19. She served **copious** amounts of food.

    (A) unequal
    (B) small
    (C) uninviting
    (D) large

20. **Credulous** most nearly means

    (A) fantastic
    (B) credit
    (C) gullible
    (D) awe-inspiring

21. **Random** most nearly means

    (A) haphazard
    (B) purpose
    (C) anger
    (D) ramble

22. State the <u>salient</u> points.

    (A) legal
    (B) conspicuous
    (C) less obvious
    (D) missed

23. <u>Tangible</u> most nearly means

    (A) illusory
    (B) tangent
    (C) concrete
    (D) tangle

24. <u>Residue</u> most nearly means

    (A) resident
    (B) part
    (C) rescue
    (D) remainder

25. <u>Catastrophe</u> most nearly means

    (A) violence
    (B) disorder
    (C) decision
    (D) disaster

26. He promised us a <u>diagnosis</u>.

    (A) analysis
    (B) decision
    (C) dialect
    (D) diagram

27. Your reaction leaves me in a <u>quandary</u>.

    (A) condition
    (B) predicament
    (C) certainty
    (D) compunction

28. <u>Stilted</u> most nearly means

    (A) bored
    (B) formal
    (C) stuffed
    (D) stifled

29. The law says you must not <u>encroach</u>.

    (A) enclose
    (B) overreach
    (C) trespass
    (D) encounter

30. <u>Deter</u> most nearly means

    (A) dissipate
    (B) detain
    (C) dispute
    (D) prevent

31. <u>Falter</u> most nearly means

    (A) die
    (B) fake
    (C) hesitate
    (D) fall

32. Our meal was a <u>meager</u> one.

    (A) sparse
    (B) rich
    (C) filling
    (D) massive

33. <u>Stifle</u> most nearly means

    (A) sign
    (B) suppress
    (C) shoot
    (D) stiff

34. <u>Dearth</u> most nearly means

    (A) lack
    (B) passing
    (C) ground
    (D) overabundance

35. <u>Accord</u> most nearly means

    (A) belief
    (B) accurate
    (C) settle
    (D) harmony

PARAGRAPH COMPREHENSION

> _Directions:_ This is a test of your ability to understand what you read. In this section you will find one or more paragraphs of reading material followed by incomplete statements or questions. You are to read the paragraph and select one of four lettered choices that best completes the statement or answers the question. When you have selected your answer, blacken in the correct numbered letter on your answer sheet.

SAMPLE QUESTION

In certain areas water is so scarce that every attempt is made to conserve it. For instance, on one oasis in the Sahara Desert the amount of water necessary for each date palm tree has been carefully determined.

1. How much water is each tree given?

    (A) no water at all
    (B) exactly the amount required
    (C) water only if it is healthy
    (D) water on alternate days

The amount of water each tree requires has been carefully determined, so answer B is correct.

Your score on this test will be based on the number of questions you answer correctly. You should try to answer every question. Do not spend too much time on any one question.

The actual test will say:
Do not turn this page until told to do so.

Paragraph Comprehension

1. History tells us that Christopher Columbus once saved his own life because he knew from his almanac that there was going to be an eclipse of the moon. In 1504 Columbus was marooned in Jamaica with no food and unfriendly natives confronting him. The explorer threatened to turn off the light in the sky if the natives refused to give him food. Columbus kept his word; the natives gave him food.

   The main idea of this paragraph is that

   (A) natives rarely own almanacs or understand scientific facts.
   (B) Christopher Columbus was in Jamaica in 1504 on his third voyage from Spain.
   (C) on his arrival in Jamaica, Christopher Columbus had no food.
   (D) Columbus saved his own life because he knew when there was going to be an eclipse of the moon.

2. One implied warranty required by state law is the "warranty of merchantability." This means that the seller promises that the product will do what it is supposed to do. For example,

   (A) a car will never need repairs.
   (B) a lawn mower will also cut bushes.
   (C) a toaster will toast.
   (D) your roof will last 75 to 100 years.

3. Both coasts of the American continent were joined on May 10, 1869, when a golden spike was driven to join the last rail at Promontory Point, Utah. Many immigrants moved west to take up free homestead land or purchase tracts at low prices.

   According to the passage, the settling of the American west

   (A) made immigrants very wealthy from land ownership.
   (B) followed the completion of the railroad.
   (C) made it impossible for anyone to purchase land.
   (D) was finished before the summer of 1869.

4. The most disadvantaged type in both countries was the single parent, female headed household, of which 38% in Canada and 61% in the U.S. were in need. Moreover, 44% of single females living alone in Canada and 51% in the U.S. were in housing need. By contrast, male single parents experienced about half the housing need of their female equivalents.

   You can conclude from the paragraph that needy male single parents in housing need in the U.S. numbered approximately

   (A) 61%.
   (B) 30%.
   (C) 44%.
   (D) 22%.

5. In 1973, when the OPEC nations embargoed oil exports to the United States, their action signaled an unprecedented rise in oil prices. In fact, crude oil prices quadrupled, sending oil-dependent countries into a recession.

One of the results of the oil embargo was that

(A) the United States embargoed oil exports of OPEC nations.
(B) the price of crude oil declined.
(C) the price of crude oil doubled.
(D) oil-dependent countries experienced a recession.

6. Although they last no longer than a fraction of a second, voltage variations can cause problems with your sensitive equipment. Variation in voltage causes digital clocks to blink and timers to be thrown off schedule. Computers are especially

(A) useful when you transfer data to memory.
(B) easy to protect from variations in voltage.
(C) useful in publishing.
(D) sensitive to voltage variations.

7. In 1948, the United Nations General Assembly adopted the resolution entitled the Universal Declaration of Human Rights. The resolution stresses personal, civil, political, social, cultural, and economic rights of people. In so doing, the article promotes

(A) financial well-being only.
(B) fundamental freedoms.
(C) social unrest.
(D) only one political party.

8. DNA, a nucleic acid contained in all living material, orders every cell to reproduce in a certain manner. In fact, DNA molecules determine both the form and function of all living cells.

DNA is

(A) only found in animals.
(B) one kind of cell.
(C) a nucleic acid.
(D) a nuclear device.

9. Garbage has become an alarming problem—and it won't go away. State landfills, as they are presently designed, are quickly filling up. Consequently, since 30% of trash being dumped can be recycled, it is time for communities to set up recycling programs.

Not all trash needs to be dumped. We know that

(A) a third of what we dump could be recycled.
(B) people could start their own landfills.
(C) recycling will never take place.
(D) 70% of trash can be recycled.

10. Sometimes a state legislature asks the voters to approve or reject a proposal called a referendum. The proposal may be a constitutional amendment, a plan for long-term borrowing, or a special law affecting a city. In effect, the question is "referred" to the voters.

The Constitution of the United States was submitted to State conventions for approvals. From the definition above, you can say that it was

(A) approved unanimously.
(B) approved by a form of referendum.
(C) rejected by a majority of the States.
(D) referred to the President of the United States.

11. Some pollutants that render air unsafe to breathe cannot be seen or smelled. Nitric oxide, carbon monoxide, and radon gas are examples. Other pollutants, such as formaldehyde, can be smelled at high levels only, but are still unsafe to breathe even at lower levels.

You can conclude from the paragraph that formaldehyde

(A) is safer to breathe than nitric oxide.
(B) can never be seen or smelled.
(C) cannot be smelled at lower levels.
(D) is not one of the pollutants that renders air unsafe to breathe.

12. Pneumonia is caused by bacteria, viruses, fungi, or mycoplasmas. Bacterial pneumonia is the main type of pneumonia to follow an attack of the flu and a major precipitator of pneumonia deaths.

Which type of pneumonia most often leads to pneumonia deaths?

(A) bacterial
(B) viral
(C) fungi
(D) flu

13. Because the temperature of ocean water changes more slowly than the temperature of air, oceans affect the world's climate. As ocean water moves past land masses, it affects the climate by warming the air in winter and cooling it in summer.

The key idea in this paragraph is that

(A) ocean water moves past land masses.
(B) ocean water cools the air in winter.
(C) ocean water warms the land masses in summer.
(D) the world's climate is affected by the temperature of the oceans.

14. Laser and incandescent lights are different in an important way. Incandescent light, from light bulbs, emits light of different wavelengths and moves in many directions. On the other hand, laser beams are monochromatic, of a single wavelength. They can travel great distances without spreading. Any comparison of laser and incandescent lights must include a discussion of

    (A) small and large light bulbs.
    (B) wavelengths.
    (C) sound waves.
    (D) echoes.

15. To get full value for your energy dollars, first arrange for an energy audit of your home. An audit will reveal such things as energy-sapping drafts, insufficient insulation, improper weatherstripping, and a need for storm windows and doors.

    Installing storm windows may be energy-saving but should be preceded by

    (A) an energy audit.
    (B) storm doors.
    (C) insulation.
    (D) proper weatherstripping.

MATHEMATICS KNOWLEDGE

> **Directions:** This is a test of your ability to solve general mathematical problems. Each problem is followed by four answer choices. Select the correct response from the choices given. Then mark the space on your answer form that has the same number and letter as your choice. Use scratch paper to do any figuring that you wish.

SAMPLE PROBLEM

1. If $x + 8 = 9$, then x is equal to

    (A) 0
    (B) 1
    (C) −1
    (D) $\dfrac{9}{8}$

The correct answer is 1, so B is the correct response.

Your score on this test will be based on the number of questions you answer correctly. You should try to answer every question. Do not spend too much time on any one question.

The actual test will say:
Do not turn this page until told to do so.

Mathematics Knowledge

Time —24 minutes
25 Questions

1. What is 4% of 0.0375?

   (A) 0.0015
   (B) 0.9375
   (C) 0.0775
   (D) 0.15

2. What number multiplied by $\frac{2}{3}$ will give a product of 1?

   (A) $-\frac{2}{3}$

   (B) $-\frac{3}{2}$

   (C) $\frac{3}{2}$

   (D) $\frac{4}{6}$

3. What is the value of the expression $x^2 - 5xy + 2y$ if $x = 3$ and $y = -2$?

   (A) −25
   (B) −27
   (C) 32
   (D) 35

4. Solve the following inequality: $x - 3 < 14$

   (A) $x < 11$
   (B) $x < 17$
   (C) $x = 11$
   (D) $x > 17$

5. Multiply $7a^3b^2c$ by $3a^2b^4c^2$.

   (A) $10a^5b^6c^3$
   (B) $21a^5b^6c^2$
   (C) $21a^6b^8c^2$
   (D) $21a^5b^6c^3$

6. A floor is made up of hexagonal tiles, some of which are black and some of which are white. Every black tile is completely surrounded by white tiles. How many white tiles are there around each black tile?

    (A) 4
    (B) 5
    (C) 6
    (D) 8

7. The value of $8°$ is

    (A) 8
    (B) 0
    (C) 1
    (D) $\dfrac{1}{8}$

8. If $2x - 3 = 37$, what is the value of x?

    (A) 17
    (B) 38
    (C) 20
    (D) 80

9. An audience consists of M people. $\dfrac{2}{3}$ of the audience are adults. Of the adults, $\dfrac{1}{2}$ are males. How many adult males are in the audience?

    (A) $\dfrac{1}{6}M$

    (B) $M - \dfrac{2}{3} - \dfrac{1}{2}$

    (C) $\dfrac{1}{3}M$

    (D) $M - \dfrac{1}{3}$

10. What is the value of $(0.2)^3$?

    (A) 0.008
    (B) 0.8
    (C) 0.006
    (D) 0.6

11. If $x^2 + x = 6$, what is the value of x?

    (A) 6 or –1
    (B) 1 or –6
    (C) 2 or –3
    (D) 3 or –2

12. What is the number of square inches in the area of a circle whose diameter is 28 inches? (Use $\frac{22}{7}$ for the value of π.)

(A) 616
(B) 88
(C) 44
(D) 1,232

13. The expression $\frac{x^2 + 2x - 3}{x + 3}$ cannot be evaluated if x has a value of

(A) 0
(B) −1
(C) 3
(D) −3

14. If $\sqrt{x + 11} = 9$, what is the value of x?

(A) −2
(B) −8
(C) 70
(D) 7

15. The points $A(2,7)$ and $B(5,11)$ are plotted on coordinate graph paper. What is the distance from A to B?

(A) 7
(B) 5
(C) 25
(D) $\sqrt{14}$

16. Solve the following equation for y: $ay - bx = 2$

(A) $\dfrac{bx + 2}{a}$

(B) $2 + bx - a$

(C) $\dfrac{2}{a - bx}$

(D) $\dfrac{2}{a} - bx$

17. For a special mission, a man is to be chosen at random from among three infantrymen, two artillerymen, and five armored corpsmen. What is the probability that an infantryman will be chosen?

(A) $\dfrac{3}{10}$

(B) $\dfrac{1}{10}$

(C) $\dfrac{1}{3}$

(D) $\dfrac{3}{7}$

18. A cylindrical post has a cross section that is a circle with a radius of 3 inches. A piece of cord can be wound around it exactly seven times. How long is the piece of cord? (Use $\dfrac{22}{7}$ as the value of π.)

(A) 66 inches.
(B) 42 inches.
(C) 198 inches.
(D) 132 inches.

19. A naval task force is to be made up of a destroyer, a supply ship, and a submarine. If four destroyers, two supply ships, and three submarines are available from which to choose, how many different combinations are possible for the task force?

(A) 9
(B) 24
(C) 8
(D) 12

20. The basis of a cylindrical can is a circle whose diameter is 2 inches. Its height is 7 inches. How many cubic inches are there in the volume of the can? (Use $\dfrac{22}{7}$ for the value of π.)

(A) $12\dfrac{4}{7}$
(B) 22
(C) 44
(D) 88

21. A rectangular vegetable garden 16 yards long and 4 yards wide is completely enclosed by a fence. To reduce the amount of fencing used, the owner replaced the garden with a square one having the same area. How many yards of fencing did he save?

    (A) 4
    (B) 6
    (C) 8
    (D) 16

22. The value of $\sqrt{164}$ to the nearest integer is

    (A) 18
    (B) 108
    (C) 42
    (D) 13

23. What is the maximum number of boxes, each measuring 3 inches by 4 inches by 5 inches, that can be packed into a storage space measuring 1 foot by 2 feet by 2 feet, 1 inch?

    (A) 120
    (B) 60
    (C) 15
    (D) 48

24. A circle passes through the four vertices of a rectangle that is 8 feet long and 6 feet wide. How many feet are there in the radius of the circle?

    (A) 14
    (B) $2\frac{1}{2}$
    (C) 10
    (D) 5

25. There are 12 liters of a mixture of acetone in alcohol that is $33\frac{1}{3}\%$ acetone. How many liters of alcohol must be added to the mixture to reduce it to a mixture containing 25% acetone?

    (A) 1
    (B) 2
    (C) 4
    (D) 6

ANSWER KEYS AND ANSWER EXPLANATIONS

Arithmetic Reasoning

Answer Key

1. **B**	6. **C**	11. **D**	16. **D**	21. **C**	26. **C**
2. **C**	7. **D**	12. **C**	17. **A**	22. **A**	27. **A**
3. **B**	8. **D**	13. **A**	18. **C**	23. **B**	28. **A**
4. **B**	9. **A**	14. **D**	19. **B**	24. **B**	29. **D**
5. **D**	10. **B**	15. **B**	20. **D**	25. **B**	30. **B**

Answer Explanations

1. **(B)** The number of men in the company divided by the number in each platoon gives the number of platoons.

    $$132 \div 11 = 12$$

    12 noncommissioned officers are needed, one for each position.

2. **(C)** Find the total of all the amounts withheld.

    $$\$27.75 + \$5.65 + \$9.29 + \$3.58 = \$46.27$$

    Net pay is the salary for the week minus the total of all the withholdings.

    Net pay = $350.00 − $46.27

            = $303.73

3. **(B)** The average is the sum of the high and low temperatures divided by 2.

    $$\text{Average} = \frac{-4° + 16°}{2} = \frac{12°}{2} = 6°$$

4. **(B)** If $\frac{1}{4}$ inch represents 1 foot, then $\frac{3}{4}$ inch will represent 3 feet.

    $\frac{1}{2}$ foot will be represented by one-half of $\frac{1}{4}$ inch, or $\frac{1}{8}$ inch. Thus,

    $3\frac{1}{2}$ feet will be represented by $\frac{3}{4}$ inch plus $\frac{1}{8}$ inch.

    $$\frac{3}{4} + \frac{1}{8} = \frac{6}{8} + \frac{1}{8} = \frac{7}{8}$$

5. **(D)** The rebate will be 15% (or 0.15) of the list price, $13,600.

    $$
    \begin{array}{r}
    \$13,620 \\
    \underline{\times \quad 0.15} \\
    681.00 \\
    \underline{1,362.00} \\
    \$2,043.00 \quad = \text{rebate}
    \end{array}
    $$

6. **(C)** Find the rise in price by subtracting the original price from the new price per gallon.

   Rise in price = $2.08 – $1.90 = $0.18

   The percent of increase is the rise in price divided by the original price.

   $$= \frac{0.18}{1.90} = \frac{18}{190} = \frac{2}{21} = 9.5\%$$

7. **(D)** The number of games won is 70% (or 0.70) of the number of games played, 40.

   Number of games won = 0.70(40) = 28.00 = 28

   The number of games lost is the total number played minus the number won.

   Number of games lost = 40 – 28 = 12

8. **(D)** The time of arrival is 2 hours and 55 minutes after the departure time of 3:50 P.M. By 4:00 P.M., the flight has taken 10 minutes of the total flight time of 2 hours and 55 minutes. 2 hours and 45 minutes remain, and 2 hours and 45 minutes after 4:00 P.M. is 6:45 P.M.

9. **(A)** There are 16 ounces in 1 pound. Therefore, 4 of the 4-ounce candy bars will make 1 pound. A 3-pound package will hold 3 times 4 or 12 bars.

10. **(B)** Find the relationship between each pair of successive numbers in the series. It is helpful to change $3\frac{1}{2}$ to $3\frac{1}{6}$ in order to see the relationships.

    For $\left(2\frac{5}{6}, 3\frac{1}{2}\right)$: $3\frac{1}{2} - 2\frac{5}{6} = 3\frac{3}{6} - 2\frac{5}{6} = \frac{4}{6}$

    For $\left(3\frac{1}{2}, 4\frac{1}{6}\right)$: $4\frac{1}{6} - 3\frac{1}{2} = 4\frac{1}{6} - 3\frac{3}{6} = \frac{4}{6}$

    For $\left(4\frac{1}{6}, 4\frac{5}{6}\right)$: $4\frac{5}{6} - 4\frac{1}{6} = \frac{4}{6}$

    Each term of the series is obtained by adding $\frac{4}{6}$ to the preceding term. The fifth term is

    $$4\frac{5}{6} + \frac{4}{6} = 4\frac{9}{6}$$
    $$= 4 + \frac{6}{6} + \frac{3}{6}$$
    $$= 4 + 1 + \frac{1}{2}$$
    $$= 5\frac{1}{2}$$

11. **(D)** First add the prices of the 3 items ordered to get the cost of the meal before the tax.

$10.50 + $1.50 + $.50 = $12.50

The tax is 6% (or 0.06) of the cost of the meal.

0.06 × $12.50 = $.7500 = $.75

12. **(C)** There are 4 quarts in 1 gallon. A 55-gallon drum holds 4 × 55 quarts.

$$4 \times 455 \text{ quarts} = 220 \text{ quarts}$$

If each can holds 2 quarts, the number of cans filled is 220 divided by 2.

$$220 + 2 = 110 \text{ cans}$$

13. **(A)** The number of minutes required to finish 1 spindle is the number of minutes, 45, taken for all 9 spindles, divided by their number, 9.

$$45 \div 9 = 5 \text{ minutes per spindle}$$

The number of minutes to finish 96 spindles will be 96 times as much.

$$5 \times 96 = 480 \text{ minutes}$$

There are 60 minutes in 1 hour. Divide the number of minutes by 60 to convert their number to hours.

$$480 \div 60 = 8 \text{ hours}$$

14. **(D)** The perimeter, 40 feet, is the sum of the lengths of all three sides. The sum of the lengths of the two equal sides is the difference between the perimeter and the length of the third side.

Sum of lengths of 2 equal sides

$$= 40 \text{ feet} - 13 \text{ feet, 2 inches}$$
$$= 39 \text{ feet, 12 inches} - 13 \text{ feet, 2 inches}$$
$$= 26 \text{ feet, 10 inches}$$

The length of one side is obtained by dividing the sum by 2.

Length of one equal side

$$= \frac{26 \text{ feet, 10 inches}}{2}$$
$$= 13 \text{ feet, 5 inches}$$

15. **(B)** Since 3 feet = 1 yard, convert the length and width to yards by dividing their dimensions in feet by 3.

$$\text{Width} = \frac{21}{3} = 7 \text{ yards}$$

$$\text{Length} = \frac{39}{3} = 13 \text{ yards}$$

The area of a rectangle is the product of its length and width.

Area = 7 × 13 = 91 square yards

The cost for the entire lawn is obtained by multiplying the area in square yards by the cost per square yard.

$$91 \times \$.40 = \$36.40$$

16. **(D)** Find the number of miles traveled by multiplying the rate, 48 m.p.h., by the time, 7 hours.

$$48 \times 7 = 336 \text{ miles}$$

The number of gallons of gas used is the number of miles driven divided by the number of miles per gallon.

$$\frac{326}{21} = \frac{112}{7} = 16 \text{ gallons}$$

17. **(A)** If the profits are shared in the ratio 5:4, one partner gets $\frac{5}{9}$ of the profits and the other gets $\frac{4}{9}$. Note that $\frac{5}{9} + \frac{4}{9} = 1$, the whole profit.

The larger share is $\frac{5}{9}$ of the profit, $63,000.

$$\frac{5}{9} \times \frac{\$63,000}{1} = \frac{5}{1} \times \frac{\$7,000}{1}$$
$$= \$35,000$$

18. **(C)** Consider the original price as 100%. Then the price after an increase of 4% is 104%. To find the original price, divide the price after the increase, $17.16, by 104% (or 1.04).

$$
\begin{array}{r}
\$\ \ 16.50 = \text{original price} \\
104\overline{)1716.00} \\
\underline{104} \\
676 \\
\underline{624} \\
520 \\
520 \\
\end{array}
$$

19. **(B)** 5 workers making 6 garments each = 30 garments per day
3 workers making 4 garments each = 12 garments per day

$\frac{1}{9}$ workers making 12 garments = $\frac{12}{54}$ garments per day

Add the number of workers and the number of garments per day.
9 workers make 54 garments per day
To find the average number of garments per worker per day, divide the number of garments per day by the number of workers.

$$\frac{54}{9} = 6 \text{ garments per worker per day}$$

20. **(D)** The distance traveled by driving at 45 m.p.h. for 2 hours is 2 × 45, or 90 miles.
The remainder of the 255 mile trip is 255 – 90, or 165 miles.

To finish the trip in 5 hours, the man has 5 – 2, or 3, hours still to drive. To find the rate of travel for a distance of 165 miles driven in 3 hours, divide the distance by the time.

$$\frac{165}{3} = 55 \text{ miles per hour}$$

21. **(C)** Cost of masonry materials and labor = $\frac{1}{10} \times$ \$300,000 = \$30,000

Cost of lumber and carpentry = $\frac{1}{3} \times$ \$300,000 = \$100,000

Cost of plumbing and heating = $\frac{1}{5} \times$ \$300,000 = \$60,000

Cost of electrcial and lighting work = $\frac{1}{6} \times$ \$300,000 = \$50,000

Total costs \$240,000

Profit = total bid, \$300,000, minus total costs.

Profit = \$300,000 – \$240,000 = \$60,000

22. **(A)** The first discount of 20% means that a customer actually pays 80% (or $\frac{4}{5}$) of the list price. The second successive discount of 30% means that a customer actually pays 70% (or $\frac{3}{10}$) of the price determined after the first discount.

The price the customer actually pays is the list price multiplied by the portions determined from each discount.

$$\overset{\overset{13}{\cancel{65}}}{\cancel{\$325}}_{1} \times \frac{\overset{2}{\cancel{4}}}{\cancel{5}_{1}} \times \frac{7}{\cancel{10}_{\cancel{5}_{1}}} = \frac{26 \times 7}{1} = \$182$$

23. **(B)** At 2 quarts for \$1.99, each quart costs

$$\frac{\$1.99}{2} = \$.99\frac{1}{2}$$

At 6 quarts for \$5.43, each quart costs

$$\frac{\$5.43}{6} = \$.90\frac{1}{2}$$

The saving per quart is

$$\$.99\frac{1}{2} - \$.90\frac{1}{2} = \$.09$$

24. **(B)** For the regular 40 hours, the worker earns $7.20 × 40 = $288.00. If the regular wage is $7.20 per hour, then overtime paid at time and

    one half is $7.20 × $1\frac{1}{2}$ or $7.20 × $\frac{3}{2}$.

$$\overset{3.60}{\cancel{\$7.20}} \times \frac{3}{\underset{1}{\cancel{2}}} = \frac{\$10.80}{1} = \$10.80 \text{ per hour}$$

    If 43 hours are worked, 3 hours are overtime.

    Overtime pay = $10.80 × 3 = $32.40.

    Add the regular pay for 40 hours to the overtime pay to find the total amount earned for the week.

    $288.00 + $32.40 = $320.40 = total pay.

25. **(B)** The ratio of the heights of the two trees will be the same as the ratio of the lengths of their shadows.

    The ratio of the length of the shadow of the second tree to the length

    of the shadow of the first tree is $\frac{6}{8}$ or $\frac{3}{4}$.

    Thus, the height of the second tree is $\frac{3}{4}$ of the height of the

    36 foot tree.

$$\frac{3}{\underset{1}{\cancel{4}}} \times \frac{\overset{9}{\cancel{36}}}{1} = \frac{27}{1} = 27 \text{ feet}$$

26. **(C)** Add the portion spent on newspaper ads and radio commercials.

$$\frac{3}{5} + \frac{1}{3} = \frac{9}{15} + \frac{5}{15} = \frac{14}{15}$$

    The portion left for TV commercials is the entire budget, 1, minus the

    portion spent on newspaper and radio, $\frac{14}{15}$.

$$1 - \frac{14}{5} = \frac{15}{15} - \frac{14}{15} = \frac{1}{15}$$

27. **(A)** A half-hour is 30 minutes.

    The portion of 180 minutes that is represented by 30 minutes is

    $\frac{30}{180}$ or $\frac{1}{6}$. As a percent, $\frac{1}{6}$ is $16\frac{2}{3}$%

28. **(A)** 5 pounds of cashew nuts at $1.80 per pound is worth

    5 × $1.80 = $9.00.

    4 pounds of peanuts at $1.62 per pound is worth 4 × $1.62 = $6.48.

The total value of the 9-pound mixture is $9.00 + $6.48 = $15.48. The value of the mixture per pound is found by dividing the total value by the number of pounds.

$$\frac{\$15.48}{9} = \$1.72$$

29. **(D)** If there are four pieces of wallpaper, each 7 feet, 8 inches long, the total length of the wallpaper is 4 × 7 feet, 8 inches, or 28 feet, 32 inches.

Since 12 inches = 1 foot, 32 inches = 2 feet, 8 inches. Thus, 28 feet, 32 inches = 30 feet, 8 inches.

30. **(B)** From 9:00 P.M. to 5:00 A.M. is a tour of duty of 8 hours.

Since 60 minutes = 1 hour, when the watchman checks in every

40 minutes he checks in every $\frac{40}{60}$, or every $\frac{2}{3}$, of an hour

$$\frac{8}{1} \div \frac{2}{3} = \frac{\overset{4}{\cancel{8}}}{1} \times \frac{3}{\underset{1}{\cancel{2}}} = \frac{12}{1} = 12$$

The watchman must check in once at the beginning of each of the twelve 40-minute periods, or 12 times. But he must also check in at the end of the last period. Thus, he checks in 12 + 1, or 13, times.

Word Knowledge

Answer Key

1. **D**	6. **A**	11. **D**	16. **C**	21. **A**	26. **A**	31. **C**
2. **B**	7. **D**	12. **C**	17. **B**	22. **B**	27. **B**	32. **A**
3. **A**	8. **C**	13. **A**	18. **C**	23. **C**	28. **B**	33. **B**
4. **B**	9. **B**	14. **A**	19. **D**	24. **D**	29. **C**	34. **A**
5. **C**	10. **B**	15. **D**	20. **C**	25. **D**	30. **D**	35. **D**

Answer Explanations

1. **(D)** **Pinnacle**, like *summit*, means the highest point.
2. **(B)** **Brawl**, like *fight*, means a noisy quarrel.
3. **(A)** A **pauper** is an extremely poor person.
4. **(B)** **Punctual**, like *prompt*, means arriving or doing something exactly at the appointed time.
5. **(C)** **Segment**, like *part*, means a portion.

6. **(A) Revere**, like *esteem*, means to regard someone or something with great respect.
7. **(D) Brevity**, like *conciseness*, means of short duration.
8. **(C) Illogical**, like *fallacious*, means senseless.
9. **(B) Excerpt**, like *extract*, means something picked out from the total.
10. **(B) Sheen**, like *luster*, means shininess or brightness.
11. **(D) Divulge**, like *tell*, means to disclose or make known.
12. **(C) Cite**, like *specify*, means to bring information forward as proof.
13. **(A) Allay**, like *ease*, means to relieve.
14. **(A) Vitality**, like *liveliness*, means vigor or energy.
15. **(D) Defer**, like *delay*, means to postpone someone from doing something.
16. **(C) Deplore**, like *regret*, means to feel or express disapproval.
17. **(B) Concur**, like *agree*, means to have the same opinion.
18. **(C) Refute**, like *disprove*, means to prove an argument or statement wrong.
19. **(D) Copious**, like *large*, means an ample or plentiful supply.
20. **(C) Credulous**, like *gullible*, means able to believe too readily.
21. **(A) Random**, like *haphazard*, means having no clear pattern.
22. **(B) Salient**, like *conspicuous*, means prominent or pronounced.
23. **(C) Tangible**, like *concrete*, means capable of being touched.
24. **(D) Residue**, like *remainder*, means what is left after the removal of something.
25. **(D) Catastrophe**, like *disaster*, means a great calamity or tragedy.
26. **(A) Diagnosis**, like *analysis*, means the opinion derived from examining the nature of something.
27. **(B) Quandary**, like *predicament*, means a dilemma or state of uncertainty.
28. **(B) Stilted**, like *formal*, means stiffly dignified.
29. **(C) Encroach**, like *trespass*, means to intrude.
30. **(D) Deter**, like *prevent*, means to restrain someone from doing something.
31. **(C) Falter**, like *hesitate*, means to waver.
32. **(A) Meager**, like *sparse*, means skimpy or scant.
33. **(B) Stifle**, like *suppress*, means to restrict.
34. **(A) Dearth**, like *lack*, means scarcity.
35. **(D) Accord**, like *harmony*, means agreement.

Paragraph Comprehension

Answer Key

1. **D**	6. **D**	11. **C**
2. **C**	7. **B**	12. **A**
3. **B**	8. **C**	13. **D**
4. **B**	9. **A**	14. **B**
5. **D**	10. **B**	15. **A**

Answer Explanations

1. **(D)** The main idea is stated in the first sentence of the paragraph. All of the other sentences contribute to the main idea by describing the circumstances under which Columbus was able to save his own life.

2. **(C)** When you apply the "warranty of merchantability," i.e., that the product will do what it is supposed to do, you see that only one answer states a product (a toaster) and what it does (toasts).

3. **(B)** According to the passage, the settling of the American West took place after both coasts were joined by the completion of the railroad.

4. **(B)** The paragraph states that 61% of single female parents were in housing need and that single male parents experienced half that housing need. Half of 61% is approximately 30%.

5. **(D)** The embargo caused the price of crude oil to quadruple. This increase, in turn, caused oil-dependent countries to experience a recession. Answers A, B, and C are all incorrect details.

6. **(D)** The paragraph talks about the effect of voltage variations on sensitive equipment. It is logical to conclude that computers, which are also sensitive equipment, would be affected by voltage variation.

7. **(B)** Answer B, fundamental freedoms, summarizes all the rights listed in the paragraph.

8. **(C)** The fact that DNA is a nucleic acid is stated in the first sentence. Answers A, B, and D are all incorrect details.

9. **(A)** The paragraph states that 30% of trash being dumped can be recycled. Another way of stating that detail is to say that a *third* of what we dump could be recycled.

10. **(B)** According to the paragraph's definition of a referendum, submitting the constitution of the United States to the state conventions for approvals was a form of referendum.

11. **(C)** The paragraph states that unlike the other pollutants mentioned, formaldehyde can be smelled at high levels only. You can conclude that it cannot be smelled at lower levels.

12. **(A)** Sentence 2 states that bacterial pneumonia is a major precipitator (cause) of pneumonia deaths. Answers B, C, and D are all incorrect details.

13. **(D)** The key idea is found in the first sentence: the temperature of ocean water changes more slowly than the air; therefore, the oceans affect the world's climate.

14. **(B)** The purpose of the paragraph is to make a comparison between laser and incandescent light. The two are compared in one way, i.e., in terms of their different wavelengths.

15. **(A)** The main idea of the paragraph is that an energy audit should be done as a first step to saving energy dollars. The details that follow are some of the items an audit concentrates on. The question, however, asks you to identify what precedes, or comes before, the installation of an energy-saving device.

Mathematics Knowledge

Answer Key

1. **A**	6. **C**	11. **C**	16. **A**	21. **C**
2. **C**	7. **C**	12. **A**	17. **A**	22. **D**
3. **D**	8. **C**	13. **D**	18. **D**	23. **A**
4. **B**	9. **C**	14. **C**	19. **B**	24. **D**
5. **D**	10. **A**	15. **B**	20. **B**	25. **C**

Answer Explanations

1. **(A)** Multiply 0.0375 by 4% (or 0.04).
   $0.0375 \times 0.04 = 0.001500 = 0.0015$
   Note that the product has as many decimal places as there are in the multiplicand and multiplier combined, but the two final zeros may be dropped since they are to the right of the decimal point and at the end.

2. **(C)** If a number is multiplied by its reciprocal (also called its multiplicative inverse), the product is 1. The reciprocal of a fraction is found by inverting the fraction.

   The reciprocal of $\frac{2}{3}$ is $\frac{3}{2}$, that is,

   $$\frac{2}{3} \times \frac{3}{2} = 1$$

3. **(D)** Substitute 3 for x and -2 for y in the expression $x^2 - 5xy + 2y$.
$$(3)^2 - 5(3)(-2) + 2(-2)$$
$$9 - 15(-2) - 4$$
$$9 + 30 - 4$$
$$35$$

4. **(B)** $x - 3 < 14$ is an inequality that states that x minus 3 is less than 14. To solve the inequality, add 3 to both sides of it.
$$x - 3 + 3 < 14 + 3$$
$$x < 17$$
The result says that the inequality is true for any value of x less than 17. Try it for some value of x less than 17, for example, $x = 10$.
$$10 - 3 < 14$$
$$7 < 14 \text{ is a true statement}$$

5. **(D)** To multiply $7a^3b^2c$ by $3a^2b^4c^2$, first multiply the numerical coefficients, 7 and 3.
$$7 \times 3 = 21$$
Powers of the same base, such as a^3 and a^2, are multiplied by adding their exponents; thus, $a^3 \times a^2 = a^5$.
$$(a^3b^2c) \times (a^2b^4c^2) = a^5b^6c^3$$
Note that c should be regarded as c^1 when adding exponents.
The combined result for $(7a^3b^2c) \times (3a^2b^4c^2) = 21\,a^5b^6c^3$

6. **(C)**

A hexagon has six sides. Each of the six sides of the black tile must touch a side of a white tile, so there are six white tiles surrounding each black tile.

7. **(C)** x^0 is defined as always equal to 1, provided that x does not equal 0. Therefore $8^0 = 1$.

8. **(C)** The equation $2x - 3 = 37$ means that "twice a number minus 3 is equal to 37." To arrive at a value for x, we first eliminate -3 on the left side. This can be done by adding 3 to both sides of the equation, thus undoing the subtraction.
$$2x - 3 + 3 = 37 + 3$$
$$2x = 40$$

To eliminate the 2 that multiplies x, we undo the multiplication by dividing both sides of the equation by 2.

$$\frac{2x}{x} = \frac{40}{2}$$
$$x = 20$$

9. **(C)** If $\frac{2}{3}$ of M people are adults, then $\frac{2}{3} M$ represents the number of adults. If $\frac{1}{2}$ of $\frac{2}{3} M$ are males, then $\frac{1}{2} \times \frac{2}{3} M$ represents the number of adult males.

$$\frac{1}{\cancel{2}} \times \frac{\cancel{2}}{3} M = \frac{1}{3} M$$

10. **(A)** $(0.2)^3$ means $0.2 \times 0.2 \times 0.2$.
Multiply the first two numbers:
$$0.2 \times 0.2 \times 0.2 = 0.04 \times 0.2$$
Now multiply the remaining two numbers: $0.04 \times 0.2 = 0.008$.

11. **(C)** Rewrite the equation as $x^3 + x - 6 = 0$. The left side of the equation can now be factored:
$$(x + 3)(x - 2) = 0$$
This result states that the product of two factors, $(x + 3)$ and $(x - 2)$, equals 0. But if the product of two factors equals 0, then either or both must equal 0:
$$x + 3 = 0 \text{ or } x - 2 = 0$$
Subtract 3 from both sides of the left equation to isolate x on one side, and add 2 to both sides of the right equation to accomplish the same result:

$$x + 3 - 3 = 0 \qquad\qquad x - 2 + 2 = 0 + 2$$
$$x = -3 \qquad\qquad\qquad x = 2$$

12. **(A)** The area of a circle is πr^2 where $\pi = \frac{22}{7}$ and r represents the length of the radius. A radius is one-half the length of a diameter. Therefore, if the diameter is 28 inches, the radius of the circle is 14 inches.

$$\text{Area of circle} = \frac{22}{7} \times \frac{14}{1} \times \frac{14}{1}$$
$$= \frac{22}{\cancel{7}} \times \frac{\cancel{14}}{1} \times \frac{14}{1}$$
$$= \frac{44}{1} \times \frac{14}{1}$$
$$= \frac{616}{1}$$
$$= 616 \text{ square inches}$$

13. **(D)** If $x = -3$, the denominator of

$$\frac{x^2 + 2x - 3}{x + 3}$$

will equal 0. Division of 0 is undefined, so x cannot equal -3.

14. **(C)** The given equation means that a number is added to 11 and then the square root of the result is taken and it equals 9. The square root sign (or radical sign) can be removed by squaring both sides of the equation.

$$\left(\sqrt{x+11}\right)^2 = 9^2$$

$$x + 11 = 81$$

Isolate x on one side of the equation by subtracting 11 from both sides.

$$x + 11 - 11 = 81 - 11$$

$$x = 70$$

15. **(B)**

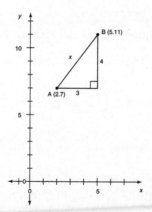

Plot the points. When a pair of numbers is given as the coordinates of a point, the first number is the x-value (or distance right or left from the origin). The second number is the y-value (or distance up or down). Form the right triangle shown in the diagram. The horizontal leg has a length of $5 - 2$, or 3; the vertical leg has a length of $11 - 7$, or 4. The distance A to B is the hypotenuse of the right triangle. Let $x = AB$. By the Pythagorean theorem, the square of the length of the hypotenuse equals the sum of the squares of the lengths of the legs.

$$x^2 = 3^2 + 4^2$$

$$x^2 = 9 + 16$$

$$x^2 = 25$$

The equation $x^2 = 25$ means that x times x equals 25. Therefore, $x = 5$.

16. **(A)** The given equation $ay - bx = 2$ is to be solved for y. Isolate the y-term on one side of the equation by adding bx to both sides.

$$ay - bx + bx = 2 + bx$$
$$ay = 2 + bx$$

y is multiplied by a. To obtain y alone, undo the multiplication by dividing both sides of the equation by a.

$$\frac{ay}{a} = \frac{2 + bx}{a}$$
$$y = \frac{2 + bx}{a}$$

17. **(A)** The probability of an event occurring is the number of favorable outcomes divided by the total possible number of outcomes. Since there are three possible infantrymen to choose, there are three favorable outcomes for choosing an infantryman. Since a choice may be made from among three infantrymen, two artillerymen, and five armored corpsmen, there are $3 + 2 + 5$, or 10, possible outcomes. The probability of choosing an infantryman is $\frac{3}{10}$.

18. **(D)** A length of cord that will wind around once is equal to the circumference of the circle whose radius is 3 inches. The circumference of a circle equals $2\pi r$ where $\pi = \frac{22}{7}$ and r is the radius.

$$\text{Circumference} = \frac{2}{1} \times \frac{22}{7} \times \frac{3}{1} = \frac{132}{7} \text{ inches}$$

If the cord can be wound around the post seven times, its length is seven times the length of one circumference.

$$\text{Length of cord} = \frac{132}{\overset{1}{\underset{1}{7}}} \times \frac{\overset{1}{7}}{1} = 132 \text{ inches}$$

19. **(B)** There are four possible choices for the destroyer. Each of these choices may be coupled with any of the two choices for the supply ship. Each such destroyer-supply ship combination may in turn be coupled with any of the three possible choices for the submarine. Thus, there are $4 \times 2 \times 3$, or 24, different combinations possible.

20. **(B)** The volume of a cylinder is equal to the product of its height and the area of its base. The base is a circle. The area of a circle is πr^2, where $\pi = \frac{22}{7}$ and r is the radius. Since the diameter is 2 inches, the radius (which is one-half the diameter) is 1 inch.

$$\text{Area of circular base} = \frac{22}{7} \times \frac{1}{1} \times \frac{1}{1} = \frac{22}{7} \text{ square inches}$$

The height is 7 inches.

$$\text{Volume} = \frac{22}{7} \times \frac{7}{1} = 22 \text{ cubic inches}$$

21. **(C)**

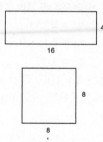

The area of the rectangular garden is equal to the product of its length and width.

Area of rectangle = 16 × 4 = 64 square yards. In order for the square to have the same area, 64 square yards, its sides must each be 8 yards long, since 8 × 8 = 64 square yards.

The fence around the rectangular garden has a length of 16 + 4 + 16 + 4, or 40, yards. The fence around the square garden has a length of 4 × 8, or 32, yards. The saving in fencing is 40 – 32, or 8, yards.

22. **(D)** $\sqrt{164}$ stands for the square root of 164, or the number that when multiplied by itself equals 164. We know that 12 × 12 = 144 and that 13 × 13 = 169. Therefore, $\sqrt{164}$ lies between 12 and 13. It is nearer to 13 since 164 is nearer to 169 than it is to 144.

23. **(A)** The storage space measurements of 1 foot by 2 feet by 2 feet, 1 inch can be converted to inches as 12 inches by 24 inches by 25 inches. Boxes measuring 3 inches by 4 inches by 5 inches can be stacked so that four of the 3-inch sides make up the 12-inch storage dimension, six of the 4-inch sides fill the 24-inch storage dimension, and five of the 5-inch sides fill the 25-inch storage dimension.

There will be 4 × 6 × 5, or 120, boxes packed into the storage space.

24. **(D)**

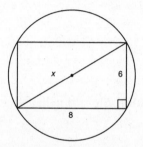

If the circle passes through all four vertices of the rectangle, its diameter will be a diagonal of the rectangle. Since a rectangle's angles are right angles, the diagonal forms a right triangle with two sides of the rectangle. Let x = the length of the diagonal. By the Pythagorean theorem, in a right triangle the square of the length of the hypotenuse is equal to the sum of the squares of the legs.

$$x^2 = 8^2 + 6^2$$
$$x^2 = 64 + 36$$
$$x^2 = 100$$

$x^2 = 100$ means that x times $x = 100$. Therefore $x = 10$ feet. But 10 is a diameter of the circle. A radius of a circle is one-half the diameter. Hence, the radius is 5 feet.

25. **(C)** If the original mixture is $33\frac{1}{3}\%$ (or $\frac{1}{3}$) acetone, then $\frac{1}{3}$ of the mixture of 12 liters, or 4 liters, is acetone. The fraction $\frac{4}{12}$ represents the ratio of acetone to total mixture. If the total mixture is increased by x liters, the ratio of acetone to total mixture becomes $\frac{4}{(12 + x)}$.

This is to be equal to 25% (or $\frac{1}{4}$).

$$\frac{4}{12 + x} = \frac{1}{4}$$

To undo the divisions on both sides of the equation, multiply both sides by 4 and also by $12 + x$.

$$\frac{4}{\overset{1}{\underset{1}{12+x}}} \times \frac{\overset{1}{4(12+x)}}{1} = \frac{1}{\underset{1}{4}} \times \frac{\overset{1}{4(12+x)}}{1}$$
$$16 = 12 + x$$

To isolate x on one side of the equation, subtract 12 from both sides.

$$16 - 12 = 12 + x - 12$$
$$4 = x$$

Mathematics Review: Arithmetic Reasoning/ Mathematics Knowledge

4

The material in this section is a review of basic terms and problem-solving methods taught in high school mathematics courses. You will find samples of math problems most often asked on the ASVAB exam, with an explanation of how to solve each. (You may find that you know one or several other ways for working out a problem.) Before you study the topics in this section, look over the following suggestions for how to do good work in mathematics.

A. Develop the habit of careful reading. As you read a problem, look for answers to these questions:

1. What is given? (the facts in the problem)
2. What is unknown? (the answer to be found)
3. What do I use? (the best method or steps for solving the problem)

B. Pay careful attention to each word, number, and symbol. In mathematics, directions and problems are compressed into very few words. Sometimes, the principal direction is expressed as a symbol.

EXAMPLE

What is the value of 6 – 3? (The minus sign tells you to subtract.)

C. The reading of mathematics also requires close attention to relationships. How does one fact or idea lead to another? Which facts or ideas are connected? Take the following example:

Mr. Brown and his partner worked for 5 hours on Monday. For his wages, Mr. Brown received $10 an hour. How much did he earn on Monday?

To solve this problem, you can ignore the day of the week and the fact that there was a partner present. Just multiply the number of hours Mr. Brown worked (5) by the amount he received each hour ($10).

$$5 \times \$10 = \$50 \text{ (Mr. Brown's earnings)}$$

LAWS AND OPERATIONS

The numbers 5 and 10 are *whole numbers*. So are 0, 1, 2, 3, 4, and so on. (By contrast, $\frac{3}{4}$ is a fraction, and $6\frac{3}{4}$ is a mixed number—a whole number plus a fraction.) In mathematics, when we combine two or more whole numbers, we perform an *operation* on them. There are two such basic operations: *addition* and *multiplication*. In addition, we combine individual numbers (23 + 4) to find an answer called the *sum*. In multiplication, we combine groups of numbers for an answer called the *product*. For example, three times four (3 × 4) means three groups of four; their product is 12.

Subtraction and *division* are really *opposite*, or *inverse*, *operations* of addition and multiplication. Subtraction is performed to undo addition, and division must be performed to undo multiplication. The answer in subtraction is called the *remainder*; in division, it is called the *quotient*. Consider these examples.

BASIC OPERATIONS	INVERSE OPERATIONS
Addition	Subtraction
23 + 4 = 27 (sum)	27 – 4 = 23 (remainder)
Multiplication	Division
4 × 3 = 12 (product)	12 ÷ 4 = 3 (quotient)

Use of Parentheses: Order of Operations

Sometimes, parentheses are used in a math problem to indicate which operation must be done first. For example, in the problem 3 + (5 × 2), you would first multiply 5 × 2, then add 3. Look at the different results you get when you work without the parentheses, and then with them.

$$
\begin{array}{ll}
3 + 5 \times 2 = & 3 + (5 \times 2) = \\
8 \times 2 = 16 & 3 + 10 \quad = 13
\end{array}
$$

Even though we read a problem from left to right, there is an order in which we must perform arithmetic operations:

1. First, do all work within parentheses.
2. Next, do all multiplications and divisions. Do these in left-to-right order.
3. Finally, do additions and subtractions.

In the following example, notice the order in which arithmetic operations are carried out.

$$(10 - 6) \times 5 - (15 \div 5) = \quad \text{(first do operations inside the parentheses)}$$
$$4 \times 5 - \quad 3 = \quad \text{(next do multiplication)}$$
$$20 - \quad 3 = 17 \quad \text{(then do subtraction)}$$

Rounding Off Numbers

Occasionally, you are asked to *round off* answers to the nearest ten, hundred, or thousand, etc. We do this in everyday speech when we say that a pair of shoes priced at $37.50 cost "about $40." Rounding off, estimating, and approximating all mean the same thing. You make a guess as to the approximate value. There is a rule for rounding off numbers. First, look at these labels and the way that the number 195,426,874 is written below them.

millions	thousands	hundreds
1 9 5,	4 2 6,	8 7 4

If you are asked to round off 195,426,874 to the nearest hundred, you would first find the number in the highest hundred place (8), and then look at the number to its right (7). If the number to the right is 5, 6, 7, 8, or 9, you round off the hundreds to the next higher number—(9) and replace the 74 with 00. It's the same as saying that 874 is about 900. Your answer would be 195,426,900.

Suppose your original amount was 195,426,834. In that case, when you check the number to the right of 8, you would find 3. Since 3 is below 5, you would leave the 8 and replace the 34 with 00. Your answer would be 195,426,800.

Prime and Composite Numbers

Whole numbers are sometimes classified as either *prime* or *composite numbers*. A prime number is one that can be divided evenly by itself and 1—but not by any other whole number.

EXAMPLES

2, 3, 5, 7, 11, 13

A composite number is one that can be divided evenly by itself, by 1, and by at least one other whole number.

EXAMPLES

4, 6, 8, 10, 15, 27

Factors

When a whole number has other divisors besides 1 and itself, we call these other divisors *factors*. In other words, factors are numbers that we multiply to form a composite (whole) number.

Sometimes you will be asked "to factor" a number—for example, 6. The factors of 6 are the numbers that you multiply to produce 6. Since 3 times 2 equals 6, the factors of 6 are 3 and 2.

Exponents

There is a short way of writing *repeated factors* in multiplication. For example we may write 5×5 as 5^2. The small 2 written to the right and slightly above the 5 is called an *exponent*. It tells us that 5 is used twice as a factor. You can read 5^2 as either "5 to the second power," or more briefly, "5 squared." Note that 5^2 does not represent "5×2." The expression 2^3 means "2 to the third power," or "2 cubed," and represents $2 \times 2 \times 2$.

---

n Factorial

Don't confuse these expressions of repeated factors with the term *factorial*. When you see "6 factorial," for example, it means "find the product of every number between 1 and 6." Thus, 6 factorial means $6 \times 5 \times 4 \times 3 \times 2 \times 1$. (The symbol for 6 factorial is 6!)

Reciprocal

You may also be asked to find the *reciprocal* of a number. To find the reciprocal of 5, look for the number that you multiply by 5 to get 1. The easiest way to work this out is to divide 1 by 5. You can express the answer either as $\frac{1}{5}$ or as 0.2 (see the following sections on fractions and decimals). Remember that the product of a number and its reciprocal is always 1: the reciprocal of $\frac{1}{4}$ is 4; the reciprocal of $\frac{2}{4}$ is 2.

Series and Sequences

There is a popular type of question involving a *series* or *sequence* of numbers. You are given several numbers arranged in a pattern, and are asked to find the number that comes next. The way to solve this is to figure out the pattern. Try the following two examples:

A. 2, 4, 6, 8, ?
B. 3, 9, 4, 8, ?

Each number in sequence A is 2 higher than the number to its left. Thus, the missing term is 10. By testing the relationships between numbers in series B, you find the following pattern:

3 (+ 6) = 9	The first step is "add 6."
9 (− 5) = 4	The next step is "subtract 5."
4 (+ 4) = 8	The next step is "add 4."

To continue the pattern, the next step will have to be "subtract 3." Thus, the missing number is 5.

FRACTIONS

Many problems in arithmetic have to do with fractions. (Decimals and percents are other ways of writing fractions.) There are at least four ways to think about fractions.

1. A fraction is a part of a whole. The fraction $\frac{2}{3}$ means that something has been divided into 3 parts, and we are working with 2 of them. The number written above the fraction line (2) is the numerator, and the number below it (3) is called the denominator.

2. A fraction is the result of a multiplication. The fraction $\frac{3}{4}$ means 3 times $\frac{1}{4}$.

3. A fraction is an expression of division. Thus $\frac{2}{5}$ is the quotient (result) when 2 is divided by 5. This can also be written as $2 \div 5$.

4. A fraction is an expression of a ratio. A ratio is a comparison between two quantities. For example, the ratio of 6 inches to 1 foot is $\frac{6}{12}$, since there are 12 inches in a foot.

USING ARITHMETIC OPERATIONS WITH FRACTIONS

There are special rules and some shortcuts, too, for multiplying, dividing, adding, and subtracting fractions and mixed numbers. (A *mixed number* is one that is made up of a whole number and a fraction—for example, $3\frac{2}{7}$.)

Multiplying Fractions

The general rule for multiplying two or more fractions is to multiply the numerators by one another, and then multiply the denominators by one another.

EXAMPLE

$$\frac{1}{2} \times \frac{3}{4} \times \frac{5}{8} = \frac{15}{64} \quad \frac{\text{(numerators)}}{\text{(denominators)}}$$

Explanation: $1 \times 3 \times 5 = 15; 2 \times 4 \times 8 = 64$

Sometimes, the product you get when you multiply two fractions can be expressed in simpler terms. When you express a fraction in its *lowest terms,* you put it in a form in which the numerator and denominator no longer have a common factor.

EXAMPLE

Reduce $\frac{24}{36}$ to lowest terms.

Step 1. Find a number which is a factor of both 24 and 36. Both numbers can be divided by 4.

Step 2. Divide 24 and then 36 by 4.

$24 \div 4 = 6$

$36 \div 4 = 9$

Thus, $\frac{24}{36} = \frac{6}{9}$

Step 3. Check again. Is there a number which is a factor of both 6 and 9? Yes, both numbers can be divided by 3. Divide 6 and then 9 by 3.

$6 \div 3 = 2$

$9 \div 3 = 3$

Thus, $\frac{6}{9} = \frac{2}{3}$

Answer: $\frac{24}{36}$ can be reduced to its lowest terms, $\frac{2}{3}$

Changing Improper Fractions to Mixed Numbers

When the numerator of a fraction is larger than its denominator, it is called an *improper fraction.* An improper fraction can be changed to a mixed number.

EXAMPLE

Change $\frac{37}{5}$ to a mixed number.

Since a fraction is also an expression of division, $\frac{37}{5}$ means $37 \div 5$.

If 37 is divided by 5, the quotient is 7, and the remainder is 2. Thus,

$$\frac{37}{5} = 7\frac{2}{5}$$

Changing Mixed Numbers to Improper Fractions

In order to multiply or divide mixed numbers, it is necessary to change them into improper fractions.

EXAMPLE

Change $8\frac{3}{5}$ to an improper fraction.

Convert the whole number, 8, to fifths: $8 = \frac{40}{5}$. $\frac{40}{5}$ and $\frac{3}{5}$ is $\frac{43}{5}$, an improper fraction. A shortcut for achieving the change from a mixed number to an improper fraction is to multiply the whole part of the mixed number by the fraction's denominator, and then add the result to the original numerator. Thus, $8\frac{3}{5} = \frac{8 \times 5 + 3}{5} = \frac{43}{5}$.

Multiplying Mixed Numbers

When multiplying or dividing with a mixed number, change the mixed number to an improper fraction before working out the problem.

EXAMPLE

$$2\frac{2}{3} \times \frac{5}{7} =$$

$$\frac{8}{3} \times \frac{5}{7} = \frac{40}{21} = 1\frac{19}{21}$$

Cancellation

Cancellation is a shortcut you can use when multiplying (or dividing) fractions. Suppose you want to multiply $\frac{8}{9}$ times $\frac{3}{16}$. If you immediately multiply the numerators by each other, and the denominators by each other, you get an answer you have to reduce to lowest terms.

$$\frac{8}{9} \times \frac{3}{16} = \frac{24}{144} = \frac{1}{6}$$

An easier way to handle the problem is to see if there is any number you can divide evenly into both a numerator and a denominator of the original example. In this case, there is. You can divide 8 into both itself and 16.

Step 1. $\dfrac{\overset{1}{\cancel{8}}}{9} \times \dfrac{3}{\underset{2}{\cancel{16}}} =$

You can also divide 3 into the numerator 3 and the denominator 9. Solve the problem by multiplying the new numerators, and then the new denominators.

Step 1. $\dfrac{\overset{1}{\cancel{8}}}{\underset{3}{\cancel{9}}} \times \dfrac{\overset{1}{\cancel{3}}}{\underset{2}{\cancel{16}}} = \dfrac{1}{16}$

Dividing Fractions

Division of fractions looks similar to their multiplication, but there is an important extra step. Dividing something by 3 is the same as multiplying it by $\dfrac{1}{3}$. Therefore we can convert the division example $\dfrac{1}{2} \div \dfrac{3}{1}$ into the multiplication example $\dfrac{1}{2} \times \dfrac{1}{3}$.

To divide with fractions, always *invert* the second term, and change the division sign to a times sign. In other words, write the second term upside down and then treat the problem as a multiplication of fractions. This is also called multiplying the first fraction by the reciprocal of the second fraction. Note that in the example below, 3 can be written as $\dfrac{3}{1}$.

$$\dfrac{1}{2} \div 3 \quad = \dfrac{1}{2} \div \dfrac{3}{1} \quad = \dfrac{1}{2} \times \dfrac{1}{3} \quad = \dfrac{1}{6}$$

Adding and Subtracting Fractions

To add or subtract fractions, follow two basic rules:

✔ Add or subtract only those fractions that have the same denominator.
✔ Add or subtract only the numerators of the fractions. Keep the same denominator.

If two fractions you want to add or subtract do not have a *common denominator*, find a way to change them so that both denominators are the same. This is easy if one of the denominators divides evenly into the other. To add $\dfrac{5}{6}$ and $\dfrac{1}{12}$, you can work with the fact that 6 goes into 12 evenly. You can change the $\dfrac{5}{6}$ to $\dfrac{10}{12}$, a fraction with the same value.

Step 1. Write the fraction you have to change. Next to it, write the new denominator you want to use.

$$\dfrac{5}{6} = \dfrac{?}{12}$$

Step 2. To find the missing numerator: (a) divide the original denominator into the new denominator (6 into 12 = 2), then (b) multiply your answer by the original numerator (2 × 5 = 10). Your new fraction is $\frac{10}{12}$. By changing $\frac{5}{6}$ to $\frac{10}{12}$, you can now add it to $\frac{1}{12}$.

$$\frac{10}{12} + \frac{1}{12} = \frac{11}{12}$$

If you cannot divide one of the denominators into the other, then you have to find a number that both will go into. If you are working with three fractions, you have to find a number that all three denominators can divide evenly.

Suppose you are asked to add $\frac{1}{4}$, $\frac{1}{5}$, and $\frac{1}{6}$. One rule for finding a common denominator for several fractions is to take the largest denominator and start multiplying it by 2, 3, etc., until you find a number that the other denominators will also divide into evenly. In this case, 6 is the largest denominator. If you multiply 6 times 2, you get 12—a number that 5 does not divide evenly. You have to keep trying until you reach 60—the first product that all three denominators divide evenly. Thus,

$$\frac{1}{4} = \frac{15}{60}$$
$$\frac{1}{5} = \frac{12}{60}$$
$$+\frac{1}{6} = \frac{10}{60}$$

By adding the converted fractions, you find that $\frac{1}{4} + \frac{1}{5} + \frac{1}{6} = \frac{37}{60}$.

To add mixed numbers, follow these three steps:

Step 1. Add the whole numbers.

Step 2. Add the fractions. If the sum of these is an improper fraction, change the sum to a mixed number.

Step 3. Add the sum of the whole numbers to the sum of the fractions.

EXAMPLE

Step 1. $3\frac{2}{3} + 12\frac{2}{3}$

Step 2. $\frac{2}{3} + \frac{2}{3} = \frac{4}{3} = 1\frac{1}{3}$

Step 3. $15 + 1\frac{1}{3} = 16\frac{1}{3}$

In subtracting mixed numbers, you may have to "borrow" as you do in subtracting whole numbers. For example, if you want to subtract $6\frac{3}{4}$ from $9\frac{1}{4}$, you realize you cannot take $\frac{3}{4}$ from $\frac{1}{4}$. (Try to get \$.75 out of a quarter!) Thus, you borrow 1 from 9, and rewrite the example.

$$9\frac{1}{4} = 8\frac{4}{4} + \frac{1}{4} = \quad 8\frac{5}{4}$$
$$-6\frac{3}{4} = \qquad\qquad -6\frac{3}{4}$$
$$\overline{\qquad\qquad} \qquad \overline{\qquad\qquad}$$
$$2\frac{2}{4} = 2\frac{1}{2}$$

DECIMALS

Decimal Fractions

Decimal fractions are special fractions whose denominators are always powers of ten. *Powers of ten* are easy to remember. The exponent tells you how many zeros there are in the power of ten. Thus,

$$10^1 = 10 \qquad = 10 \times 1$$
$$10^2 = 100 \qquad = 10 \times 10$$
$$10^3 = 1,000 \quad = 10 \times 10 \times 10$$

You can tell the denominator of a decimal fraction by counting the places in the number to the right of its decimal point. When it is written as a fraction, the denominator has the same number of zeros as this number of places. That is, it has the same power of ten. Thus,

$$0.7 = \frac{7}{10^1} \text{ or } \frac{7}{10} \qquad \text{(seven tenths)}$$

$$0.07 = \frac{7}{10^2} \text{ or } \frac{7}{100} \qquad \text{(seven hundredths)}$$

$$0.007 = \frac{7}{10^3} \text{ or } \frac{7}{1,000} \qquad \text{(seven thousandths)}$$

$$0.0007 = \frac{7}{10^4} \text{ or } \frac{7}{10,000} \qquad \text{(seven tenths)}$$

Changing Fractions to Decimals

To change a fraction to a decimal, divide the numerator by the denominator. Place a decimal point to the right of the numerator, and add a zero for each decimal place you want in your answer.

EXAMPLE

$$\frac{2}{5} = 5\overline{)2.0} \quad\quad \text{So } \frac{2}{5} = 0.4$$

$$\frac{0.4}{\underline{20}}$$

Here's a short list of common fractions, converted to decimals.

$$\frac{1}{2} = .50 \quad\quad\quad \frac{1}{3} = .33\frac{1}{3}$$

$$\frac{1}{4} = .25 \quad\quad\quad \frac{3}{4} = .75$$

$$\frac{1}{5} = .20 \quad\quad\quad \frac{3}{5} = .60$$

$$\frac{4}{5} = .80 \quad\quad\quad \frac{1}{8} = .12\frac{1}{2} \text{ (or .125)}$$

Changing Decimals to Fractions

Every decimal is really a fraction whose denominator is a power of ten. For example,

$$0.0231 \text{ is } \frac{231}{10.000}; \; 0.25 \text{ is } \frac{25}{100} \text{ or } \frac{1}{4}; \text{ and } 3.4 \text{ is } \frac{34}{10}.$$

Multiplying Decimals by Powers of 10

Here's a shortcut for multiplying a decimal by a power of ten. Suppose you want to multiply .16 by 10^3.

Step 1. Count the number of zeros in the power of ten.

$$10^3 = 1,000 \quad \text{(3 zeros)}$$

Step 2. Move the decimal in .16 to the right. Move it as many places as this number of zeros.

Sometimes, you have to add one or more zeros so that you can move the correct number of places.

$$10^3 \times .16 = 10^3 \times .160 = 160$$

Other examples: $10^2 \times 2.1 = 10^2 \times 2.10 = 210$

$$10^4 \times .43 = 10^4 \times .4300 = 4300$$

Dividing Decimals by Powers of 10

To divide a decimal by a power of ten, count the number of zeros in the power of ten, and move that many places to the left of the decimal.

EXAMPLES

$158.7 \div 10^1 = 158.7 \div 10 = 15.87$
$.32 \div 10^2 = 00.32 \div 100 = .0032$

Adding and Subtracting Decimals

To add or subtract decimals, line up the numbers so that the decimal points are directly under one another. Then add or subtract as you would with whole numbers. Write zeros at the end of decimals if you find it easier to work with place holders.

EXAMPLES

Add 3.12 + 14.3 + 205.6 + 0.0324, and subtract their sum from 1,000.55. Remember to put the decimal point in the answers.

3.1200	1,000.5500
14.3000	− 223.0524
205.6000	777.4976 (remainder)
+ 0.0324	
223.0524 (sum)	

Multiplying Decimals

Multiply two decimals as though they were whole numbers. Then use these steps to find out where to put the decimal point in your answer.

Step 1. Add the decimal places in both numbers, counting from the decimal point to the right.

Step 2. Count off this same number of places from right to left in the answer.

Step 3. Insert a decimal point where you finish counting off. Add extra zeros, if you need them, to fill out the correct number of places.

EXAMPLES

$$.02 \times .12 = .0024$$
$$30 \times 1.5 = 45.0$$

Dividing Decimals

To divide a decimal by a whole number, divide the numbers as though they were both whole numbers. Then place a decimal point in the answer directly above the decimal in the problem.

EXAMPLE

$5.117 \div 17$

$$
\begin{array}{r}
0.301 \\
17\overline{)5.117} \\
\underline{5\,1} \\
17 \\
\underline{17}
\end{array}
$$

To divide one decimal by another, begin by making the divisor a whole number. Do this by moving the decimal in the divisor all the way to the right. Count the number of places you move it. Then move the decimal in the other number (the dividend) the same number of places.

EXAMPLE

$$\frac{1.8}{0.2} = \frac{18}{2} = 9$$

Rounding Off Decimals

Many mathematical problems require a rounding off process to reach an answer. Think about 3.7 yards. Is this closer to 3 yards or to 4 yards? $3.7 = 3\frac{7}{10}$, which is closer to 4 yards. How about 3.5 yards? This is exactly midway between 3 and 4 yards. We must make an agreement on rounding off a number of this type. We agree that 3.5 yards will be rounded off to 4 yards. Now round off 3.346 to the nearest tenth. This lies between 3.3 and 3.4, but is closer to 3.3. A common mistake in rounding off is to start from the right; in this case the 6 in the thousandths place will round the 3.346 off to 3.35. This causes our rounded off number to become 3.4 instead of 3.3. To round off a decimal to the nearest tenth, look at the number in the hundredths place (just to the right of the tenths). If it is 5 or more, round off upward. If it is less than 5, drop it and all numbers following it.

PERCENTS

A *percent* is a way to express a fraction. It simply means hundredths. To use a percent in solving a problem, change it to a fraction or a decimal.

To change a percent to a fraction, drop the percent sign and multiply by $\frac{1}{100}$.

EXAMPLES

5%	means	$5 \times \frac{1}{100}$ or	$\frac{5}{100}$
20%	means	$20 \times \frac{1}{100}$ or	$\frac{20}{100}$
100%	means	$100 \times \frac{1}{100}$ or	$\frac{100}{100}$

Changing a Percent to a Decimal

To change a percent to a decimal, drop the percent sign and move the decimal point two places to the left. Add extra zeros, if you need them, to fill out the correct number of places. If the percent is given as a fraction, first change the fraction to a decimal.

EXAMPLES

3% = .03	1.2% = .012
75% = .75	$\frac{1}{4}$% = .25% = .0025
15% = .15	100% = 1.00 (or 1)

Changing a Decimal to a Percent

To change a decimal to a percent, move the decimal point two places to the right and add the percent sign.

EXAMPLES

.23 = 23%	.05 = 5%
.5 = 50%	$.66\frac{2}{3} = 66\frac{2}{3}\%$

Arithmetic Problems Using Percent

An arithmetic problem using percent usually falls into one of three categories:

1. Find a number when you are told it is a certain percent of another number. This involves multiplication.

EXAMPLE

What is the amount of the discount on a hat marked $49.95 and discounted at 20%?

Step 1. Change the rate of discount to a fraction or decimal. 20% = .2

Step 2. Multiply the marked price by the rate of discount.

$$\$49.95 \times .2 = \$9.99 \text{ (discount)}$$

---

2. Find what percent one number is of another. This involves division.

EXAMPLE

A baseball team played 20 games and won 17 of them. What percent of its games did it win?

Step 1. Express the games won by the team as a part of the total games they played. In other words, state the relationship between the two numbers by writing a fraction (a ratio).

$$\frac{17}{20}$$

Step 2. Convert this fraction to a percent. Divide the numerator by the denominator. (Add a decimal point and zeros to carry the answer out two places.)

$$\frac{17.00}{20} = 0.85$$

Step 3. Multiply the quotient by 100 to convert to percent.

$$0.85 \times 100 = 85\% \text{ (games won)}$$

---

3. Find a whole number when you know only a part of it and the percent that the part represents. This involves division.

EXAMPLE

A family pays $5,000 a year in premiums for home insurance. If the rate of insurance is $12\frac{1}{2}\%$, how much is the insurance policy worth?

Step 1. Change the percent to a decimal.

$$12\frac{1}{2}\% = 0.125 \text{ (rate of insurance)}$$

Step 2. Divide the premium by the rate of insurance.

$$\$5,000 \div 0.125 = 125\overline{)\begin{array}{c} \$40,000 \\ \$5,000,000 \\ \hline 500 \end{array}}$$

The home insurance policy is worth $40,000.

Interest

A percent problem you frequently meet has to do with interest earned on a sum of money, the *principal*. A formula for finding interest is: principal (p) × rate of interest (r) × the period of time (t) = interest (i). *Time* is always time in years.

$$i = p \times r \times t$$

EXAMPLE

How much interest will there be on $5,000 for 6 months at 5%?

Step 1. Change the rate of interest to a fraction: $5\% = \frac{5}{100}$ (or $\frac{1}{20}$)

Step 2. Express the time in terms of years. There are 12 months in a year, so 6 months is $\frac{6}{12}$, or $\frac{1}{2}$, of a year.

Step 3. Apply the formula for finding interest.

$$i = p \times r \times t$$

$$i = \frac{\$5,000}{1} \times \frac{1}{20} \times \frac{1}{2}$$

$$i = \frac{\overset{\$2,500}{\cancel{\$5,000}}}{1} \times \frac{1}{20} \times \frac{1}{\cancel{2}}$$

$$i = \frac{\overset{\$125}{\overset{\cancel{\$2,500}}{\cancel{\$5,000}}}}{1} \times \frac{1}{\underset{1}{\cancel{20}}} \times \frac{1}{\underset{1}{\cancel{2}}} = \$125$$

The interest on $5,000 for 6 months will be $125.

SQUARE ROOT

The square root of a number is one of the two equal factors that when multiplied together give that number. For example, the square root of 9 is 3 since $3 \times 3 = 9$, and the square root of 49 is 7 since $7 \times 7 = 49$.

The square root of a number may be indicated by using a radical sign. For example, $\sqrt{81}$ means the square root of 81, that is, $\sqrt{81} = 9$. Similarly, $\sqrt{25} = 5$.

Only numbers that are perfect squares have exact square roots. Some perfect squares are 1, 4, 9, 16, 25, 36, 49, 64, 81, and 100.

Finding the Square Root of a Number

You may be asked to find the square root of a number that is not a perfect square, giving your answer correct to the nearest tenth, for example. A trial-and-error procedure can be used to find a square root to the nearest decimal place. For example, suppose you are asked to find $\sqrt{29}$ to the nearest tenth: $\sqrt{29}$ is between $\sqrt{25}$, which we know is 5, and $\sqrt{36}$, which we know is 6. And $\sqrt{29}$ is nearer to $\sqrt{25}$ than it is to $\sqrt{36}$. Guess 5.3 as $\sqrt{29}$ to the nearest tenth. Divide 5.3 into 29:

$$
\begin{array}{r}
5.4 \\
53.\overline{)29\,0.0} \\
\underline{26\,5} \\
2\,50 \\
\underline{2\,12} \\
\end{array}
$$

This was a good guess. We now know that $\sqrt{29}$ is between 5.3 and 5.4. The results of multiplying 5.3×5.3 and 5.4×5.4 show that $\sqrt{29}$ is nearer to 5.4 than to 5.3:

$$
\begin{array}{r}
5.3 \\
\underline{5.3} \\
1\,59 \\
\underline{26\,5} \\
28.09 \\
\end{array}
\qquad
\begin{array}{r}
5.4 \\
\underline{5.4} \\
2\,16 \\
\underline{27\,0} \\
29.16 \\
\end{array}
$$

ALGEBRA

Algebra is a way to reduce a problem to a small set of symbols. When we can state a problem with a few symbols, letters, and numbers, it seems easier to solve. The solution we are looking for is often an *"unknown"* quantity, and we speak of "finding the unknowns."

Take an example. We know that if a sweater is priced at $20, we have to pay $20 to buy one. If we want three sweaters, we pay three times that amount, or $60. How do we find the answer, $60? We multiply two numbers to find a third number. Using the style of algebra, we can express this operation briefly. Let p equal the price of one sweater, and let c (the "unknown") equal the cost of three sweaters. Here's an algebraic expression for how we find c.

$$c = 3 \times p \text{ (or) } c = 3p$$

In this expression, the letters c and p are called *literal numbers,* meaning they are letters that stand for numbers. Another word for such letters is *variables,* meaning that the numbers they stand for can change. (If the price of the sweater is discounted to $18, then p will equal $18, and c will equal $54.)

Arithmetic Operations in Algebra

All four arithmetic operations are possible in algebra: both basic operations (addition and multiplication), and inverse operations (subtraction and division). We can express these operations algebraically:

1. The sum of two numbers x and y, is $x + y$
2. The difference between two numbers, x and y, is $x - y$
3. The product of two numbers, x and y, is $(x) \times (y)$ (or) $x \cdot y$ (or) xy
4. The quotient of two numbers, x and y, is $x \div y$ (or) $\dfrac{x}{y}$

Equations

An *equation* is a statement that two quantities are equal. This is clear when the quantities are expressed in numbers. Thus,

$$3 + 7 = 10 \qquad\qquad 7 \cdot 8 = 56$$
$$5 - 3 = 2 \qquad\qquad 18 \div 2 = 9$$

But in algebra, equations always include variables, or unknowns. Usually, you will be asked to "solve the equation" by finding the unknown number value. In this sense, the *solution* to an equation is the number which proves that the equation is true. (You show that it's true by substituting the number for the variable.) But how do you find the number?

Suppose you heard someone say, "I can't afford to buy a car for $8,000. That would leave me with only $5,000 in my bank account." How would we express his (or her) statement in algebra? (Remember, the "unknown" is the unstated amount, x, now in the bank account.) Here's one way of writing the expression:

$$x - \$8{,}000 = \$5{,}000$$

How do we solve for x?

Step 1. Think about what the expression now means: A certain number, minus $8,000, equals $5,000.

Step 2. Think of how you want to express the solution: x = (the amount in the bank)

Step 3. Think of how the statement of your solution will differ from the equation you begin with: $8,000 will no longer be on the same side of the equal sign as x.

Step 4. Now think about how to "get rid of" or "clear" the $8,000 from the side that shows x. Notice that the sign with $8,000 is a minus sign. If you add $8,000 to the left side of the equation, the two 8,000s will cancel each other. But remember that in a true equation, everything on the left side of the equal sign must have the same value as everything on the right side. If you add $8,000 to the left, you have to add it to the right. Thus,

$$x - \$8,000 = \$5,000$$
$$x - \$8,000 + \$8,000 = \$5,000 + \$8,000$$
$$x = \$13,000 \text{ (amount in bank)}$$

How is the equation solved? By performing an inverse operation on both sides of the equation.

Thus, to solve for x, we go through three steps:

Step 1. We decide to "clear for x" by removing all other operations from the side of the equation where x is found.

Step 2. We remove an operation from one side of the equal sign by performing its inverse (opposite) operation on the same side.

Step 3. We then perform the same operation on the other side of the equal sign. (That is, if we subtract 3 from one side, we subtract 3 from the other side.)

Examples of Using Inverse Operations to Solve Equations

1. The inverse of addition is subtraction.

Solve: $x + 7 = 50$
$$x + 7 - 7 = 50 - 7$$
$$x = 43 \text{ (solution of equation)}$$

2. The inverse of subtraction is addition.

Solve: $x - 3 = 4$
$$x - 3 + 3 = 4 + 3$$
$$x = 7 \text{ (solution)}$$

3. The inverse of multiplication is division.

Solve: $0.05x = 4$

$$\frac{0.05x}{0.05} = \frac{4}{0.05}$$

$x = 80$ (solution)

($0.05 \div 0.05 = 1$. When you divide 4 by 0.05, you have to clear the decimal from the divisor, first. Thus, 0.05 becomes 5, and 4 becomes 400.)

4. The inverse of division is multiplication.

Solve: $\frac{x}{2} = 72$

$$\left(\frac{x}{2}\right) = 7 \times 2$$

$x = 14$ (solution)

Inverse Operations with More Complex Equations

Sometimes, an equation shows x as part of more than one operation. There may also be negative terms (terms with a minus sign). The same basic steps are involved in finding the solution, but may have to be repeated. Remember, the goal is always to isolate x on one side of the equation.

EXAMPLE

Solve: $3x + 7 = -11$

Step 1. Perform the inverse operation of + 7.

$$3x + 7 - 7 = -11 - 7$$
$$3x = -18$$

Step 2. Perform the inverse operation of $3x (3 \cdot x)$.

$$\frac{3x}{3} = \frac{-18}{3}$$
$$x = -6 \text{ (solution)}$$

(Remember that in multiplication and division, if the signs of both terms are plus or minus, the answer is signed by a plus sign. If the two terms are different, the answer is signed by a minus sign.)

Sometimes, x appears on both sides of the original equation. In that case, the first step is to remove x from one side (or, "collect all xs on one side") of the equal sign.

EXAMPLE

Solve: $-7x = 24 - x$

Step 1. Perform the inverse operation of $-x$.

$$-7x + x = 24 - x + x$$
$$-6x = 24$$

Step 2. Perform the inverse operation of $(-6)x$.

$$\frac{-6x}{-6} = \frac{24}{-6}$$
$$x = -4 \text{ (solution)}$$

Algebraic Expressions

An *algebraic expression* is any collection of numbers and variables. This collection may have more than one variable. For example, $3x + 4y$ is an algebraic expression meaning "3 times one unknown number (x), plus 4 times another unknown number (y)."

Arithmetic Operations with Algebraic Expressions

1. To add or subtract algebraic expressions, remember that only *similar*, or *"like"* terms can be combined. (Terms are similar if they have the same variable, raised to the same power.) Thus, we can subtract $3x$ from $5x$ to get $2x$, but we cannot get x^3 by adding x and x^2, or get $9zh$ out of $4z$ and $5h$.

   EXAMPLE

   Add: $3x + 2y - 4z + 2x - 5y$
   $$3x + 2x = 5x \text{ (partial sum)}$$
   $$2y - 5y = -3y \text{ (partial sum)}$$

   Therefore, $5x - 3y - 4z$ is the sum.

2. To multiply algebraic expressions, follow these steps.

   Step 1. Multiply the numbers of similar terms.

   Step 2. Multiply the letters of similar terms. When multiplying one power of x by another power of x, just add the exponents.

EXAMPLE

$(2x^2)(3x^5)$

Step 1. $2 \times 3 = 6$ (partial product)

Step 2. $x^2 \times x^5 = x^7$ (partial product)

Thus, the product is $6x^7$

Sometimes, you are asked to multiply more complex algebraic expressions. The rules are basically the same.

EXAMPLE

In $x^2y(3x - 5y)$, the parentheses tell you that x^2y is the multiplier for both $3x$ and $-5y$.

Step 1. $x^2y \times 3x = 3x^3y$ (partial product)

Step 2. $x^2y \times -5y = -5x^2y^2$ (partial product)

The product is $3x^3y - 5x^2y^2$

EXAMPLE

In $(a + 2)(2a - 3)$, think of $(a + 2)$ as a two-place multiplier. An easy way to do this example is to set it up as an ordinary multiplication in arithmetic.

$$
\begin{array}{rl}
2a - 3 & \\
\times\ a + 2 & \\
\hline
4a - 6 & \text{Multiply } (2a - 3) \text{ by } 2 \\
2a^2 - 3a & \text{Multiply } (2a - 3) \text{ by } a \\
\hline
2a^2 + a - 6 & \text{Product}
\end{array}
$$

3. To divide algebraic expressions, follow these steps:

Step 1. Divide the number of similar terms.

Step 2. Divide the letters of similar terms. When dividing one power of x by another power of x, subtract the exponents.

EXAMPLE

$x^5 \div x^3 = x^2$

EXAMPLE

$$\frac{8x^3}{4x} = \frac{\overset{2}{\cancel{8}}}{\underset{1}{\cancel{4}}} \times \frac{\overset{x^2}{\cancel{x^3}}}{\underset{1}{\cancel{x}}} = 2 \times x^2 = 2x^2$$

Sometimes, a divisor goes into several terms.

EXAMPLE

$$\frac{\overset{3x^2}{\cancel{24x^3}} - \overset{1}{\cancel{8x}}}{\underset{1}{\cancel{8x}}} = 3x^2 - 1$$

Evaluating Algebraic Expressions

To evaluate an algebraic expression means to replace the letters with numbers, and then simplify (add, multiply, etc.).

EXAMPLE

Evaluate the expression $(a + 2b)$ if $a = 3$ and $b = 2$.

$$a + 2b$$
$$= 3 + 2(2)$$
$$= 3 + 4$$
$$= 7$$

Factoring in Algebra

Sometimes, you are given the answer to a multiplication example in algebra, and are asked to find the original multipliers. This is called *factoring*.

1. Factor the *highest common factor*. The highest common factor of an algebraic expression is the highest expression that will divide into every one of the terms of the expression.

EXAMPLE

$6x^2 + 3xy$

Step 1. The highest number that will divide into the numerical coefficients, 6 and 3, is 3.

Step 2. The highest literal factor that will divide into x^2 and xy is x. Note that y is not contained in the first term at all.

Step 3. Divide the highest common factor, $3x$, into $6x^2 + 3xy$ to find the remaining factor:

The factors are $3x(2x + y)$.

EXAMPLE

$2a^2b^3 - 4ab^2 + 6a$

The highest common factor of the three terms is $2a$, so the factors are $2a(ab^3 - 2b^2 + 3)$.

2. Factor the *difference of two squares*. In this case, your example contains the square of one number, minus the square of another number. (The square of another is the product you get when you multiply a number by itself. The *square root* of a number is the number that was multiplied by itself to produce the square.)

EXAMPLE

$x^2 - 9$

Step 1. Find the square root of x^2 and place it to the left, within each of two "empty" parentheses. The square root of x^2 is x.

$$(x\ \ )(x\ \ )$$

Step 2. Find the square root of 9 and place it to the right, within each of these parentheses. The square root of 9 is 3.

$$(x\ \ 3)(x\ \ 3)$$

Step 3. Place a plus sign between one pair of terms, and a minus sign between the other pair of terms.

$$(x + 3)(x - 3)$$

The factors of $x^2 - 9$ are $(x + 3)$, $(x - 3)$.

3. Factor a *quadratic trinomial*. A quadratic trinomial is an algebraic expression of the form $ax^2 + bx + c$, where a, b, and c are numbers and a does not equal 0. Its factors are always two pairs of terms. The terms in each pair are separated by a plus or minus sign.

EXAMPLE

Factor $x^2 - 11x + 30$.

Step 1. Find the factors of the first term in the trinomial. The factors of x^2 are x and x.

$$(x\ \ )(x\ \ )$$

Step 2. Look at the last term in the trinomial. It has a plus sign. This means that both factors of the trinomial are either plus or minus. Which one? Since the middle term ($-11x$) has a minus sign, both factors must have minus signs.

$$(x -)(x -)$$

Step 3. Find the factors of 30. There are several numbers you can multiply to get 30: 30×1, 10×3, etc. But the two multipliers you use must also combine somehow to give you 11, the middle term. When 5 and 6 are multiplied, they give you 30. When they are added, they give you 11. We know the factors have minus signs. So the factors of 30 are actually -6 and -5.

$$(x - 6)(x - 5)$$

The factors of $x^2 - 11x + 30$ are: $(x - 6)$, $(x - 5)$.

Solving Quadratic Equations

A *quadratic equation* is an equation that contains a term with the square of the unknown quantity and has no term with a higher power of the unknown. In a quadratic equation, the exponent is never higher than 2 (x^2, b^2, c^2, etc.). Examples of quadratic equations include:

$$x^2 + x - 6 = 0$$
$$3x^2 = 5x - 7$$
$$x^2 - 4 = 0$$
$$64 = x^2$$

How do we solve equations like this? Basically, we factor them, and then set each factor equal to zero. After that, it's easy to solve for x. Let's take it step by step.

EXAMPLE

Solve: $x^2 = 3x + 10$

Step 1. Place all terms on one side of the equal sign, leaving the equation equal to 0. (Remember inverse operations.)

$$x^2 - 3x - 10 = 0$$

Step 2. Factor this equation.

$$(x - 5)(x + 2) = 0$$

Step 3. Set each factor equal to zero, and solve the equations.

$$x - 5 = 0 \qquad x + 2 = 0$$
$$x = +5 \qquad x = -2$$

Step 4. To check its accuracy, substitute each answer in the original equation.

$$x^2 = 3x + 10 \qquad\qquad x^2 = 3x + 10$$
$$(5)^2 = 3(5) + 10 \qquad (-2)^2 = 3(-2) + 10$$
$$25 = 15 + 10 \qquad\qquad 4 = -6 + 10$$
$$25 = 25 \text{ (proof)} \qquad\quad 4 = 4 \text{ (proof)}$$

The solution of the quadratic equation is $x = 5, -2$.

Inequalities

Not everything in algebra is an equation! An *inequality* is a statement that two quantities are not equal to each other. With an inequality, one of these two things must be true:

1. The first quantity is greater than the second.

OR

2. The first quantity is less than the second.

A number line helps to show how this is true.

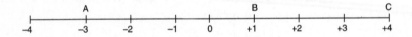

On the number line, A is to the left of B, and B is to the left of C. Whenever one variable is to the left of another on a number line, it is less than the other. Thus, −3 is less than +1, and +1 is less than +4. We can make a few general statements.

1. Any negative number is less than zero.
2. Zero is less than any positive number.
3. Any negative number is less than any positive number.

There are symbols for statements of inequality.

Symbols	Meanings
$6 \neq 7$	6 does not equal 7
$7 > 6$	7 is greater than 6
$6 < 7$	6 is less than 7
$x \geq 8$	x is greater than or equal to 8
$x \leq 8$	x is less than or equal to 8

Solving Inequalities

The rules for solving inequalities are similar to those used for solving equations with one important difference, which is illustrated in the second of the two examples below. The difference is that when both sides of an inequality are multiplied or divided by a *negative* number, the direction of the inequality sign must be reversed. To illustrate, if $8 > 5$ has each side multiplied by -2, then $-16 < -10$.

EXAMPLE

Solve: $x - 3 < 8$

"Clear" for x by transferring -3 to the other side of the inequality symbol. Do this by performing an inverse operation.

$$x - 3 + 3 < 8 + 3$$
$$x < 11 \text{ (solution)}$$

The solution means that any number less than 11 will make the original statement of inequality true. You can prove that by substituting numbers less than 11 for x. Try letting $x = 10$.

$$x - 3 < 8$$
$$10 - 3 < 8$$
$$7 < 8 \quad \text{This is certainly true!}$$

EXAMPLE

Solve: $13 - 2x < 7$

"Clear" the x term by subtracting 13 from both sides of the inequality.

$$13 - 13 - 2x < 7 - 13$$
$$-2x < -6$$

To obtain x alone, divide both sides of the inequality by -2. Since division is by a *negative* number, the direction of the inequality sign must be reversed.

$$x > 3$$

The solution means that any number greater than 3 will make the original inequality true. To prove this, substitute any number greater than 3 for x. Try letting $x = 5$.

$$13 - 2x < 7$$
$$13 - 2(5) < 7$$
$$13 - 10 < 7$$
$$3 < 7$$

This is certainly true!

GEOMETRY

Geometry has to do with the world around us. Some knowledge of geometry is necessary for everyone. Both arithmetic and algebra are used in solving geometry problems. Many geometry problems involve measurement, and use familiar words, such as line or point. An important term in geometry is *angle*.

Angles

An angle is formed by two lines meeting at a point. The point is called the *vertex* of the angle. You can name an angle in three ways.

1. By the point at the vertex (for example, angle B).

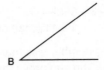

2. By the letter names of the lines that meet to form the angle, with the vertex in the middle (for example, angle ABC).

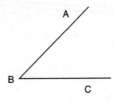

3. By a number inside the angle on a diagram (for example, angle #2).

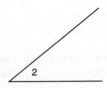

Protractor

To measure an angle, we use an instrument called a *protractor*. Angles are measured in *degrees* (°). Just as a foot is broken into 12 inches, a degree is broken into minutes (′) and seconds (″). (Don't confuse these with time!)

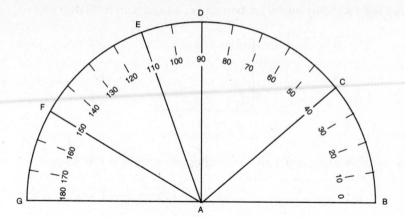

1. A *straight line* is an angle of 180 degrees.

180°

Straight Angle

2. A *right angle* is an angle of 90 degrees.

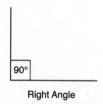

90°

Right Angle

3. An *obtuse angle* is an angle of more than 90 degrees, but less than 180 degrees.

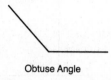

Obtuse Angle

4. An *acute angle* is an angle of more than 0 degrees and less than 90 degrees.

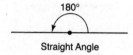

Acute Angle

5. *Complementary angles* are two angles whose sum is 90 degrees.

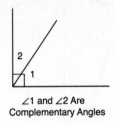

∠1 and ∠2 Are
Complementary Angles

6. *Supplementary angles* are two angles whose sum is 180 degrees.

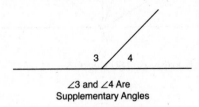

∠3 and ∠4 Are
Supplementary Angles

Lines

Parallel lines are two lines that are equally distant from one another at every point along the lines.

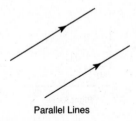

Parallel Lines

Perpendicular lines are two lines that meet to form a right angle.

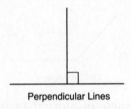

Perpendicular Lines

Polygons

A *polygon* is composed of three or more lines, connected so that an area is closed in. There are several types of polygons.

1. A *triangle* has three sides.
2. A *quadrilateral* has four sides.
3. A *pentagon* has five sides.
4. A *hexagon* has six sides.
5. An *octagon* has eight sides.
6. A *decagon* has ten sides.

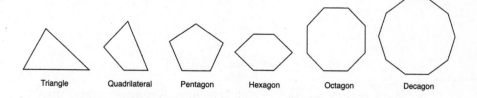

| Triangle | Quadrilateral | Pentagon | Hexagon | Octagon | Decagon |

Triangles

Most of you know that a triangle is a geometric figure with three straight lines. There are several ways to classify a triangle, but all triangles contain 180 degrees.

1. An *equilateral triangle* is one in which all three sides are equal, and all three angles are equal—60 degrees each.

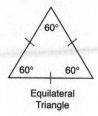

Equilateral
Triangle

2. An *isosceles triangle* is one in which two sides are equal. (The angles opposite these sides are also equal.)

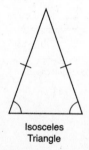

Isosceles
Triangle

3. A *scalene triangle* is one in which all the sides and all the angles are unequal.

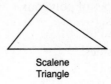

Scalene
Triangle

4. An *acute triangle* is one in which all three angles are acute (less than a right angle).

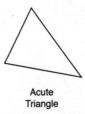

Acute
Triangle

5. An *obtuse triangle* is one in which one angle is obtuse (greater than 90 degrees).

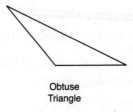

Obtuse
Triangle

6. A *right triangle* is one that includes a right angle (90 degrees). The longest side of a right triangle is called the *hypotenuse*. It is always the side opposite the right angle (side c). The other two sides are called *legs*.

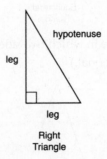

hypotenuse

leg

leg

Right
Triangle

There is a very important idea connected with right triangles. It is called the *Pythagorean Theorem*. It says that in a right triangle, the square of the hypotenuse is equal to the sum of the square of the legs. As an equation, the Pythagorean Theorem would be expressed as follows:

$$c^2 = a^2 + b^2$$

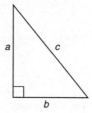

EXAMPLE

A gardener placed a 5-foot ladder against a 4-foot wall. If the top of the ladder touched the top of the wall, how far away from the base of the wall was the bottom of the ladder?

Solution

The angle formed by the base of the wall and the ground is a right angle. Therefore, we can use the Pythagorean Theorem. Since the ladder was opposite the right angle, let $c = 5$.

$$c^2 = a^2 + b^2$$
$$5^2 = 4^2 + x^2 \text{ (Clear for } x.)$$
$$5^2 - 4^2 = 4^2 - 4^2 + x^2$$
$$25 - 16 = x^2$$
$$9 = x^2 \text{ (Find the square roots.)}$$
$$3 = x$$

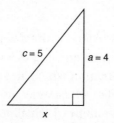

7. *Congruent triangles* are alike in every respect. All three sides and all three angles of one triangle are exactly the same as those of the other.

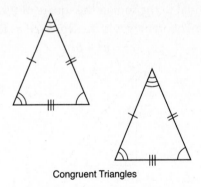

Congruent Triangles

8. *Similar triangles* are triangles with exactly the same shape, but not necessarily the same size. The angles of two similar triangles are the same.

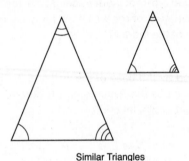

Similar Triangles

Quadrilaterals

There are several types of quadrilaterals, but all quadrilaterals contain 360 degrees.

1. A *parallelogram* is a quadrilateral with its opposite sides parallel. In a parallelogram the opposite sides and angles are also equal.
2. A *rectangle* is a parallelogram in which all angles are right angles.
3. A *square* is a rectangle all of whose sides are equal.
4. A *rhombus* is a parallelogram in which all four sides are equal.
5. A *trapezoid* is a quadrilateral with two sides parallel, and two sides not parallel.

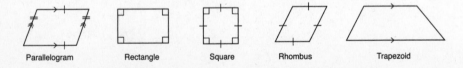

Parallelogram   Rectangle   Square   Rhombus   Trapezoid

Perimeter and Area

The *perimeter* of a polygon is the sum of all its sides.

EXAMPLE

Find the perimeter of a triangle whose sides measure 3 feet, 4 feet, and 5 feet.

3' + 4' + 5' = 12' (perimeter)

EXAMPLE

Find the perimeter of a square whose side is 9 yards.

9 + 9 + 9 + 9 = 36 yds (perimeter)

Since all four sides of a square are equal, you can use the rule "perimeter (P) of a square equals four times a side (s)": P = 4s.

The *area* of a polygon is the space enclosed by its sides.

1. The area of a parallelogram is base times height.

A = bh

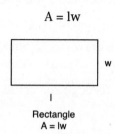

b
Parallelogram
A = bh

2. The area of a rectangle is length times width.

A = lw

w

l
Rectangle
A = lw

3. The area of a square is one side "squared."

$$A = s^2$$

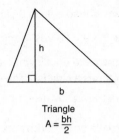

s
Square
$A = s^2$

4. The area of a triangle is one-half the base times the height.

h

b

Triangle
$A = \dfrac{bh}{2}$

EXAMPLE

Find the area of a room whose length is 20 feet and whose width is 18 feet.

$$A = lw$$
$$x = 20' \times 18'$$
$$x = 360 \text{ square feet (area)}$$

Circles

A *circle* is a closed curved line, all of whose points are equally distant from the center. A circle contains 360 degrees. There are several special "parts" to a circle.

The *circumference* of a circle is its "length"—once around the rim.

The *radius* of a circle is a line drawn from the center to any point on the circumference.

The *diameter* is a line passing through the center of a circle, and is equal to twice the radius.

Circle

Perimeter and Area of a Circle

To find the circumference (perimeter) of a circle, we use a new number, Pi (π). Pi is actually a Greek letter. In geometry it expresses an unchanging relationship between the circumference of a circle and its diameter. In other words, the circumference is always Pi times the diameter. Since the diameter is twice the radius, we can also say that the circumference of a circle is Pi times twice the radius. Thus,

$$C = (\pi)d \text{ OR } C = (\pi)2r$$

When we do arithmetic operations with Pi, we use either 3.14 or $3\frac{1}{7}$ for Pi.

EXAMPLE

Find the circumference of an ice rink whose radius is 70 yards.

$C = (\pi)2r$

$C = (\pi)\,(2 \times 70)$

$C = 3\frac{1}{7} \times 140$

$C = \dfrac{22}{\overset{}{\underset{1}{7}}} \times \overset{20}{\cancel{140}}$

$C = 22 \times 20 = 440$ yards

The area of a circle also has a fixed relationship to Pi. The area equals Pi times the square of the radius. Thus,

$$A = (\pi)r^2$$

EXAMPLE

Find the area of a circular tract of land whose diameter is 20 miles.

Step 1. Find the radius (one-half of the diameter).

$20 \div 2 = 10$ miles (radius)

Step 2. Apply the formula for the area of a circle.

$A = (\pi)r^2$

$A = 3.14 \times 10^2$

$A = 3.14 \times 100$

$A = 314$ square miles (area)

Volume

Volume is the space occupied by a solid figure. A *solid*, or three-dimensional object, has a flat base and height (sometimes called depth). Volume is measured in cubic units.

A *rectangular solid* has length, width, and height. The formula for finding its cubic measure is length times width times height. Thus,

$$V = lwh.$$

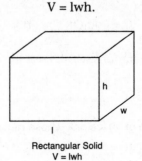

Rectangular Solid
$V = lwh$

A *cube* is a solid whose length, width, and height are the same. The volume of a cube is one side "cubed"—or one side raised to the third power. Thus,

$$V = s^3.$$

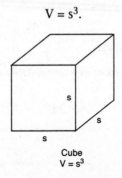

Cube
$V = s^3$

A solid in which both bases are circles in parallel planes is called a *cylinder.* The volume of a cylinder is the area of its base (a circle) times its height. Thus,

$$V = (\pi)r^2h.$$

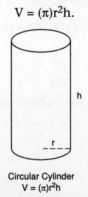

Circular Cylinder
$V = (\pi)r^2h$

EXAMPLE

Find the difference between the capacity of a rectangular solid measuring 3' by 5' by 10' and a cylinder with a radius of 7' and a height of 3'.

Step 1. Find the volume of the rectangular solid.

$$V = lwh$$
$$V = 3' \times 5' \times 10'$$
$$V = 150 \text{ cubic feet}$$

Step 2. Find the volume of the cylinder.

$$V = (\pi)r^2h$$
$$V = 3\frac{1}{7} \times 7^2 \times 3$$
$$V = \frac{22}{\underset{1}{\cancel{7}}} \times \cancel{49}^{\,7} \times 3$$
$$V = 22 \times 7 \times 3$$
$$V = 462 \text{ cubic feet}$$

Step 3. Find the difference between both volumes.

$$462 - 150 = 312 \text{ cubic feet}$$

Verbal Review: Word Knowledge/Paragraph Comprehension | 5

▶▶▶▶▶▶▶▶▶▶▶▶▶▶▶▶▶▶▶▶▶▶▶▶▶▶

WORD KNOWLEDGE AND HOW TO BUILD A VOCABULARY

Why Vocabulary

In a classic study conducted by Johnson O'Connor of the Human Engineering Institute and reported in an article called "Vocabulary and Success," the main finding was that a good vocabulary was more frequently to be found among successful persons (persons in important positions) than any other single factor. That doesn't mean that everyone with a good vocabulary is necessarily successful, but it is generally true that successful people have good vocabularies.

This discovery should really come as no surprise. A vocabulary is not merely a collection of words. It is all the ideas for which words stand. Take, for example, the following words taken from the study of government.

anarchy	fascism
autocracy	federal
autonomy	oligarchy
democracy	republic
dictatorship	totalitarian

These words all identify systems of government. Anyone who knows the meanings of these ten words has an understanding of the most widely known kinds of government and what each represents. Or, to choose a more technical (and a more dramatic) area, that of space exploration, any knowledgeable person will have as part of his vocabulary such words as

abort	injection
apogee	orbit
burnout	perigee
cislunar	phasing
docking	telemetry

among others. The point is that the person with a good vocabulary has more ideas (about government, for example) and more knowledge (about space exploration, for example) and such persons are always in demand in business and in the professions.

How to Add a Word to Your Vocabulary

The best way to find words to build your vocabulary is by reading, and not the most difficult books either. Research has shown that, to build your vocabulary, it is better to read books just a little bit more difficult than the level you find to be easy. A few new words a page are better than many. Let us take a few examples of how reading can help you add words to your vocabulary.

A fine American short story starts with the sentence:

"It was late in the afternoon, and the light was *waning*."

The sentence itself provides a clue to the meaning of the word "waning." "Late in the afternoon" the light grows dim. Reference to the dictionary confirms this guess at the meaning from the clues provided in the sentence. One definition reads: "to grow dim, as a light." It would be helpful to fix the meaning of the word if you jotted it down in a small pocket vocabulary notebook. The notation should include the following:

Word (correctly spelled)	Meaning	Example of use
wane	grow dim	The light began to *wane*.

The final clincher is your own proper use of the word in another sentence. One possibility might be: "His eyesight began to *wane*."

In the above example, you can find the five steps to take if you wish to master a word.

1. Find the word as it is used in the company of other words on the printed page. Reading is the best way to do this.
2. Make a temporary judgment as to the meaning of the word from the clues contained in the sentence where it is found.
3. Check your opinion of its meaning by referring to a dictionary at your first opportunity.
4. If possible, add the word to a continuing list you develop in a small pocket-size notebook. Include the meaning and a typical context (the sentence in which it was found).
5. Use it yourself in the same or, preferably, in a new context (word setting).

Now try your hand at the next example.

This is taken from another fine American short story.

"It was a *desolate* country in those days; geographers still described it as The Great American Desert, and in looks it deserved the title."

How would you master the word "desolate"?

A temporary judgment as to its meaning would be based on the clue in the sentence that it was similar to a desert. But what quality or characteristic of a desert does it stand for? You find out by checking with the dictionary. The entry is found on the page with the guide words desecrate—detach. It is in its alphabetical place between Des Moines and desolation. Four meanings are given and you start with the first: "lonely; solitary." That is the original meaning and the most precise. It is best to choose the first definition in preference to the others if it fits the sentence. In this case, the others are all possible extensions of the main meaning "lonely": uninhabited; laid waste; forlorn. Your notebook notation might read something like this:

Word	Meaning	Example of use
desolate	lonely	The station was in a desolate part of the city.

There is one more important dictionary clue in the entry for *desolate.* The origin of the word is given [>L. *de*- intens. + *solus,* alone]. The word comes to us from the Latin. *De* is an intensive, meaning *very,* but the important clue is the Latin word *solus,* meaning *alone.* Other English words use forms of the Latin word "solus." These are some that might occur to you: sole, solitaire, solitary, solitude, solo.

Study the Parts of a Word

This means of vocabulary building requires you to work with three elements of a word: the root, prefixes, and suffixes.

The one essential part of any word is the root. It may be a word in itself (for example, *flex*) or a word element from which other words are formed (for example, *aud*). Knowing many word roots is one way of multiplying your vocabulary, for each root can lead you to several words. We shall show you how, after we define the other two elements; prefixes and suffixes.

A prefix is a word (a syllable or group of syllables) added to the beginning of a word that changes its meaning. Let us return to the example *flex.* By itself, it means to bend or contract. The context is the human body. You can flex an arm; you can flex a muscle. If you add the syllable *re* to the beginning of the root, *flex,* that is, if you add the prefix *re,* you get a new word, *reflex,* with a new meaning. *Reflex* describes an action that you cannot control, such as a sneeze.

We can further change the meaning of the root *flex* by adding a suffix. A suffix is a word part (a syllable or group of syllables) added to the end of a word that changes its meaning. If you add the syllables *ible* to the end of the root, that is, if you add the suffix *ible*, you get another new word, *flexible*, with a new meaning. *Flexible* means *able to bend without breaking* or, in a broader meaning, *able to adjust to change*.

It is also possible to add both a prefix and a suffix to a root and get still another word. If you add both the prefix *in* meaning *not* and the suffix *ible* meaning *able*, you get a new word, *inflexible*. *Inflexible* means *unbending* or, in a broader meaning, *stubborn* and *unable to adjust to change*.

To give you some idea of the *flex* family of words, here are a number of other words (*flect* is another form of *flex*).

flexibility	reflection
deflect	circumflex
inflection	genuflect

Here is a list of widely used prefixes in English. Make up at least one word using each prefix and check your accuracy in the dictionary.

Prefix	Meaning	Word
a	no, not	
ab	away, from	
ad	to	
amphi	both	
ante	before	
anti	against	
be	completely	
circum	around	
contra	against	
de	from, away	
dia	across	
eu	well	
ex	out of	
extra	beyond	
fore	before	
hyper	above	
hypo	below, under	
in	into	
in	not	
inter	between	
intra	within	
mis	wrong	
ob	against	
out	from, beyond	
over	above, too much	
para	beside	
peri	around	

Prefix	Meaning	Word
poly	many	
post	after	
pre	before	
pro	forward	
re	back, again	
retro	back	
se	apart	
sub	under	
super	above, beyond	
syn	together, with	
trans	across	
ultra	beyond	
un	not	
under	below	

Here is a list of widely used word roots. Make up at least one word using each root and check your word in the dictionary. Try to combine the root with one of the prefixes we have listed for you.

Prefix	Meaning	Word
act	do	
anim	spirit, life	
anthro	man	
ann(u)	year	
aqua	water	
aud	hear	
bene	well	
cas	fall	
chrom	color	
chron	time	
ced(e)	go	
cid(e)	kill	
clud(e)	close	
cor	heart	
corp	body	
cred	believe	
curr	run	
dem	people	
dic(t)	say	
do(n)	give	
duc(t)	lead	
fac(t)	make	
fer	carry	
fin	end	
flect	bend	
flu(x)	flow	
fract	break	
frater	brother	
graph	write	

Prefix	Meaning	Word
gress	walk	
hetero	different	
homo	same	
hydro(o)	water	
ject	throw	
jur(e)	swear	
litera	letter	
lith	stone	
magn	large, great	
mal	evil	
man(u)	hand	
mar	sea	
mater	mother	
ment	mind	
met(er)	measure	
micro	small	
mit	send	
mono	one	
mort	death	
mot	move	
multi	many	
nom(y)	science of	
norm	rule	
nov	new	
ortho	right	
pan	all	
pater	father	
path	suffer, feel	
ped	foot	
pend	hang	
phil	love	
phon	sound	
psych	mind	
pugn	fight	
rupt	break	
sci	know	
scrib	write	
sect	cut	
sol	alone	
soph	wise	
spect	look	
struct	build	
tele	far	
temp	time	
tract	draw	
vad	go	
ven(t)	come	
vert	turn	
vis	see	
vict	conquer	
voc, voke	call	
volv	turn	

The following is a list of prefixes, both in Greek and Latin, that indicate a number. Find one word for each prefix and add it to your vocabulary.

Meaning	Latin		Greek	
half	semi	....	hemi	....
one	uni	....	mono	....
two	bi	....	di	....
three	tri	....	tri	....
four	quadr	....	tetra	....
five	quint	....	penta	....
six	sex	....	hexa	....
seven	sept	....	hepta	....
eight	oct	....	octa	....
nine	nona	....	rarely used	....
ten	dec	....	deca	....
hundred	cent	....	rarely used	....
thousand	mill	....	kilo	....

Learn the Synonyms and Antonyms of a Word

A synonym is a word that has the same or nearly the same meaning as another word in the language. An antonym is a word that has the opposite or nearly the opposite meaning from another word in a language. You may ask, "How do I find these synonyms and antonyms?" The answer is again: "In the dictionary." The paperback pocket-size dictionary, because of its size, will give you little help in this particular technique. You must resort to a desk-size dictionary.

Let us take *Webster's New World Dictionary of the American Language*, College Edition's listing of synonyms for the word *happy*.

SYN.—happy generally suggests a feeling of great pleasure, contentment, etc. (a *happy* marriage); glad implies more strongly an exultant feeling of joy (your letter made her so *glad*), but both glad and happy are commonly used in merely polite formulas expressing gratification (I'm *glad*, or *happy*, that you could come); cheerful implies a steady display of bright spirits, optimism, etc. (He's always *cheerful* in the morning); joyful and joyous both imply great elation and rejoicing, the former generally because of a particular event, and the latter as a matter of usual temperament (the *joyful* throngs, a *joyous* family). See also *lucky.*—*ANT.* sad

---

In addition to giving you four synonyms for *happy*, the entry distinguishes among them. It also gives you a context (group of words in which the synonym appears) for each synonym. And it refers you to *lucky*, under which you find two more synonyms—*fortunate* and *providential*. Finally, it gives you one antonym, *sad*, which itself becomes a clue to five other antonyms—*sorrowful, melancholy, dejected, depressed,* and *doleful.* From the one word, *happy,* the dictionary has led us to seven synonyms and five antonyms, an additional dozen words.

Similarly, the word *large* will lead you to synonyms *big* and *great* and to antonyms *small, little, diminutive, minute, tiny, miniature,* and *petite.*

Learn to Associate Words by Topic or Idea

One of the most helpful aids to vocabulary building is a book based on this principle. It is called *Roget's International Thesaurus* or the treasury (of words) of Peter Mark Roget, the man who first thought out the organization of words into 1000 related groups. The *Thesaurus* of Roget cannot be used by itself. It must be used together with a dictionary since the *Thesaurus* merely lists the words by idea. For example, under the idea of GREATNESS, the word *consummate* is listed as one of the adjectives. The word *consummate* fits into the general idea of greatness, but it refers to great mastery of a skill, both to be admired or to be disapproved of, as in "with consummate artistry" or "a consummate liar." That is why the *Thesaurus must* be used together with a dictionary.

While we are on the subject of association as a way of learning new words, there is another kind of association that you can make: associate words that deal with a specific topic or subject. A good place to start is your own interests. Let's try foods and food preparation. Words such as the following come to mind: *aspic, baste, sauté, truss, buffet, entrée, ragout, simmer, braise, compote, cuisine, curried, garnish, soufflé, meringue, hors d'oeuvres.*

Now for a subject that concerns all of us—health. The following words are the stock in trade of the medical doctor: *abscess, allergy, anemia, cataract, cyst, eczema, embolism, gangrene, hemorrhage, hepatitis, metabolism, neuralgia, pleurisy, sciatica, stroke, tumor.*

And anyone with an interest in motors and tools should be familiar with the terms *carburetor, condenser, compression, gear ratio, piston, socket wrench, dynamometer, emission, vacuum.*

Many books have glossaries, lists of difficult words with definitions. When you read a book on a particular subject, see if it has a glossary, and if it does, study the new words and their definitions.

A BASIC 1100-WORD VOCABULARY

To help you build your vocabulary, we have selected 1100 words which every high school graduate should know. They are grouped into lists of nouns, verbs, and adjectives. You should use these lists and the definitions together with a good dictionary such as *Webster's New World Dictionary of the American Language*. For each word, we have provided a definition which is most widely used but is often far removed from the first or literal meaning. You may wish to study other meanings of each word. We have also provided many words, sentences, or phrases to show you how the particular word should be used.

300 Useful Nouns

access (means of) approach or admittance (e.g. to records)

accord agreement

adage proverb (as "Better late than never")

affluence abundance; wealth (e.g. age of ___)

agenda list of things to be done or discussed (e.g. at a meeting)

alacrity brisk willingness (e.g. agreed with ___)

alias assumed name (e.g. Fred Henry, John Doe)

animosity great hatred (e.g. toward strangers)

anthology collection of writings or other creative work such as songs

apathy indifference (e.g. toward poverty)

apex the highest point (e.g. ___ of a triangle)

atlas book of maps

audacity boldness

avarice greed for wealth

awe feeling of respect and wonder (e.g. in ___ of someone's power)

beacon guiding light (e.g. of knowledge)

benediction blessing

bigotry unwillingness to allow others to have different opinions and beliefs from one's own

blemish defect (e.g. on one's record)

bondage slavery

boon benefit (e.g. a ___ to business)

brawl noisy fight

brevity shortness

brochure pamphlet (e.g. a travel ___)

bulwark strong protection (e.g. a ___ against corruption)

caliber quality (e.g. a person of high ___)

camouflage disguise, usually in war, changing the appearance of persons or equipment

caste social class or distinction

catastrophe sudden disaster (e.g. an earthquake)

chagrin feeling of deep disappointment

chronicle historical record

clamor uproar

clemency mercy (e.g. toward a prisoner)

condolence expression of sympathy (e.g. extended ___ to a bereaved)

connoisseur expert judge (e.g. of paintings, food)

consensus general agreement

context words or ideas just before or after a given word or idea (e.g. meaning of a word in a given ____)

criterion standard of judgment (e.g. good or poor by this ____)

crux the essential point (e.g. the ____ of the matter)

cynic one who doubts the good intentions of others

data known facts (e.g. ____ were found through research)

dearth scarcity (e.g. of talent)

debacle general defeat (e.g. in a battle)

debut first appearance before an audience (e.g. actor, pianist)

deluge great flood (e.g. rain or, in a special sense, mail)

depot warehouse

destiny predetermined fate

detriment damage or loss (e.g. it was to his ____)

diagnosis determining the nature of a disease or a situation

diction manner in which words are used in speech (e.g. The radio announcer's ____ was excellent.)

dilemma situation requiring a choice between two unpleasant courses of action (e.g. He was in a ____.)

din loud continuing noise

directive a general order (e.g. from an executive or military commander)

discord disagreement

discrepancy inconsistency (e.g. in accounts, in testimony)

discretion freedom of choice (e.g. He was given ____ to spend the money as he saw fit.)

dissent difference of opinion (e.g. from a decision)

drought long spell of dry weather

egotist one who judges everything only as it affects his own interest; a self-centered person

elite choice part (e.g. of society)

enterprise an important project

environment surrounding influences or conditions

epitome typical representation (e.g. She was the ____ of beauty.)

epoch period of time identified by an important person or event (e.g. the ____ of space flight)

era period of time marked by an important person or event (e.g. the Napoleonic ____)

essence basic nature (e.g. of the matter)

etiquette rules of social behavior which are generally accepted

excerpt passage from a book or a document

exodus departure, usually of large numbers

facet side or aspect (e.g. of a problem)

facsimile exact copy

fallacy mistaken idea; reasoning which contains an error

fantasy imagination (e.g. He indulged in ____.)

feud continued deadly hatred (e.g. between two families)

fiasco complete, humiliating failure

fiend inhumanly cruel person

finale last part of a performance

flair natural talent (e.g. for sports)

flaw defect

focus central point (e.g. of attention)

foe enemy

format physical appearance or arrangement (e.g. of a book)

forte one's strong point (e.g. math, sports)

fortitude steady courage (e.g. when in trouble)

forum a gathering for the discussion of public issues

foyer entrance hall (e.g. to a building or dwelling)

fraud deliberate deception

friction rubbing of the surface of one thing against the surface of another

function purpose served by a person, object, or organization

furor outburst of excitement (e.g. over a discovery)

gamut the whole range (e.g. of experiences)

gazetteer geographical dictionary, usually accompanying an atlas

genesis origin (e.g. of a plan)

ghetto section of a city where members of a particular group (formerly religious, now racial) live

gist essential content (e.g. of a speech or an article)

glutton one who overeats or who indulges in anything to excess

grievance complaint made against someone responsible for a situation believed to be unjust

havoc great damage and destruction (e.g. wreak ____ on)

hazard danger

heritage inheritance either of real wealth or of a tradition

hoax deliberate attempt to trick someone either seriously or as a joke

horde crowd

horizon limit (of knowledge, experience, or ambition)

hue shade of color

hysteria wild emotional outburst

idiom expression peculiar to a language which has a different

meaning from the words which make it up (e.g. hit the road)

illusion idea or impression different from reality

image likeness or reflected impression of a person or object

impetus moving force

incentive spur or motive to do something (e.g. profit ____)

incumbent present holder of an office

infirmity physical defect

influx flowing in (e.g. of money into banks, tourists into a country)

infraction violation of a rule or a law

initiative desire or ability to take the first step in carrying out some action (often a new plan or idea)

innovation introduction of a new idea or method

integrity moral and intellectual honesty and uprightness

interim meantime (e.g. in the ____)

interlude period of time between two events (e.g. ____ between the acts of a play)

intrigue secret plot

intuition knowledge through instinct rather than thought

iota very small amount

itinerary route followed on a trip, actual or planned

jeopardy risk of harm (e.g. put into ____)

keynote main theme (e.g. He sounded the ____ of the convention)

larceny theft (e.g. They couldn't decide whether it was grand or petty ____)

layman one who is not a member of a particular profession (e.g. from the point of view of a ____)

legacy material or spiritual inheritance (e.g. ____ from a parent)

legend story or stories passed on from generation to generation and often considered to be true

legion large number

liaison contact between two or more groups (e.g. ____ between headquarters and field units)

lore body of traditional knowledge (e.g. nature ____)

malady disease (e.g. incurable ____)

maneuver skillful move (e.g. a clever ____)

mania abnormal absorption (e.g. She had a ____ for clothes.)

marathon contest requiring endurance

maverick one who acts independently rather than according to an organizational pattern

maxim saying which provides a rule of conduct (e.g. Look before you leap.)

medium means of communication (e.g. ____ of radio)

memento object which serves as a reminder (e.g. a ____ of the war)

metropolis main city of a state or region (or any large city)

milieu surroundings

morale state of mind as it affects possible future action (e.g. The troops had good ____.)

mores well-established customs (e.g. the ____ of a society)

multitude a large number

myriad a large number of varied people or things

myth a story which is a traditional explanation of some occurrence, usually in nature (e.g. the ____ of Atlas holding up the heavens)

niche a suitable and desirable place (e.g. he found his ____ in the business organization.)

nomad wanderer

nostalgia desire to return to past experiences or associations

oasis a place which provides relief from the usual conditions (e.g. an ____ of peace in a troubled world)

oblivion place or condition in which one is completely forgotten

odyssey long journey

omen something which is believed to predict a future event (e.g. an evil ____)

optimum the best possible quantity or quality (e.g. He participated to the ____.)

ovation enthusiastic reception usually accompanied by generous applause (e.g. He received a tumultuous ____.)

oversight failure to include something through carelessness (e.g. His name was omitted because of an ____.)

overture first step, which is intended to lead to others in either action or discussion (e.g. He made a peace ____.)

pageant public spectacle in the form of a stage performance or a parade (e.g. a historical ____)

panacea something considered a cure for all diseases or problems

panorama a clear view of a very broad area

paradox statement of a truth which appears to contradict itself (e.g. a 20-year-old who had only five birthdays because he was born on February 29).

pastime way of spending leisure time (e.g. He took up golf as a ____.)

paucity scarcity (e.g. a ____ of nuclear scientists)

pauper very poor person

peer an equal as to age, social standing, ability, or other feature

phenomenon a natural occurrence such as the tides

phobia fear of something which is so great as to be unreasonable (e.g. ____ toward cats)

physique build (of the human body)

pilgrimage long trip to some place worthy of respect or devotion

pinnacle highest point (e.g. the ____ of power)

pitfall trap

pittance very small sum of money (e.g. He survived on a ____.)

plateau area of level land located at a height

plight condition, usually unfavorable (e.g. the sorry ____ of the refugees)

poise calm and controlled manner of behavior (e.g. He showed ____ in difficult situations.)

populace the common people

posterity future generations (e.g. leave a peaceful world to our ____)

precedent event or regulation which serves as an example or provides the basis for approval of a later action (e.g. set a ____)

predicament unpleasant situation from which it is difficult to free oneself (e.g. He found himself in a ____.)

preface introductory statement to a book or speech

prelude something which is preliminary to some act or work which is more important

premise statement from which a conclusion is logically drawn (e.g.

granted the ____ that ..., we may conclude ....)

premium amount added to the usual payment or charge (e.g. He paid a ____ for the seats.)

prestige respect achieved through rank, achievement, or reputation

pretext reason given as a cover-up for the true purpose of an action (e.g. He gave as a ____ for stealing it his sentimental attachment to the ring.)

priority something which comes before others in importance (e.g. He gave ____ to his studies.)

process step-by-step system for accomplishing some purpose (e.g. the ____ of legislation)

prospect outlook for the future (e.g. the ____ of peace)

proviso requirement that something be done, usually made in writing

prowess superior ability (e.g. ____ in athletics)

proximity nearness

pseudonym assumed name, usually by an author (e.g. Mark Twain, ____ of Samuel Clemens)

pun play on words depending on two different meanings or sounds of the same word (e.g. Whether life is worth living depends on the liver.)

qualm uneasy doubt about some action (e.g. He had a ____ about running for office.)

quandary uncertainty over a choice between two courses of action (e.g. He was in a ____ between the careers of law and medicine.)

query question

quest search (e.g. ____ for knowledge)

rapport harmonious relationship (e.g. ____ between teacher and pupil)

rarity something not commonly found (e.g. A talent like his is a ____.)

refuge place to which one can go for protection (e.g. He found ____ in the church.)

remnant remaining part (e.g. ____ of the troops)

remorse deep feeling of guilt for some bad act (e.g. He felt ____ at having insulted his friend.)

rendezvous a meeting or a place for meeting

renown fame (e.g. an actor of great ____)

repast meal

replica an exact copy (e.g. ____ of a painting)

reprimand severe criticism in the form of a scolding (e.g. He received a ____ from his superior.)

reprisal return of something in kind (e.g. ____ for an injury—"An eye for an eye")

residue remainder

resources assets, either material or spiritual, which are available for use

respite temporary break which brings relief (e.g. ____ from work)

résumé summary

reverence feeling of great respect (e.g. ____ for life)

robot one who acts mechanically or like a mechanical man

roster list of names (e.g. ____ of guests)

sabotage deliberate damage to vital services of production and supply, usually to those of an enemy in wartime

saga long tale, usually of heroic deeds

salutation greeting, written or spoken (e.g. The ____ of a letter may be "Dear Sir.")

sanction approval, usually by proper authority

sarcasm use of cutting remarks

satire attack upon evil or foolish behavior by showing it to be ridiculous

scapegoat someone who is blamed for the bad deeds of others

scent distinctive smell

scope entire area of action or thought (e.g. the ____ of the plan)

scroll roll of paper or parchment containing writing

sect group of people having the same beliefs, usually religious

segment part or section of a whole (e.g. ____ of a population)

semblance outward appearance (e.g. He gave the ____ of a scholar.)

sequel something that follows from what happened or was written before (e.g. ____ to a novel)

sham false imitation (e.g. His devotion was a ____ of true love.)

sheaf bundle either of grain or of papers

sheen luster (e.g. of furniture)

silhoutte outline drawing in black

site location of an object or an action (e.g. original ____ of a building)

slander untruth spoken or spread about someone which damages his reputation

slogan motto which is associated with an action or a cause (e.g. Pike's Peak or bust!)

slope slant (e.g. ____ of a line)

snare trap

solace comfort (e.g. She found ____ in work.)

sponsor one who endorses and supports a person or an activity

spur something which moves one to act (e.g. a ____ to sacrifice)

stamina ability to fight off physical difficulties such as fatigue

stature height reached physically or morally (e.g. a man of great ____)

status standing, social or professional

stigma mark of disgrace

stimulus any encouragement to act

strategy skillful planning and execution (e.g. the ____ in a battle)

strife conflict (e.g. ____ between labor and management)

summit the highest point (e.g. the ____ of his career)

supplement amount added to complete something (e.g. ____ to a budget)

survey broad study of a topic (e.g. a ____ of employment)

suspense tenseness brought about by uncertainty as to what will happen

symbol something which is used to stand for something else (e.g. Uncle Sam is a ____ of the United States.)

symptom indication of something (e.g. ____ of disease)

synopsis brief summary

tact ability to say and do the right thing socially

tactics skillful actions to achieve some purpose (e.g. The ____ he used to win were unfair.)

tally record of a score or an account (e.g. the ____ of the receipts)

tang strong taste or flavor

technique method or skill in doing work (e.g. the ____ of an artist)

temperament natural disposition, often to act in a contrary manner (e.g. He displayed a changeable ____.)

tempo pace of activity (e.g. The ____ of life is increasing.)

tension mental or emotional strain (e.g. He was under great ____.)

theme topic of a written work or a talk

threshold the starting point (e.g. the ____ of a career)

thrift ability to save money (e.g. He became wealthy because of ____.)

tint a shade of color

token sign which stands for some object or feeling (e.g. a ____ of esteem)

tonic something which is a source of energy or vigor

tradition customs and beliefs which are received by one generation from another

trait distinguishing feature (e.g. ____ of character)

transition movement from one situation to another (e.g. ____ from dictatorship to democracy)

tribunal place of judgment, such as a court

tribute showing of respect or gratitude (e.g. He paid a ____ to his parents.)

turmoil disturbance (e.g. great ____ at the meeting)

tutor a private teacher

tycoon wealthy and powerful businessman

ultimatum a final condition or demand ("Take it or leave it!")

unrest restless dissatisfaction

upheaval sudden overthrow, often violent

usage established practice or custom

utensil implement which is of use (e.g. a kitchen ____)

utopia ideal place or society

valor courage

venture something involving risk
vicinity neighborhood
victor winner
vigor vitality
vim energy
vow solemn pledge
wager bet
whim sudden notion or desire

woe great sorrow (e.g. He brought ____ to his friends.)
wrath intense anger (e.g. He poured his ____ on his enemies.)
zeal eager desire
zenith the highest point
zest keen enthusiasm (e.g. ____ for competition)

300 Useful Verbs

abhor hate
absolve free from guilt (e.g. for a crime)
accede agree to (e.g. a request)
accelerate speed up
accost go up and speak to
adhere give support to (e.g. a cause)
adjourn put off to a later time (e.g. a meeting)
advocate act in support of (e.g. revolution)
allay calm (e.g. fears)
allege claim
allot assign (e.g. a share)
allude refer to (e.g. a book)
alter change
assent agree
atone make up for (e.g. a sin)
augment add to
avert prevent
baffle puzzle
ban forbid
bar exclude
befall happen to
berate scold
beseech plead
bestow grant (used with on or upon)
cede give up (e.g. territory)
censure blame
char scorch
chastise punish
chide scold

cite mention in order to prove something
coerce force
collaborate work with someone
commend praise
comply act in answer to (e.g. a request)
concede admit that something is true (e.g. an argument)
concur agree
constrict squeeze
cull pick out
curtail cut short or reduce
deduce come to a conclusion from given facts
deem consider
defer postpone
defray pay (e.g. the costs)
delete remove or erase (e.g. a word)
delve investigate
deplete use up
deplore be sorry about
deprive keep someone from having or getting something
despise scorn
detain delay temporarily
detect uncover something that is not obvious
deter keep someone from doing something
detest hate
detract take away from

devour eat up greedily

digress depart from the subject under consideration

dilute weaken by adding something less strong to the original (e.g. a mixture)

disburse pay out

discern make out clearly (e.g. a pattern)

disdain look down on with scorn

disintegrate fall apart

dismay dishearten

dispel drive away

disperse scatter

disrupt break up

distort present incorrectly (e.g. facts)

diverge go in different directions

divert turn from a course (e.g. a stream)

divulge reveal

don put on (e.g. clothing)

efface blot out

effect bring about

eject throw out

elate make happy

emit give forth (e.g. sounds)

encounter meet

encroach intrude on (e.g. property)

endeavor try

endow provide with (e.g. a desirable quality)

enhance increase the value of

ensue follow as a result

entreat plead

err make a mistake

erupt break out

esteem value

evade avoid or escape from someone or something

evict expel

exalt raise to greater heights

exceed surpass

expedite speed up the handling of

exploit take advantage of a situation or a person

extol praise highly

falter stumble

famish starve

feign pretend

flaunt show off

flourish thrive

flout defy mockingly

foil prevent

forgo do without

forsake abandon

frustrate prevent someone from achieving something

gauge estimate

harass disturb constantly

heave lift and throw

heed pay attention to (e.g. advice)

hinder keep back

hover hang in the air above a certain spot

hurl throw with force

ignite set fire to

immerse plunge into a liquid

impair damage

impede stand in the way of

imply suggest

incite arouse

incur bring upon oneself (e.g. criticism)

induce persuade

indulge satisfy (e.g. a desire)

infer come to a conclusion based on something known

inhibit restrain

instigate spur to action

instill put a feeling into someone gradually (e.g. fear)

intercept interrupt something (or someone) which is on its (his/her) way

interrogate question

intimidate frighten by making threats

invoke call upon

irk annoy

jar shake up (e.g. as in a collision)

jeer poke fun at (e.g. as by sarcastic remarks)

lament feel sorrow for

launch set in motion

loom appear in a threatening manner

lop cut off

lure tempt

lurk remain hidden

magnify make larger

maim cripple

mimic imitate

mock ridicule

molest bother

narrate tell (e.g. a story)

navigate steer (e.g. a ship)

negate deny

orient adjust oneself or someone to a situation

oust expel

parch make dry

peer look closely

pend remain undecided

perfect complete

perplex puzzle

persevere continue on a course of action despite difficulties

pertain have reference to

perturb upset to a great extent

peruse read carefully

pine long for

placate make calm

ponder think through thoroughly

preclude prevent something from happening

prescribe order (e.g. for use or as a course of action)

presume take for granted

prevail win out over

probe investigate thoroughly

procure obtain

profess claim with doubtful sincerity

prosper be successful

protrude project

provoke arouse to action out of irritation

pry look closely into

quell subdue

ravage ruin

rebate give back, usually part of an amount paid

rebuff repulse

rebuke disapprove sharply

recede move backward

recompense repay

reconcile bring together by settling differences

recoup make up for (e.g. something lost)

rectify correct

recur happen again

redeem buy back; make good a promise

refrain keep from

refute prove false

reimburse pay back

reiterate repeat

reject refuse to take

relinquish give up

reminisce recall past happenings

remit send (e.g. money)

remunerate pay for work done

renounce give up (e.g. a claim)

renovate restore (e.g. a house)

repent feel regret for (e.g. a sin)

replenish make full again

repose rest

repress hold back (e.g. a feeling)

reproach blame

repudiate refuse to recognize

repulse drive back

rescind cancel (e.g. a rule or regulation)

respire breathe

restrain hold back

retain keep

retaliate return in kind (e.g. a blow for a blow)

retard delay

retort answer sharply

retract take back (e.g. something said)

retrieve get back

revere have deep respect for

revert go back to a former condition

revoke withdraw (e.g. a law)

rupture break

salvage save something out of a disaster such as fire

scald burn painfully with steam or hot liquid

scan look at closely

scoff mock

scorn treat with contempt

scour clean thoroughly; move about widely in a search

scowl make an angry look

seclude keep away from other people

seep ooze

seethe boil

sever divide

shear cut with a sharp instrument

shed throw off (e.g. clothing)

shirk seek to avoid (e.g. duty or work)

shrivel contract and wrinkle

shun avoid

shunt turn aside

sift sort out through careful examination (e.g. evidence)

signify mean

singe burn slightly

skim read over quickly

smite hit hard

smolder burn or give off smoke after the fire is out

snarl tangle

soar fly high in the air

sojourn live temporarily in a place

solicit plead for (e.g. help)

spurn reject scornfully

startle surprise

stifle suppress (e.g. feelings)

strew scatter

strive try hard

stun daze

subside lessen in activity

subsist continue to live with difficulty

succumb yield to

suffice be enough

suppress put down (e.g. a revolt)

surge increase suddenly

surmount overcome (e.g. an obstacle)

sustain support

swarm move in great numbers

sway move back and forth

tamper meddle with

tarnish discolor

taunt reproach mockingly

thaw melt

thrash defeat thoroughly

thrive prosper

throb beat insistently

throttle choke

thrust push forcefully and suddenly

thwart prevent someone from achieving something

tinge color slightly

torment afflict with pain

transform change the appearance of

transmit send along

transpire come to light

traverse cross over

trudge walk with difficulty

undergo experience

undo return to condition before something was done

usurp seize power illegally

utilize make use of

utter speak

vacate make empty

vanquish conquer

vary change

vend sell

verge be on the point of

verify prove the truth of

vex annoy

vibrate move back and forth

violate break (e.g. a law)

vouch guarantee

waive give up (e.g. a right or privilege)

wane decrease in strength

warp twist out of shape

waver sway back and forth

whet sharpen

wield put to use (e.g. power or a tool such as a club)

wilt become limp

wither dry up (e.g. a flower)

withstand hold out against (e.g. pressure)

wrest pull violently

wring force out by squeezing

writhe twist and turn about

yearn long for

yield give up

500 Useful Adjectives

acrid sharp to taste or smell (e.g. odor)

adamant unyielding

adept skilled

adroit skillful

aesthetic having to do with beauty

agile nimble

ambidextrous equally skilled at using both hands

amenable disposed to follow (e.g. advice)

amiable friendly

apt suitable

aquatic living in or practiced on water

ardent passionate

arrogant overly proud

articulate able to express oneself clearly (e.g. a person)

astute shrewd

auspicious favorable (e.g. circumstances)

austere harsh

authentic genuine

auxiliary helping

barren unfruitful

bizarre strange

bland gentle

blatant overly loud

boisterous rambunctious

brusque rudely brief

callous unfeeling

candid honest

casual offhand

chic stylish

chronic continuing over a long period of time

civic municipal

civil courteous

cogent convincing (e.g. argument)

coherent clearly holding together

colloquial conversational

colossal huge

compatible capable of getting along together

complacent satisfied with oneself

concise brief but complete
copious plentiful
crafty sly
credible believable
credulous given to believing anything too easily
cumbersome bulky
cursory done quickly but only on the surface (e.g. an examination)
curt rudely brief
deft skillful
defunct dead
demure overly modest
derogatory belittling
desolate lonely
despondent depressed
destitute poverty-stricken
detergent cleansing
devious indirect
devoid completely free of (e.g. feeling)
devout very religious
diffident shy
diminutive tiny
dire dreadful
discreet careful
discrete distinctly separate
disinterested impartial
dismal gloomy
distraught driven to distraction
diverse varied
docile easily led
dogmatic stubbornly positive (e.g. opinion)
domestic having to do with the home
dominant ruling
dormant sleeping
drastic extreme (e.g. changes)
dreary gloomy
dubious doubtful
durable lasting

dynamic energetic
earnest intensely serious
ebony black
eccentric peculiar (e.g. behavior)
edible fit to be eaten
eerie weird
elegant tastefully fine
eloquent powerfully fluent in writing or speech
elusive hard to get hold of
eminent distinguished (e.g. author)
epic heroic in size
erratic not regular
eternal everlasting
ethnic having to do with race
exorbitant unreasonable (e.g. price)
exotic foreign
expedient suitable in a given situation but not necessarily correct
explicit clearly indicated
exquisite extremely beautiful
extemporaneous spoken or accomplished with little preparation
extensive broad
extinct no longer existing
extraneous having nothing to do with the subject at hand
fanatic extremely emotionally enthusiastic
feasible possible to carry out (e.g. a plan)
feeble weak
fertile productive
fervent warmly felt
festive in the spirit of a holiday (e.g. celebration)
fickle changeable
flagrant noticeably bad (e.g. violation)
fleet swift

flimsy not strong (e.g. platform)
fluent smooth (e.g. speech)
forlorn hopeless
formidable fear-inspiring because of size or strength (e.g. enemy)
fragile easily broken
frail delicate
frank outspoken
fraternal brotherly
frigid extremely cold
frugal thrifty
futile useless
gala festive
gallant courteously brave (e.g. conduct)
gaudy tastelessly showy
gaunt overly thin and weary-looking
genial kindly
germane pertinent
ghastly frightful (e.g. appearance)
gigantic huge
glib fluent but insincere
glum gloomy
gory bloody
graphic vividly realistic
gratis free
grievous causing sorrow
grim sternly forbidding (e.g. future)
gross glaringly bad (e.g. injustice)
grotesque distorted in appearance
gruesome horrifying
gullible easily fooled
guttural throaty (e.g. sound)
haggard worn-looking
hale healthy
haphazard chance
hardy having endurance
harsh disagreeably rough
haughty overly proud
hearty friendly (e.g. welcome)
hectic feverish
heinous outrageous (e.g. crime)
hideous extremely ugly

hilarious very gay
homogenous of like kind (e.g. group)
horrendous horrible
hostile unfriendly (e.g. unwelcome)
humane merciful
humble modest
humid damp
illicit illegal
immaculate spotlessly clean
immense very large
imminent about to happen (e.g. storm)
impartial unbiased
imperative necessary
impertinent rude
impetuous acting on impulse
implicit implied
impromptu without any preparation (e.g. remarks)
impudent rudely bold
inane silly
incendiary causing fire (e.g. bomb)
incessant uninterrupted
inclement rough (e.g. weather)
incognito with real identity hidden
incoherent not clearly connected
indelible unable to be erased
indifferent showing no interest
indigent poor
indignant very angry
indispensable absolutely necessary
industrious hard-working
inept ineffective
infallible unable to make a mistake
infamous having a bad reputation
infinite endless
infinitesimal very, very small
inflexible unbending
ingenious clever
ingenuous naturally simple
inherent existing in someone or something

innate inborn
innocuous harmless
insipid uninteresting (e.g. conversation)
insolent boldly rude
integral essential to the whole
intensive thorough (e.g. study)
intermittent starting and stopping (e.g. rain)
intolerant unwilling or unable to respect others or their beliefs
intricate complicated
invincible unable to be conquered
irate angry
irrational unreasonable
jovial good-humored
jubilant joyous
judicious showing good judgment (e.g. decision)
laborious demanding a lot of work
lank tall and thin
latent hidden (e.g. talent)
laudable worthy of praise
lavish extremely generous (e.g. praise)
lax loose (e.g. discipline)
legible easily read (e.g. print)
legitimate lawful (e.g. claim)
lethal fatal
listless lacking in spirit
literal following the exact words or intended meaning of the original (e.g. translation)
literate educated to the point of being able to read and write (e.g. person)
livid discolored by a bruise (e.g. flesh)
loath reluctant
lofty very high
loquacious talkative
lucid clear
lucrative profitable (e.g. business)
ludicrous ridiculous

lurid shockingly sensational (e.g. story)
lusty vigorous
majestic grand (e.g. building)
malicious spiteful
malignant harmful
mammoth gigantic
mandatory required
manifest evident
manual done by the hands (e.g. labor)
marine of the sea (e.g. life)
martial warlike
massive bulky and heavy
meager scanty
menial lowly (e.g. task)
mercenary working only for financial gain (e.g. soldier)
meticulous extremely careful
militant aggressive
mobile movable (e.g. home)
moot debatable (e.g. question)
morbid unhealthily gloomy
mutual reciprocal (e.g. admiration)
naive innocently simple
nauseous disgusting
nautical having to do with ships and sailing
negligent neglectful
neurotic describing the behavior of a person suffering from an emotional disorder
nimble moving quickly and easily
nocturnal of the night (e.g. animal)
nominal small in comparison with service or value received (e.g. fee)
nonchalant casual and unexcited
notable important (e.g. person)
notorious well-known in an unfavorable way (e.g. criminal)
null having no effect
obese overly fat

objective free from prejudice (e.g. analysis)

oblique indirectly indicated (e.g. suggestion)

obnoxious extremely unpleasant (e.g. behavior)

obsolete out-of-date (e.g. machine)

obstinate stubborn

ominous threatening (e.g. clouds)

onerous burdensome (e.g. task)

opportune timely

opulent wealthy

ornate elaborately decorated

orthodox usually approved (e.g. religious beliefs)

ostensible apparent

outright complete

overt open

paltry insignificant (e.g. sum of money)

paramount chief (e.g. importance)

passive not active (e.g. participation)

patent obvious

pathetic pitiful

pedestrian unimaginative (e.g. ideas)

peevish irritable

penitent repentant

pensive thoughtful

perennial lasting for a long time (e.g. problem)

perilous dangerous

pertinent relevant

petty relatively unimportant

picayune petty

pious devoutly religious

placid calm (e.g. waters)

plausible apparently true (e.g. argument)

pliable flexible

poignant keenly painful to the emotions

pompous self-important (e.g. person)

portable capable of being carried (e.g. radio)

posthumous taking place after a person's death (e.g. award)

potent powerful (e.g. drug)

potential possible (e.g. greatness)

practicable capable of being done

pragmatic practical

precarious risky

precise exact

precocious advanced to a level earlier than is to be expected (e.g. child)

predominant prevailing

preposterous ridiculous

prevalent widespread

primary fundamental (e.g. reason)

prime first in importance or quality

primitive crude (e.g. tools)

prior previous (e.g. appointment)

prodigious extraordinary in size or amount (e.g. effort)

proficient skilled

profuse abundantly given (e.g. praise)

prolific producing large amounts (e.g. author)

prone disposed to (e.g. accident)

prosaic ordinary

prostrate laid low (e.g. by grief)

provincial narrow (e.g. view of a matter)

prudent discreet (e.g. advice)

pugnacious quarrelsome (e.g. person)

pungent sharp to taste or smell (e.g. odor)

punitive inflicting punishment (e.g. action)

puny small in size or strength (e.g. effort)

putrid rotten

quaint pleasantly odd (e.g. custom)

radiant brightly shining

rampant spreading unchecked (e.g. violence)

rancid having the bad taste or smell of stale food (e.g. butter)

random decided by chance (e.g. choice)

rank complete (e.g. incompetency)

rash reckless

raucous harsh (e.g. sound)

ravenous extremely hungry

reflex of an involuntary response (e.g. action)

regal royal

relentless persistent (e.g. chase)

relevant pertinent

remiss careless (e.g. in one's duty)

remote far distant (e.g. time or place)

replete filled (e.g. with thrills)

repugnant extremely distasteful

repulsive disgusting

reputable respectable (e.g. doctor)

resigned submitting passively to (e.g. to one's fate)

resolute firmly determined

resonant resounding (e.g. sound)

restive restless (e.g. pupils)

reticent speaking little (e.g. child)

rigid stiff

robust strong and healthy

rowdy rough and disorderly (e.g. mob)

rugged rough

rustic of the country (e.g. life)

ruthless pitiless (e.g. dictator)

sage wise (e.g. advice)

salient prominent (e.g. points)

salutary healthful (e.g. climate)

sane mentally sound

sanguinary bloody

sanguine cheerfully hopeful

scanty meager

scholastic having to do with school and education (e.g. record)

scrawny thin

scrupulous careful and honest (e.g. accounting)

secretive given to secrecy

secular not religious (e.g. education)

sedate dignified

serene calm

sheer very thin (e.g. stockings); utter (e.g. nonsense)

shiftless lazy

shifty tricky

shoddy inferior in quality (e.g. material)

shrewd clever in one's dealings (e.g. businessman)

simultaneous happening at the same time (e.g. events)

singular remarkable; strange (e.g. behavior)

sinister threatening evil

skeptical showing doubt (e.g. attitude)

slack not busy (e.g. business season); loose (e.g. rope)

sleek smooth and glossy (e.g. appearance)

slender small in size or amount (e.g. contribution)

slovenly untidy

sluggish slow-moving

smug self-satisfied

snug comfortable

sober serious

solemn grave (e.g. occasion)

solitary lone

somber dark and gloomy (e.g. outlook)

sophisticated wise in the ways of the world

sordid wretched (e.g. condition)

sparse thinly scattered

spirited lively

spiritual of the spirit or soul

spontaneous happening as a result of natural impulse (e.g. reaction)

sporadic happening at irregular times (e.g. shooting)

spry nimble

staccato with breaks between successive sounds

stagnant dirty from lack of movement (e.g. water)

stalwart robust

staunch firm (e.g. friend)

stark bleak (e.g. outlook)

stately dignified

static stationary

stationary not moving

steadfast firm

stern severe (e.g. look)

stocky short and heavily built

stodgy uninteresting

stoical unmoved emotionally

stout fat; firm (e.g. resistance)

straightforward honest (e.g. answer)

strenuous demanding great energy (e.g. exercise)

stupendous amazing (e.g. effort)

sturdy strongly built

suave smoothly polite (e.g. manner)

sublime inspiring admiration because of noble quality (e.g. music)

subsidiary of less importance (e.g. rank)

substantial of considerable numbers or size

subtle suggested delicately (e.g. hint)

sullen resentful

sultry extremely hot and humid (e.g. weather)

sumptuous costly (e.g. meal)

sundry various

superb of a high degree of excellence

superficial not going beyond the obvious (e.g. examination)

superfluous beyond what is needed

superlative superior to all others (e.g. performance)

supple limber (e.g. body)

surly offensively rude

susceptible easily affected by (e.g. to colds)

swarthy dark-skinned

tacit not openly said but implied (e.g. approval)

tangible capable of being touched; actual (e.g. results)

tardy late (e.g. student)

tart having a sharp taste (e.g. food)

taut tightly stretched (e.g. rope)

tedious long and tiresome (e.g. study)

temperate moderate (e.g. climate)

tenacious holding fast (e.g. grip)

tentative for a temporary period of trial (e.g. agreement)

tepid lukewarm (e.g. water)

terminal concluding

terse brief but expressing a good deal (e.g. comment)

thankless unappreciated (e.g. task)

tidy neat (e.g. appearance)

timeless eternal (e.g. beauty)

timely happening at a desirable time (e.g. arrival)

timid shy

tiresome tiring

titanic of enormous size or strength

torrid intensely hot

tranquil calm (e.g. waters)

transient passing away after a brief time

trifling of little importance

trite ordinary (e.g. remark)
trivial insignificant
turbulent agitated
ultimate final (e.g. conclusion)
unanimous in complete agreement (e.g. decision)
unassuming modest
uncanny unnatural (e.g. accuracy)
unconditional absolute (e.g. surrender)
uncouth crude and clumsy (e.g. adolescent)
undaunted not discouraged
underhanded sly
unduly overly (e.g. concerned)
uneasy disturbed
ungainly awkward (e.g. youth)
unique only one of its kind (e.g. specimen)
unkempt not combed
unruly disorderly (e.g. crowd)
unscathed uninjured
unwieldy clumsy to use, usually because of size (e.g. implement)
upright honest (e.g. citizen)
utmost most extreme (e.g. in distance, height, or size)
utter complete (e.g. failure)
vain futile (e.g. attempt); conceited (e.g. person)
valiant brave
valid (legally) sound (e.g. argument)
vast very large in extent or size (e.g. distances)
vehement violent in feeling (e.g. protest)

verbatim word for word (e.g. report)
versatile able to perform many tasks well (e.g. athlete)
vigilant watchful (e.g. sentry)
vile highly disgusting (e.g. conduct)
visible able to be seen (e.g. object)
vital essential (e.g. contribution)
vivacious lively
vivid bright (e.g. color)
void not binding legally (e.g. contract)
voluminous very great in size (e.g. writings)
voracious greedy for food (e.g. appetite)
vulnerable open to attack (e.g. position)
wary cautious
weary tired
wee very small
weighty important (e.g. decision)
wholesome causing a feeling of well-being (e.g. entertainment)
wily cunning (e.g. magician)
wishful showing desire that something be so (e.g. thinking)
witty amusingly clever (e.g. remark)
wordy using too many words (e.g. reply)
worldly enjoying the pleasures and experiences of this world (e.g. person)
worthy deserving (e.g. choice)
wretched miserable

PARAGRAPH COMPREHENSION

The paragraph comprehension part of the ASVAB tests your ability to understand what you read. It does this by asking multiple-choice questions based on passages that vary in length from one to five paragraphs of about 30 to 120 words. Each passage is used for from one to five questions.

Reading comprehension involves several abilities: the ability to recognize main ideas, the ability to recall details, the ability to make inferences about the material in a passage, the ability to apply the material in the passage to other material, the ability to recognize and understand sequential, cause/effect, and comparative relationships, and the ability to paraphrase or summarize a passage.

Finding the Main Idea

The main idea is the most important point the author wants the reader to understand about the subject matter of a paragraph or passage. Sometimes the main idea is stated directly by the author and sometimes it is implied rather than stated.

Whenever you are asked to determine a passage's main idea, always check the opening and closing sentences of each paragraph. Authors typically provide readers with a "topic sentence" that expresses a paragraph's main idea succinctly. Although such topic sentences may appear anywhere in the paragraph, they often are the opening or closing sentence.

EXAMPLE

The world faces a serious problem of overpopulation. Right now many people starve from lack of adequate food. Efforts are being made to increase the rate of food production, but the number of people to be fed increases at a faster rate.

In this paragraph, the main idea is stated directly in the opening sentence. You know that the passage will be about "a serious problem of overpopulation." Like a heading or caption, the topic sentence sets the stage or gets your mind ready for what follows in the paragraph.

EXAMPLE

During the later years of the American Revolution, the Articles of Confederation government was formed. This government suffered severely from a lack of power. Each state distrusted the others and gave little authority to the central, or federal, government. The Articles of Confederation produced a government which could not raise money from taxes, prevent Indian raids, or force the British out of the United States.

What is the topic sentence in the preceding paragraph? Certainly the paragraph is about the Articles of Confederation. However, is the key idea in the first sentence or in the second sentence? In this instance, the *second* sentence does a better job of giving you the key to this paragraph—the lack of centralized power that characterized the Articles of Confederation. The sentences that complete the paragraph relate more to the idea of "lack of power" than to the time when the government was formed. Do not assume that the topic sentence is always the first sentence of a paragraph.

EXAMPLE

> They had fewer men available as soldiers. Less than one third of the railroads and only a small portion of the nation's industrial production was theirs. For most of the war their coastline was blockaded by Northern ships. It is a tribute to Southern leadership and the courage of the people that they were not defeated for four years.

In this case you will note that the passage builds up to its main point. The topic sentence is the last one.

As we mentioned previously, you may also find that the main idea is not expressed directly at all, but can only be inferred from the selection as a whole.

EXAMPLE

> The plane landed at 4 P.M. As the door opened, the crowd burst into a long, noisy demonstration. The waiting mob surged against the police guard lines. Women were screaming. Teenagers were yelling for autographs or souvenirs. The visitor smiled and waved at his fans.

The main idea of the paragraph is not expressed, but it is clear that some popular hero or famous personality is being welcomed enthusiastically at the airport.

To help find the main idea in a reading passage on the test, ask yourself these questions:

1. Who or what is this paragraph about?
2. What aspect of this subject is the author talking about?
3. What is the author trying to get across about this aspect of the subject?

In addition, look for signal words in the passage—words like *again, also, as well as, furthermore, moreover,* and *significantly.* These signal words may call your attention to the main idea.

Finding Details

In developing the main idea of a passage, a writer will make statements to support his or her point. The writer may give examples to illustrate the idea, or facts and statistics to support it. She may give reasons why the statement that is the main idea is true, or arguments for or against a position stated as the main idea. The writer may also define a complex term, or give a number of qualities of a complicated belief (such as democracy). He may also classify a number of objects within a larger category, or use descriptive details to develop an idea and to help the reader envision the situation. Finally, the writer may compare two ideas or objects (show how they are similar) or contrast them (show how they are different).

Note how the author of the following paragraph uses supporting details.

Episodic memories relate to our individual lives, recalling what we have done and the kinds of experiences we have had. When you recall your first date, the time you fell off your bicycle, or what you felt like when you graduated from high school, you are recalling episodic memories. The information in episodic memory is connected with specific times and places....

To help you understand the term *episodic memory*, the author gives three examples in the second sentence. These examples are supporting details.

To answer questions about supporting details, you *must* find a word or group of words in the passage that supports your choice of answer. The following techniques should help:

1. Look for key words (nouns and verbs) in the question stem and the answer choices.
2. Run your eye down the passage, looking for those key words or their synonyms.
3. Reread the part of the paragraph or passage that contains the key word or its synonym.

Making Inferences

You make inferences by putting together ideas that are expressed by the author to arrive at other ideas that are not. In other words, you draw conclusions from the information the author presents. You do this by locating relevant details and determining their relationships (time sequence, place sequence, cause and effect, etc.).

In inference questions you must put two and two together and see what you get; the passage never tells you directly what the answer is. Inference questions require you to use your own judgment. You must not take anything directly stated by the author as an inference. Instead, you must look for clues in the passage that you can use in coming up with your own conclusion. You should choose as your answer a statement that is a logical development of the information the author has provided. Remember that in answering inference questions you must go beyond the obvious, beyond what the author explicitly states, to look for logical implications of what the author says.

Let's try to apply these skills to representative passages you will encounter in the paragraph comprehension part of the test.

> Family camping has been described as the "biggest single growth industry in the booming travel/leisure market." Camping ranges from backpacking to living in motor homes with complete creature comforts. It is both an end in itself and a magic carpet to a wide variety of other forms of outdoor recreation.

It can be inferred from the passage that the LEAST luxurious form of camping is

A backpacking
B travel trailers
C camping trailers
D motor homes

The answer is A. This question requires you to make an inference from the information in the passage. The second sentence in the paragraph refers to the range of camping—from backpacking to the "creature comforts" of rolling homes. From this it can be inferred that backpacking is the least luxurious form of camping.

Understanding the Organization of the Material

Questions on a reading passage may also test your understanding of the organization of the ideas presented and their relationship to one another. Authors generally organize material in predictable and logical ways to make it easier for the reader to understand. Recognizing common patterns of organization increases understanding, recall, and speed.

Ideas may be organized in a sequential or spatial pattern, or a cause-and-effect relationship can be expressed. Ideas may also be compared or contrasted with one another, perhaps in an arguable or opposing position. A reading passage may also present a solution to a problem or problems mentioned, or a conclusion may be drawn from ideas stated or implied.

Sequential Organization

A *sequence is a series of steps or events in which order is important.* If the sequence is chronological, or time-based, the events are described or mentioned in the order in which they occurred. Clues to sequential organization of ideas include cardinal numbers (*1, 2, 3,* etc.), ordinal numbers (*first, second, third,* etc.), transition words (*next, later, then, finally*), and dates or other words referring to time (*next year, the following winter, in 1992, ten weeks later,* etc.).

EXAMPLE

If you are stung by a bee, first remove the stinger. Next, apply a paste of baking soda and water. Then, apply ice or cold water to help reduce the pain. If the pain is severe or the person is allergic to the insect, seek medical help immediately.

Spatial Organization

When the organization is spatial, the physical arrangement of a place or object is described. Clue words include, *above, below, next to, in front of, in back of, to the right of, to the left of.*

EXAMPLE

Taste buds are distributed across the tongue, but the distribution is uneven, and certain areas of the tongue are more sensitive to certain fundamental tastes than other areas.... The tip of the tongue is most sensitive to sweetness, but the portion just behind the tip is most sensitive to salty tastes. Only the sides of the tongue are very sensitive to sour tastes, and the rear specializes in bitter tastes.

Cause and Effect

A reading passage may include reasons why something happened and the results that occurred. For example, a history passage may present the events leading up to a war, or a science passage may list causes of the greenhouse effect and its effect, in turn, on global climate. Often, the relationship is presented as a *chain of events,* with one or more events leading to or resulting in another. Clue words include *for this reason, resulted in, because, consequently, since, thus.*

EXAMPLE

By the year 2020, there will be approximately one retired American for every two working Americans. In these large numbers, older Americans will become an increasingly powerful political force, and political issues of concern to the elderly, such as special housing, medical benefits, and reduced levels of employment, will become issues taken more seriously by elected officials.

Opposing or Similar Ideas

A reading passage may present the similarities or differences between ideas, people, places, or other things. The presentation may focus on similarities in a *comparison*; clue words include *like, similarly, likewise, in like manner, also.* Or, the presentation may focus on differences in presenting a *contrast*; clue words include *however, unlike, in contrast, on the other hand, versus, nevertheless.*

EXAMPLE

The American farm problem often centers on supply exceeding demand and farm policies that foster surplus production. This is not true in most other parts of the world, where countries cannot produce enough food to support their own population and must import food or face famine.

Solution to a Problem

In this organization pattern, the author presents a problem or describes a situation that is causing difficulty and presents or suggests solutions or remedies. Clue words include *problem, cause, effects, answers, remedies.*

EXAMPLE

In one study, students who lived in dormitories near an area in which earthquakes occurred frequently simply denied the seriousness of the situation and the possible danger they were in.

(In this case, the solution—an unrealistic one—was simply to ignore the problem.)

Drawing a Conclusion

A conclusion is a logical inference based on information presented or implied. If you read a passage critically, you follow the author's train of thought and arrive at logical conclusions. An author may expect a reader to draw the conclusion, or he or she may state it, often using clue words such as *thus, therefore, in conclusion,* or *hence.*

The sample passage that follows is about disabled Americans. The reader can conclude that legislation has made progress in moving the disabled into society's mainstream, although the author does not say so directly. Incidentally, you should note the sequence pattern in this passage.

EXAMPLE

A major goal for the disabled is easier access to the mainstream of society. The 1973 Rehabilitation Act has moved them toward this goal. So has the Education for All Handicapped Children Act of 1975, which mandates that all children, however severe their disability, receive a free, appropriate education. Before the legislation, one million handicapped children were receiving no education and another three million were receiving an inappropriate one (as in the case of a blind child who is not taught Braille or is not provided with instructional materials in Braille). In 1987 Congress enacted the Employment Opportunities for Disabled Americans Act, which allows disabled individuals to earn a moderate income without losing their Medicaid health coverage.

PART THREE
OVERVIEW OF ADDITIONAL SUBJECT AREAS

with Practice Questions and Answer Explanations

General Science Review

6

INTRODUCTION

Science can be divided into life, physical, and earth sciences. *Biology* is the general term for the study of life. It covers topics dealing with human health and medicine, and is closely related to the study of *botany* (the study of plants) and *zoology* (the study of animals). *Earth science* covers conditions affecting the earth (weather, climate, relation of people to their environment). *Chemistry* is a physical science that investigates the composition, structure, and properties of matter. It is also concerned with changes in matter and the energy released during those changes. *Physics*, like chemistry, is a physical science that deals with matter and energy. However, in physics, more attention is given to mechanical and electrical forces in areas such as light, sound, heat, motion, and magnetism.

The Scientific Method

Scientific problem solving depends upon accuracy of observation, precision of method, and orderliness. Scientific problem solving follows a pattern of actions which are collectively known as the *scientific method*. Each of the sciences uses this way of solving problems. It involves several steps:

1. **Observation.** In a sense, the true scientist is always involved in this step. It requires the accurate sighting and recording of a particular occurrence. The accuracy of one observation is proved when a number of independent observers agree that they see the same set of circumstances occurring under the same conditions many times.

2. **Hypothesis.** A temporary set of conclusions drawn from a set of observations is known as a hypothesis. It is usually a very general statement, and suggests the need for a particular experiment.

3. **Experiment.** To test a specific hypothesis, scientists perform experiments. The purpose of the experiments is to answer questions about data truthfully and carefully. Reliable experiments require controlled conditions.

4. Theory. When a hypothesis is supported by data obtained from experiments, the hypothesis becomes a theory.

5. Law, or principle. When a theory stands up under the test of time and repeated experiments, it may be called a "law" or principle.

PRACTICE QUESTIONS AND ANSWER EXPLANATIONS

The General Science test in the ASVAB consists of 25 questions. You will be allowed 11 minutes to complete it. Try to answer the following Practice Questions within that time period, by circling the correct answer for each question. Then check your answers with the Answer Key immediately following, and review all of the Answer Explanations.

Practice Questions

1. Sound travels fastest through

    (A) air.
    (B) steel.
    (C) water.
    (D) a vacuum.

2. In order to use sea water on board ship for boilers, the water must first be

    (A) distilled.
    (B) aerated.
    (C) chlorinated.
    (D) refined.

3. The most abundant metal in a free state in the earth's crust is

    (A) nitrogen.
    (B) aluminum.
    (C) copper.
    (D) iron.

4. An object will most effectively absorb the sun's rays if it is

    (A) polished, and dark in color.
    (B) polished, and light in color.
    (C) rough, and light in color.
    (D) rough, and dark in color.

5. The most effective farming method for returning minerals to the soil is

    (A) crop rotation.
    (B) strip farming.
    (C) contour plowing.
    (D) furrowing.

6. An example of a lever is the

    (A) wedge.
    (B) crowbar.
    (C) saw.
    (D) escalator.

7. A lunar eclipse occurs when the

    (A) earth casts its shadow on the sun.
    (B) sun casts its shadow on the moon.
    (C) earth casts its shadow on the moon.
    (D) moon casts its shadow on the earth.

8. The part of the body that would suffer most from a diet deficient in calcium is the

    (A) pancreas.
    (B) stomach.
    (C) skeleton.
    (D) skin.

9. Which of the following is found in greatest quantities in automobile exhaust gases?

    (A) sulfur dioxide
    (B) sulfur trioxide
    (C) carbon monoxide
    (D) water

10. Which common electrical device contains an electric magnet?

    (A) flatiron
    (B) lamp
    (C) telephone
    (D) toaster

11. In a vacuum, radio waves and visible light waves must have the same

    (A) intensity.
    (B) frequency.
    (C) wavelength.
    (D) speed.

12. The most accurate description of the earth's atmosphere is that it consists

    (A) mostly of oxygen, argon, carbon dioxide, and water vapor.
    (B) entirely of ozone, nitrogen, and water vapor.
    (C) of a mixture of gases, liquid droplets, and minute solid particles.
    (D) of gases which cannot be compressed.

13. Object A with a mass of 2 kilograms and object B with a mass of 4 kilograms are dropped simultaneously from rest near the surface of the earth. Neglecting air resistance, at the end of 3 seconds, what is the ratio of the speed of object A to the speed of object B?

    (A) 1:4
    (B) 1:2
    (C) 1:1
    (D) 2:1

14. In June, a weather station in a New England city reports a falling barometer and southeast winds. The best weather forecast is probably

    (A) fair and warmer.
    (B) fair and colder.
    (C) rain and warmer.
    (D) rain and colder.

15. Which substance can be removed from water by filtration?

    (A) sand
    (B) ink
    (C) alcohol
    (D) sugar

16. As a balloon rises, the gas within it

    (A) solidifies.
    (B) freezes.
    (C) condenses.
    (D) expands.

17. The best estimate of the age of the earth comes from the study of

    (A) the salt content of the oceans.
    (B) the thickness of sedimentary rock.
    (C) radioactive material.
    (D) the rate of erosion of the land.

18. The presence of coal deposits in Alaska shows that, at one time, Alaska

   (A) was covered with ice.
   (B) was connected to Asia.
   (C) was connected to Europe.
   (D) had a tropical climate.

19. When an airplane is in flight, the air pressure on the top surface of the wing is

   (A) less than on the bottom surface.
   (B) the same as on the bottom surface.
   (C) slightly more than on the bottom surface.
   (D) more or less than on the bottom surface, depending on the shape of the wing.

20. In the human eye, which structure is like the film in a camera?

   (A) pupil
   (B) retina
   (C) lens
   (D) cornea

21. When water is taken apart by electricity, what two substances are formed?

   (A) carbon and oxygen
   (B) hydrogen and oxygen
   (C) oxygen and nitrogen
   (D) hydrogen and nitrogen

22. Which of the following statements is true for the right side of this equation?

$$Fe + H_2SO_4 \rightarrow FeSO_4 + H_2 \uparrow$$

   (A) There are two elements on the right side.
   (B) There are two compounds on the right side.
   (C) There are an element and a gas on the right side.
   (D) There are a compound and an element on the right side.

23. The three elements found most commonly in commercial fertilizers are

   (A) calcium, phosphorus, iron.
   (B) phosphorus, nitrogen, sulfur.
   (C) nitrogen, phosphorus, potassium.
   (D) magnesium, iron, calcium.

24. Two non-porous rocks seem to lose the same weight when a string is attached to each and they are submerged in water. These two rocks must have the same

    (A) weight in air.
    (B) weight in water.
    (C) volume.
    (D) chemical and physical properties.

25. The thermos bottle is most similar in principle to

    (A) storm windows.
    (B) the freezing unit in an electric refrigerator.
    (C) solar heating systems.
    (D) radiant heaters.

Answer Key

1. **B**	6. **B**	11. **D**	16. **D**	21. **B**
2. **A**	7. **C**	12. **C**	17. **C**	22. **D**
3. **C**	8. **C**	13. **C**	18. **D**	23. **C**
4. **D**	9. **D**	14. **C**	19. **A**	24. **C**
5. **A**	10. **C**	15. **A**	20. **B**	25. **A**

Answer Explanations

1. **(B)** Sound travels fastest in the densest, or heaviest, materials. The molecules in heavy materials are closer together and transmit sound vibrations more rapidly than the molecules in light materials. Sound does not travel through a vacuum.

2. **(A)** In the process of distillation, a liquid is evaporated by heat and then condensed by cooling. When sea water is distilled, the salt remains behind as a residue, and the distilled water is very pure. Sea water is distilled before it is used in a ship's boilers in order to get rid of the salt, which would form a scale and ruin the boilers.

3. **(C)** Nitrogen is a gas. Iron is seldom found in a free state, aluminum occurs in combination with other elements in the earth's crust. Copper is found in combination with other elements and also in a free state.

4. **(D)** When the sun's rays strike a surface that is smooth, shiny, or light in color, the rays are reflected. When the sun's rays strike a surface that is rough and dark, the rays are absorbed.

5. **(A)** In crop rotation, plants such as legumes are planted periodically to add nitrogen to the soil, after other crops have exhausted it. None of the other methods returns minerals to the soil.

6. **(B)** The crowbar is a form of lever. By placing a crowbar over a support, you can exert pressure on one end and overcome resistance at the other. A crowbar could be balanced on the surface of one rock, for example, and then pressed hard to dislodge another rock on top.

7. **(C)** The lunar surface is darkened when the earth comes between the sun and the moon. This is caused by the fact that the shadow of the earth falls on the moon's surface.

8. **(C)** Calcium is a very important constituent of bone. Without it, the bones in our skeleton become brittle.

9. **(D)** The oxidation of the gasoline, which contains hydrogen, produces moisture. There is also an oxidation of the carbon in gasoline, which produces carbon dioxide (not mentioned in the question) and traces of car-

bon monoxide. These traces can be dangerous when the engine of a car is running in a confined, poorly ventilated place.

10. **(C)** The telephone receiver has an electromagnet with a metal diaphragm mounted close to it. The metal diaphragm vibrates (moves back and forth) and reproduces the sounds spoken into the transmitter. The sound waves produced by the speaker's voice cause the transmitter to make the current in the wires weaker and stronger. These changes occur thousands of times per second.

   These changes in current affect the electromagnet in the receiver at the other end of the phone call. The receiving electromagnet affects its diaphragm strongly or weakly as the current changes. This in turn reproduces the sound waves made originally by the speaker's voice.

11. **(D)** Radio and light waves are two forms of electromagnetic radiation. In a vacuum, all electromagnetic waves have the same speed—that is, the speed of light.

12. **(C)** The earth's atmosphere consists of a mixture of nitrogen (about 78% by volume); oxygen (about 21%); carbon dioxide (about 0.03%); small amounts of rare gases such as neon, xenon, krypton, and helium; and some water vapor and dust particles.

13. **(C)** All freely falling objects, regardless of their masses near the earth, fall toward the earth with equal acceleration. Any two objects at rest that begin to fall at the same instant will have equal velocities at the end of 3 seconds, or at any other time interval. Thus the ratio of their speeds will be 1:1.

14. **(C)** A falling barometer indicates the approach of low pressure and rising air. The rising of warm, moist air usually results in precipitation. We have reason to assume that the air is warm since we know that the southeast winds come from lower latitudes where the air was warmed, picking up moisture when it passed over the Atlantic Ocean.

15. **(A)** Sand particles are visible and comparatively large. They can be caught in the small holes of a filter. Sugar, alcohol, and most inks form true solutions in which the particles are of molecular size. These will pass through filters.

16. **(D)** Barometric pressure decreases one inch for every 900 feet of altitude. The gas in the balloon expands because it enters regions of lower and lower pressure. Balloons being prepared for ascent are only partially filled with helium. The balloonist knows that the gas will expand and fill the balloon completely at higher altitudes.

17. **(C)** The analysis of radioactive material has given scientists an accurate estimate of the age of the earth.

18. **(D)** Coal deposits were formed when layers of giant ferns as well as other vegetation were compressed into layers of coal by the earth's movement. Its coal deposits tell us that Alaska must have had a tropical climate.

19. **(A)** The curve in the top of an airplane wing forces the air to flow faster over the top of the wing than below it. This faster flowing air results in less pressure above the wing. The principle behind this was first described by Bernoulli. In any flowing liquid, the pressure becomes less as the speed of the flowing liquid becomes greater.

20. **(B)** The lens focuses the light on the retina, which "records the image," sending impulses along the optic nerve to the brain. The cornea is the transparent tissue covering the eyeball. The pupil is the opening through which light enters the eye.

21. **(B)** When water is decomposed by electrolysis, the water breaks up into hydrogen and oxygen; the ratio is two volumes of hydrogen to one of oxygen.

$$2H_2O \rightarrow 2H_2 \uparrow + O_2 \uparrow$$

22. **(D)** $FeSO_4$ is a compound of three different elements—iron (Fe), sulfur (S), and oxygen (O). Hydrogen (H) is a separate element.

23. **(C)** Nitrogen is needed most by plants. They also have some need for phosphorus and potassium. Only traces of the other elements are needed by plants; they are not a major concern for companies that produce fertilizers.

24. **(C)** When an object is placed in water, it loses the exact same weight as the weight of the water it displaces. If two objects that are placed in water appear to lose the same weight, then they must have both displaced the same amount of water. That means that they are equal in size, or "volume."

25. **(A)** A thermos is made with a vacuum between its double walls. In this vacuum, there are no molecules to receive the transfer of heat energy from the wall near the contents of the thermos. Thus, the vacuum prevents the loss of heat. Even though a storm window allows some air between it and the "year-round" window, it is the closest match to a thermos, among the choices given.

Electronics Information

7

INTRODUCTION

The early Greeks are believed to have discovered electricity in the process of conducting some experiments with amber. Those experiments led, in 1600, to the work of the Englishman William Gilbert (sometimes called the Father of Electricity) with friction and static electricity. Over the years, modern scientists learned more about the phenomenon and how its properties can be described in certain principles. They also learned how to generate, distribute, and use electricity. *Electronics* is the application of the principles of electricity.

To prepare for this portion of the ASVAB, you may wish to review and add to your knowledge of some of the following areas: atomic structures, magnetism, circuits, vacuum tubes and transistors, and the operations of motors, AM and FM receivers, transducers, and television.

PRACTICE QUESTIONS AND ANSWER EXPLANATIONS

The Electronics Information test in the ASVAB consists of 20 questions. You will be allowed 9 minutes to complete it. Try to answer the following Practice Questions within that time period, by circling the correct answer for each question. Then check your answers with the Answer Key immediately following, and review all of the Answer Explanations.

Practice Questions

1. A 9-volt transistor contains how many cells?

    (A) 1
    (B) 4
    (C) 6
    (D) 9

2. Compared to a number 12 wire a number 22 wire is

    (A) longer.
    (B) shorter.
    (C) larger in diameter.
    (D) smaller in diameter.

3. A resistor marked 1.5K Ω would have a value of

    (A) 1.5 ohms.
    (B) 105 ohms.
    (C) 1,500 ohms.
    (D) 1,500 watts.

4. An equivalent term for "electromotive force" is

    (A) voltage.
    (B) current.
    (C) resistance.
    (D) reactance.

5. The property of a circuit that opposes any change in voltage is

    (A) conductance.
    (B) capacitance.
    (C) resistance.
    (D) inductance.

6. The composition of 60/40 rosin core solder is

    (A) 60% lead, 40% tin.
    (B) 60% tin, 40% lead.
    (C) 60% silver, 40% rosin.
    (D) 60% lead, 40% silver.

7. A hair dryer is rated at 1200 watts. Assuming it is operated at 120 volts, how much current will this appliance draw?

(A) 10 amps
(B) 100 amps
(C) 1000 amps
(D) 144,000 amps

8. Another term for "cycles per second" is

(A) hertz.
(B) henry.
(C) kilo.
(D) mega.

9. A crystal microphone is an example of what electrical phenomenon?

(A) thermoionic emission
(B) piezoelectric effect
(C) inductance
(D) hysteresis

10. The process of transmitting voice by varying the height of a carrier wave is known as

(A) frequency modulation.
(B) amplitude modulation.
(C) demodulation.
(D) detection.

11. The primary of a transformer is connected to 120 volts. The voltage across the secondary is 40 volts. This transformer has a turns ratio of

(A) 1:1
(B) 1:4
(C) 1:3
(D) 3:1

12. A carbon resistor marked with the color bands of red, red, red, gold is of what value and tolerance?

(A) 2,000 ohms ± 5%
(B) 222 ohms ± 5%
(C) 2,200 ohms ± 5%
(D) 6 ohms ± 5%

13. Which is the correct schematic symbol of a tetrode tube?

(A)

(B)

(C)

(D)

14. What is the total resistance in this circuit if all resistors are 500 ohms?

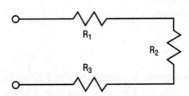

(A) 1,500 watts
(B) 1,500 ohms
(C) 1.5 ohms
(D) 500 ohms

15.

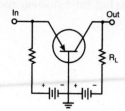

The above schematic represents which transistor configuration?

(A) common gate
(B) common collector
(C) common base
(D) common emitter

16. Which choice correctly identifies the waveform pictured?

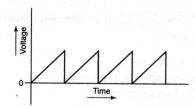

(A) sine wave
(B) square wave
(C) sawtooth wave
(D) pure DC

17. Of the choices illustrated, which is the correct schematic symbol for a potentiometer?

(A) -\/\/\-

(B) -\/\/\-

(C) ─┬─
    ─┴─

(D)

18. A component on a parts list has the following specifications, "1µF, 50 wvdc." The component specified is a

   (A) potentiometer.
   (B) coil.
   (C) transistor.
   (D) capacitor.

19.

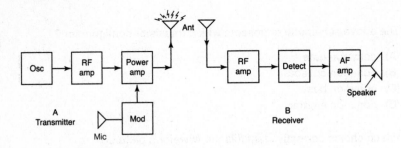

The illustration is a block diagram of a transmitter and receiver. What is the purpose of the oscillator?

   (A) to generate a radio frequency
   (B) to produce a carrier wave for the intelligence
   (C) to produce a high frequency current
   (D) all of the above choices

20. Referring to the schematic in question 19, what is the purpose of the detector stage?

   (A) to amplify the audio signal
   (B) to tune in the carrier wave
   (C) to separate the audio from the radio wave
   (D) to amplify the radio frequency

Answer Key

1. **C**	6. **B**	11. **D**	16. **C**
2. **D**	7. **A**	12. **C**	17. **B**
3. **C**	8. **A**	13. **C**	18. **D**
4. **A**	9. **B**	14. **B**	19. **D**
5. **B**	10. **B**	15. **C**	20. **C**

Answer Explanations

1. **(C)** A cell has a voltage of approximately 1.5 volts. A nine-volt battery would therefore contain 6 cells, or 1.5V $\times$ 6 = 9V.

2. **(D)** The higher the gage number of a wire, the smaller its diameter.

3. **(C)** The symbol "K" represents "kilo" or one thousand. A 1.5 K ohm resistor would therefore have a value of 1.5 $\times$ 1,000 or 1,500 ohms. Choice D is incorrect because the unit of measurement for resistance is ohm. Watts is a unit of measurement for power.

4. **(A)** The interchangeable terms for voltage are electrical pressure, electromotive force, potential difference, difference of potential, and electrical force. The other choices are incorrect because they represent other circuit properties that may not be substituted for the property of voltage.

5. **(B)** Capacitance can be defined as the circuit property that opposes any change in voltage. Inductance is the circuit property that opposes any change in current. Resistance is the circuit property that opposes the flow of electrons and reactance is the opposition to the flow of an alternating current as a result of inductance or capacitance present in a circuit.

6. **(B)** Choice A has the quantities reversed and choices C & D are incorrect because the amount of silver present in solder is minute, and rosin is a substance in the center of solder added to aid in the soldering process.

7. **(A)** To calculate the current requirement of an appliance, the power law may be applied.

Power = Current $\times$ Voltage

$P = I \times E$

$I = \dfrac{P}{E}$

$I = \dfrac{1200 \text{ watts}}{120 \text{ volts}}$

$I = 10$ amperes.

8. **(A)** Henry is the unit of measurement for inductance. Kilo represents a quantity of one thousand and mega represents a quantity of a million.

9. **(B)** The piezoelectric effect is the property of certain crystalline substances to change shape when a voltage is impressed upon them as in the crystal microphone. Thermoionic emission is the escape of electrons from a surface due to the presence of heat. Inductance is the circuit property that opposes any change in current and hysteresis is the property of a magnetic substance that causes magnetization to lag behind the force that produces it.

10. **(B)** The height of a wave is known as the wave's amplitude. Varying the height of a carrier wave is known as AM or amplitude modulation. Frequency modulation would transmit intelligence by varying the frequency of the carrier wave. Demodulation is the process of separating the intelligence from the carrier wave. Another term for this process is detection.

11. **(D)** The primary of this transformer has three times the voltage of its secondary. Therefore, the primary must have three times as many turns of wire as the secondary, or a turns ratio of 3:1. If its turns ratio was 1:1 the primary and secondary would have the same voltage. In choice B, a turns ratio of 1:4 would result in an output voltage of 480V. In choice C a turns ratio of 1:3 would result in a secondary voltage of 360V.

12. **(C)** Reading the resistor color code, the first two bands indicate numbers; the third band is the multiplier or the number of zeros to write after the first two numbers. The fourth band indicates the tolerance of the resistor. Following the color code, the value of this resistor is 2,200 ohms ± 5%. Red, representing a number value of 2 and a multiplier value of 100 (or two zeros to write after the first two numbers) would indicate a resistor coded as follows:

$$\frac{2}{\text{Band 1 – red}} \qquad \frac{2}{\text{Band 2 – red}}$$

$$\frac{00}{\text{Band 3 – red}} \qquad \frac{\pm 5\%}{\text{Band 4 – red}}$$

The tolerance of a fixed carbon resistor is a ± value. Gold represents 5% tolerance.

13. **(C)** Choice A = diode, choice B = triode, choice D = pentode.

14. **(B)** In a series circuit, the total resistance is equal to the sum of the individual resistors, or $R_T = R_1 + R_2 + R_3...R_n$. As all resistors have a value of 500 ohms, the total resistance in this circuit is equal to:

    $R_T = R_1 + R_2 + R_3$ or

    $R_T = 500 + 500 + 500$

    $R_T = 1,500$ ohms

    Choice A is incorrect because watts is a unit of power, not a unit of resistance.

15. **(C)** The base element is common or shared by both circuits. Choice A is not a transistor circuit configuration as there is no gate element in a transistor.

16. **(C)** The waveforms corresponding to the other choices are given in the review section on waveforms.

17. **(B)** A potentiometer is a variable resistor. Choice A is the symbol for a fixed resistor and choice B is the symbol for a variable resistor; note the arrow connected to the fixed symbol. Choice C is a fixed capacitor and choice D is the symbol for a variable capacitor.

18. **(D)** The unit of measurement for capacitance is the FARAD, abbreviated F. A potentiometer would be specified in ohms, a coil in henrys, and a transistor by its type or generic number.

19. **(D)** The purpose of the local oscillator is to generate a high frequency, also known as a radio or carrier wave.

20. **(C)** A detector demodulates a signal. This is the process of separating the audio or intelligence from the radio wave. The AF amp is used to amplify the audio signal and the RF amp is used to amplify the radio frequency. A tuner would be used to tune in a frequency, making choices A, B, and D incorrect.

Automotive
Information

8

INTRODUCTION

Automobiles are the basis of our transportation system and a necessary part of our whole way of life. The bright and colorful finish of the new car, the closed body, solid top, and glass windows—all this bears little resemblance to the early cars. Electronic ignition, automatic transmission, soft springs and comfortable seats, fuel-efficient engines—these and many other items of safety and convenience have increased the numbers of people able and eager to drive.

PARTS OF AN AUTOMOBILE

Fundamentally the automobile is a compartment mounted on wheels with some self-contained means for propelling it over ground. Of course, today's autombiles consist of a great deal more than that—easy riding suspension systems, soft comfortable seats, headlights for night-driving, windshield wipers, rear-view mirrors, and many other driver conveniences and safety features. If these were lacking we would feel that the car was quite incomplete. Yet the fundamentals are still there, and there was a time when many of these "extras" were unknown to builders of autombiles.

To prepare for this portion of the ASVAB, you should acquaint yourself with the parts of an automobile, make sure you understand the operation of the drive and braking systems, and review the functions of the internal combustion engine.

PRACTICE QUESTIONS AND ANSWER EXPLANATIONS

On the computerized version of the test, the Automotive Information subtest consists of 11 questions. You will be allowed 6 minutes to complete it. On the paper version it is combined with the Shop Information subtest. Circle the correct answer for each of the following Practice Questions, then check your answers with the Answer Key immediately following and review all of the Answer Explanations.

Practice Questions

1. Which is the right side of an engine?
   (A) The right side when you stand in front and look at the engine.
   (B) The side that the distributor is on.
   (C) It depends on the manufacturer.
   (D) The right side when you stand in the back and look at the engine.

2. The letter and numbers, G 78-14, printed on a tire refer to

   (A) load, width, diameter.
   (B) diameter and air pressure.
   (C) cubic inch displacement.
   (D) price code.

3. "Tracking," in terms of front-end alignment, means that

   (A) each wheel travels independently of the other.
   (B) the wheels follow well on ice or in snow.
   (C) the front tires leave stronger tracks than the rear tires.
   (D) the rear wheels follow the front wheels correctly.

4. A car with worn-out shock absorbers

   (A) cannot carry a heavy load.
   (B) will bounce a lot on a rough road.
   (C) sags very low to the ground.
   (D) will have no traction on a wet road.

5. In a three-speed transmission, the cluster gear is supported by the

   (A) pinion shaft.
   (B) countershaft.
   (C) main shaft.
   (D) output shaft.

6. A clutch release bearing

   (A) rotates whenever the engine is turning.
   (B) rotates when only the clutch is engaged.
   (C) rotates whenever the clutch pedal is depressed.
   (D) holds the clutch shaft in alignment.

7. The general procedure to follow when adjusting a band on an automatic transmission is

(A) loosen, tighten to a specified torque, loosen a specified number of turns, and lock.
(B) tighten to a specified torque with a torque wrench and lock.
(C) tighten to a specified torque, loosen 5 turns, and lock.
(D) loosen, tighten to a specified torque, and lock.

8. The purpose of the drive shaft is to connect the

(A) piston to the transmission.
(B) differential to the transmission.
(C) flywheel to the crankshaft.
(D) camshaft to the crankshaft.

9. The order in which the spark plugs in the engine fire is established by the order in which the

(A) plugs are mounted in the engine.
(B) plug leads are connected to the distributor cap.
(C) condenser is connected.
(D) contact points are opened.

10. The terminals exposed on the ignition induction coil are

(A) two secondary and one primary.
(B) one secondary and one primary.
(C) one secondary and two primary.
(D) two secondary and two primary.

11. Battery electrolyte is a mixture of distilled water and

(A) baking soda.
(B) sulfuric acid.
(C) lead peroxide.
(D) carbon particles.

Answer Key

1. **D**	3. **D**	5. **B**	7. **A**	9. **B**	11. **B**
2. **A**	4. **B**	6. **C**	8. **B**	10. **C**	

Answer Explanations

1. **(D)** When viewed from the rear, the side to your right is the right side of an engine. This method is used by all manufacturers.

2. **(A)** "G" indicates the load carrying capacity of a tire. "78" is the aspect ratio. The aspect ratio is the relationship between the tire height and width. When a tire is marked 78, the height is 78% of the width. "14" indicates that the tire will fit a 14-inch rim.

3. **(D)** Tracking is correct when both rear wheels are parallel to, and the same distance from, the vehicle center line (an imaginary line drawn through the center of the vehicle). A bent frame or twisted body structure will cause improper tracking.

4. **(B)** Shock absorbers control spring oscillation. Original equipment shocks that do not use air or spring assist are not designed to control vehicle height.

5. **(B)** The countershaft is pressed into the transmission case and supports the cluster gear. The main shaft or output shaft is splined with the driveshaft.

6. **(C)** When a clutch pedal is depressed, the release bearing comes in contact with the fingers of the clutch pressure plate and rotates.

7. **(A)** To properly adjust an automatic transmission band, loosen the adjusting screw locknut. Then tighten the adjusting screw to the specified torque with a torque wrench. Next, loosen the adjusting screw the specified number of turns. Complete the job by holding the adjusting screw and tightening the locknut.

8. **(B)** On a rear-wheel drive vehicle, the driveshaft transmits power from the transmission to the differential. The flywheel is bolted directly to the crankshaft.

9. **(B)** The spark plug leads must be installed in the correct tower of the cap to insure the proper firing order. The firing order is the order that the spark plugs ignite the air/fuel mixture in the combustion chamber. A typical firing order for a six-cylinder engine is 1-5-3-6-2-4.

10. **(C)** On a conventional ignition coil the center tower is the secondary or high-voltage terminal. The two small studs at the top of the coil are primary or low-voltage terminals.

11. **(B)** Battery electrolyte is a mixture of approximately 60% distilled water and 40% sulfuric acid.

Shop Information

9

INTRODUCTION

A person interested in making or repairing things is lost without tools. Tools make the difference between a person who works efficiently and one who struggles laboriously. There are some tools that are basic to any home shop and are generally used for simple carpentry work. Others are used for more specialized purposes.

SHOP KNOWLEDGE

General shop knowledge involves a basic understanding of tools, materials, and the processes of implementing an idea to achieve a finished product.

Common hand tools may be grouped under several headings: measuring and layout tools, cutting and shaping tools, drilling or boring tools, fasteners and fastening tools, clamping tools, pliers and wrenches, digging tools, grinding and sanding tools, and specialized tools like plumbers' or electricians' tools. Various materials are used in general shop and construction work. Among the materials most often used are concrete, wood, metal, glass, plastics, and adhesives. Blueprints, layouts, templates, and patterns are some of the means used in design and layout work.

PRACTICE QUESTIONS AND ANSWER EXPLANATIONS

On the computerized version of the ASVAB, this subtest consists of 11 questions, which you will have 5 minutes to complete. On the paper version, it is combined with the Automotive Information subtest. Circle the correct answer for each question, then check your answers with the Answer Key immediately following and review all of the Answer Explanations.

Practice Questions

1. A coping saw blade is placed in the saw

   (A) with the teeth pointing upward.
   (B) with the teeth pointing toward the handle.
   (C) so it cuts with the wood grain.
   (D) so it cuts across the wood grain.

2. Carpenters use

   (A) ball peen hammers.
   (B) chisel point hammers.
   (C) claw hammers.
   (D) planishing hammers.

3. The term *penny* is used

   (A) to designate the cost of a nail.
   (B) to designate the size of a nail.
   (C) to indicate a rosin-coated nail.
   (D) to indicate a galvanized nail.

4. A tool used to cut sheet metal is a

   (A) bar folder.
   (B) box and pan brake.
   (C) slip roll.
   (D) squaring shear.

5. One of the most common ways to fasten sheet metal today is to

   (A) solder it.
   (B) braze it.
   (C) spot-weld it.
   (D) glue it.

6. A welding torch can also be used as a

   (A) light source.
   (B) burning tool.
   (C) cutting torch.
   (D) pipe wrench.

7. Tubing cutters are smaller versions of

(A) pipe cutters.
(B) ring cutters.
(C) hole cutters.
(D) glass cutters.

8. If you "overwork" concrete, it will cause

(A) loss of a smooth surface.
(B) separation and create a less durable surface.
(C) loss of strength throughout the slab.
(D) puddles in the middle of the slab.

9. Concrete reaches 98% of its strength in

(A) 3 days.
(B) 50 days.
(C) 28 days.
(D) 10 days.

10. Deciduous trees produce

(A) softwood.
(B) deadwood.
(C) hardwood.
(D) conifers.

11. The combination square is used to lay out angles of what measurement?

(A) 90 and 180 degreees
(B) 45 and 90 degrees
(C) 45, 90, and 135 degrees
(D) π and 2π

Answer Key

1. **B**   3. **B**   5. **C**   7. **A**   9. **C**   11. **B**
2. **C**   4. **D**   6. **C**   8. **B**   10. **C**

Answer Explanations

1. **(B)** A coping saw blade is placed in the saw with the teeth of the blade facing the handle. That means that you cut with a coping saw on the downward stroke. It also calls for a special type of vise to hold whatever it is you are cutting.

2. **(C)** Carpenters use claw hammers so they can remove nails if they don't go where they belong or are bent on the way into the wood. Machinists use ball peen hammers. Planishing hammers are used by people trying to flatten or shape sheet metal. There is no such thing as a chisel point hammer.

3. **(B)** The term *penny* is an old English way to designate the size of a nail. It has no definite relation to today's measuring units. You can, however, keep in mind that the larger the number, the larger the nail.

4. **(D)** A squaring shear is used to shear or cut sheet metal.

5. **(C)** One of the most common ways to fasten sheet metal is by spot-welding it. This is done with the bodies of automobiles to make them sturdier.

6. **(C)** A welding torch can be used as a cutting torch when the proper amount of oxygen is used.

7. **(A)** A tubing cutter is nothing more than a smaller version of a pipe cutter.

8. **(B)** If you overwork concrete, it brings up all the water to the surface and the cement comes to the surface also. The heavier particles settle farther down into the slab, and you wind up with separation and create a less durable surface when it is dry.

9. **(C)** Concrete reaches 98% of its strength in 28 days.

10. **(C)** Deciduous trees are those that produce leaves that drop off in the fall. The wood produced by this type of tree is usually hard when properly dried.

11. **(B)** A combination square is used to lay out 45- and 90-degree angles of measurement.

Mechanical Comprehension

10

INTRODUCTION

The ASVAB subtest on Mechanical Comprehension tests knowledge of basic mechanical and physical principles and the ability to visualize how illustrated objects and simple machines work. You may prepare for the test by reviewing some basic principles of physics and simple machines and their functions.

FORCE

One of the basic concepts of physics is the concept of force. Force is something that can change the velocity of an object by making it start, stop, speed up, slow down, or change direction. Let's think for a minute of a car. When you take your foot off the gas pedal, your car does not suddenly come to a stop. It coasts on, only gradually losing its velocity. If you want the car to stop, you have to do something to it. That is what your brakes are for: to exert a force that decreases the car's velocity. A spacecraft also illustrates the point. *Voyager* has been coasting through the solar system for years. Nothing is pushing it. However, when we want it to speed up, slow down, or change direction, we send it signals that fire control rockets—or, in other words, we exert a force on it to change its velocity.

There are many types of force, including friction, gravity, elastic recoil, and buoyancy. Others include magnetism, which attracts iron nails to a red horseshoe, and electric force, which makes a nylon shirt cling to you when you try to take it off, or which refuses to release the dust particles from your favorite CD. Airplanes stay up because of the lift force generated by the flow of air across their wings. A rocket takes off because of the force generated by the gases expanding in it. These forces are all fundamental to physics and mechanical functions.

SIMPLE MACHINES

There are devices that make work easier. These devices are known as simple machines. Without thinking about it, everybody uses a hundred simple machines every day—a light switch, a doorknob, a pencil sharpener, to name just a few.

Simple machines include the screw (the vise, for example), the block-and-tackle (a pulley), the lever (crowbar), inclined plane (a loading ramp), and spinning machines (a winch).

The function of simple machines is not to increase your power, but to make work manageable, by spreading it out.

PRACTICE QUESTIONS AND ANSWER EXPLANATIONS

The Mechanical Comprehension test in the ASVAB consists of 25 questions. You will be allowed 19 minutes to complete it. Try to answer the following Practice Questions within that time period, by circling the correct answer for each question. Then check your answers with the Answer Key immediately following, and review all of the Answer Explanations.

Practice Questions

1. Cap screws are ordered by

    (A) wrench size.
    (B) diameter and wrench size.
    (C) diameter and number of threads.
    (D) wrench size and kind of threads.

2. A round piece of stock having a different type of thread at each end is called a

    (A) head bolt.
    (B) stud.
    (C) screw.
    (D) cap screw.

3. The measurement across the flats of a cap screw head determines the

    (A) wrench size.
    (B) bolt size.
    (C) thread size.
    (D) diameter.

4. Ring and pinion backlash is checked with

    (A) a micrometer.
    (B) a round feeler gauge.
    (C) Prussian blue.
    (D) a dial indicator.

5. The clutch aligning arbor is used to align the clutch disc to the

   (A) transmission.
   (B) pilot bearing.
   (C) pressure plate.
   (D) main drive gear.

6. An oscilloscope is used to diagnose problems in which automotive system?

   (A) charging
   (B) starting
   (C) fuel
   (D) ignition

7. Which tool is used to adjust the preload on a front wheel bearing?

   (A) pliers
   (B) torque wrench
   (C) dial indicator
   (D) bearing cup driver

8. Which device measures electrical resistance?

   (A) an ammeter
   (B) a voltmeter
   (C) an ohmmeter
   (D) a hydrometer

9. The tool used to tighten a cylinder head bolt is a

   (A) box wrench.
   (B) breaker bar.
   (C) ratchet.
   (D) torque wrench.

10. The strength of the antifreeze solution is tested with a

    (A) thermometer.
    (B) thermostat.
    (C) voltmeter.
    (D) hydrometer.

11. Helical gears have

    (A) slanted teeth.
    (B) straight teeth.
    (C) curved teeth.
    (D) beveled teeth.

12. The gear train that uses a sun gear, internal gear, and three pinion gears is known as

    (A) bevel spiral pinion.
    (B) worm and sector.
    (C) planetary gears.
    (D) differential gears.

13. Reciprocating motion is changed into rotary motion by which one of the following engine parts?

    (A) camshaft
    (B) connecting rod bearings
    (C) pistons
    (D) crankshaft

14. Moisture forming on the inner surface of a windshield on a cold day is an example of

    (A) vaporization.
    (B) evaporation.
    (C) distillation.
    (D) condensation.

15. Which of the following statements concerning the poles of a magnet is correct?

    (A) South repels north.
    (B) Like poles attract.
    (C) North attracts north.
    (D) Unlike poles attract.

16. Torque means

    (A) number of cylinders.
    (B) turning effort.
    (C) ratio of drive shaft to rear axle.
    (D) drive shaft.

17. Water in an automobile engine may cause damage in cold weather because

    (A) ice is a poor conductor of heat.
    (B) water expands as it freezes.
    (C) cold water is compressible.
    (D) ice is denser than water.

18. What is the rear axle ratio in a standard differential with eleven teeth on the pinion gear and forty-three teeth on the ring gear?

(A) 4.10 to 1
(B) 3.90 to 1
(C) 3.73 to 1
(D) 3.54 to 1

19. Gear B is intended to mesh with

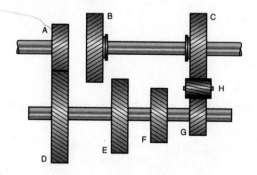

(A) gear A only.
(B) gear D only.
(C) gear E only.
(D) all of the above gears.

20. As cam A makes one complete turn, the setscrew will hit the contact point

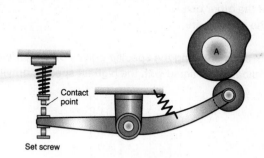

(A) once.
(B) twice.
(C) three times.
(D) not at all.

21. If gear A makes 14 revolutions, gear B will make

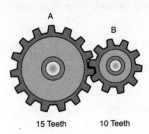

15 Teeth   10 Teeth

(A) 21.
(B) 17.
(C) 14.
(D) 9.

22. Which of the other gears is moving in the same direction as gear 2?

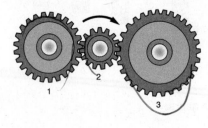

(A) gear 1
(B) gear 3
(C) neither of the other gears
(D) both of the other gears

23. Floats X and Y are measuring the specific gravity of two different liquids. Which float indicates the liquid with the highest specific gravity?

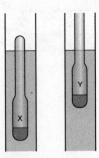

(A) Y
(B) X
(C) neither X nor Y
(D) both X and Y are the same

24. Which vacuum gauge will indicate the highest vacuum as air passes through the carburetor bore?

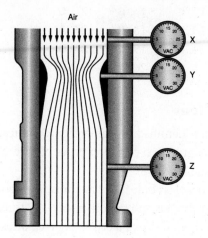

(A) X
(B) Y
(C) Z
(D) X and Z

25. The wheelbarrow is an example of a

(A) first class lever.
(B) second class lever.
(C) third class lever.
(D) first and third class lever.

Answer Key

1. **C**	6. **D**	11. **A**	16. **B**	21. **A**
2. **B**	7. **B**	12. **C**	17. **B**	22. **C**
3. **A**	8. **C**	13. **D**	18. **B**	23. **A**
4. **D**	9. **D**	14. **D**	19. **C**	24. **B**
5. **B**	10. **D**	15. **D**	20. **A**	25. **B**

Answer Explanations

1. **(C)** Cap screws are identified by diameter, pitch (threads per inch), material, hardness, and length. Two common types of thread are National Coarse (NC) and National Fine (NF).

2. **(B)** A stud is a headless bolt that has threads on both ends. Usually one side will have NF threads and the other side, NC threads.

3. **(A)** To find the wrench size of a cap screw, etc., measure across the flats of its hexagon head.

4. **(D)** The dial indicator uses a gauge to register movement. It is used to measure variations in dimensions and backlash (clearance) between two meshed gears.

5. **(B)** A pilot bearing is pressed into a hole at the end of the engine crankshaft. The purpose of the bearing is to support the tip of the transmission input (clutch) shaft. During the installation of a new clutch assembly, it is necessary to line up the clutch disc with the pilot bearing. If these parts are not aligned, the transmission will not slide into place on the engine.

6. **(D)** The oscilloscope, or scope, is a special type of voltmeter that displays traces and oscillations on a TV type picture tube. The scope has the capability of showing the rapid changes in voltage that occur in the ignition system. This is helpful in diagnosing problems in the circuit.

7. **(B)** A torque wrench is a special type of turning tool that is equipped with a gauge. It is used to tighten nuts and bolts to a specified torque or tightness.

8. **(C)** An ohmmeter is a test instrument that measures the resistance in an electrical circuit. Resistance is the opposition to the flow of current through a circuit.

9. **(D)** A cylinder head must be tightened in a specific sequence using a torque wrench. Failure to tighten the head properly can result in a blown head gasket. Note: see the answer to question 7 for additional information.

10. **(D)** The specific gravity of antifreeze solution is tested with a special hydrometer. It compares the weight of the antifreeze solution to water.

11. **(A)** Spur gears have straight teeth. Hypoid and spiral gears have curved or beveled teeth.

12. **(C)** Planetary gears are used in an automatic transmission. The three members are in constant mesh and provide gear reduction and reverse without shifting. To obtain a gear reduction or reverse, one member must be held stationary by a band or clutch assembly.

    Worm and sector gears are used in some types of steering gear assemblies. Differential or spider gears are used in a rear end assembly.

13. **(D)** The crankshaft changes the reciprocating (up and down) motion of the piston to rotary motion.

14. **(D)** Condensation takes place when a gas or vapor changes to a liquid. Moisture on the windshield is the result of water vapor in the air changing back to liquid.

15. **(D)** Unlike poles attract, like poles repel.

16. **(B)** The differential, which connects the driveshaft to the rear axle, increases engine torque through gear reduction. Engine torque is increased because the driveshaft turns faster than the rear axles.

17. **(B)** Water expands as it freezes. Water is not compressible.

18. **(B)** To calculate the gear ratio of a rear axle assembly, divide the number of teeth on the pinion gear into the number of teeth on the ring gear. 43 divided by 11 = 3.90.

19. **(C)** A and D are in constant mesh and F is too small.

20. **(A)** When the lobe (high spot) on cam A makes contact with the follower (roller) on the contact arm, the contacts will close. Since cam A has only one lobe, the contacts will close one time per revolution.

21. **(A)** To calculate the revolutions of gear B, use this formula: $r = D \times R$ divided by d.

    D = number of teeth on gear A
    R = revolutions of gear A
    d = number of teeth on gear B
    r = revolutions of gear B
    $r = D \times R$ divided by d

    $$r = \frac{15 \times 14}{10}$$

    $$r = \frac{210}{10}$$

    $$r = 21$$

22. **(C)** Gears that are meshed turn in opposite directions. Gear 2 is turning clockwise; 1 and 3 are turning counterclockwise.

23. **(A)** Hydrometers use floats to measure specific gravity. Specific gravity is the weight of a liquid compared to the weight of water. The liquid with the highest specific gravity will cause the float to rise higher in the glass tube.

24. **(B)** Vacuum is greatest at the narrow or restricted area of an air passage. The narrow area is called a venturi. Gauge Z will also indicate a vacuum, but it will read lower than Y.

25. **(B)** On a second class lever, the fulcrum is at one end, the effort is at the other end, and the load is between.

Assembling Objects

11

INTRODUCTION

The Assembling Objects (AO) subtest, a relatively recent addition to the ASVAB, tests *spatial apperception*, also known as *visualizing spatial relationships*—your ability to visualize how an object will look when its parts are put together, or how different objects will look when connected.

As of this writing, only the Navy uses the AO score to specifically qualify service members for a particular specialty (operational and some mechanical jobs), but that could and probably will change. And, if you are thinking about trying to become a pilot or getting into some other aircraft-related specialty later on, you will definitely need to develop your ability to visualize spatial relationships. All the services test their prospective pilots in this area—for more information and examples, see *Barron's Military Flight Aptitude Tests.*

Much of what needs to be done mentally when taking this subtest will seem to be intuitive—either you'll get it right away, or you won't. It's a proven fact that some people are just naturally better at seeing patterns, grasping spatial relationships, and so forth. But it's also a proven fact that most of the rest of us can learn to get better at these skills, too—so keep trying.

The Assembling Objects subtest has two types of problems. In both types, you will be shown five drawings. The first drawing will contain some uncon-nected shapes, and the remaining four drawings will each try to persuade you that they are the final result of correctly assembling the shapes.

We're going to call the first type of problem jigsaw puzzle-piece assembly. The ASVAB doesn't call them by that name—it just presents you both types of problems in the AO subtest and expects you to answer them correctly. For our ease of reference and your analysis, though, we'll call them jigsaw puzzle-piece assembly.

And, for that same ease of reference, we're going to call the second type of problem line-connector assembly problems.

Let's examine how to solve the jigsaw puzzle-piece assembly problems.

JIGSAW PUZZLE-PIECE ASSEMBLY PROBLEMS

EXAMPLE

Which figure best shows how the objects in the group on the left will appear if they are fitted together?

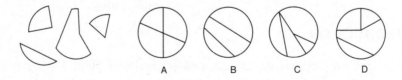

In this example, the correct answer is "D."

For those who aren't naturally good at jigsaw puzzles—who don't or can't immediately and consistently come up with the right answers to these kinds of questions (and maybe for some of those who can)—here are some suggestions:

1. **Don't try to assemble the pieces in your head—let the test do it for you.** There is more than one way to assemble the pieces the test shows you, but only one of the choices is one of those ways—only one choice is correct. Therefore, what you have to do is disqualify three out of the four choices and then confirm that the remaining choice is, in fact, one way to assemble the parts you started out with.

2. **See which of the choices has the right amount of area or mass.** Potential choices that are much bigger or smaller than the pieces given to you to assemble are usually pretty easy to identify. This doesn't help you in the first example problem above, because all the choices have about the same overall size or volume—but it can happen on other problems.

3. **Disqualify the choices that have a shape, external curve, or angle that is not in the pieces given to you to assemble.** In the example above, Choice A has two very wide "pie slice" shapes, and two more pie slices that are more "medium" size. The pieces you have to work with include only one wide and one small pie slice—so Choice A is out.

4. **Disqualify the choices that don't have an unusual or distinct curve or angle represented in the pieces given to you to assemble.** In the example above, the pieces given to you to assemble include one fairly distinctive shape:

Look for this shape in Choices B, C, and D (you've already discarded Choice A). Yep, it's right there in the middle of Choice D. So, there's your answer.

5. **Expect that some or all of the pieces to assemble are rotated to some degree.** In the example above, two of the four pieces in the initial group have to be rotated to fit together with the other shapes. Imagine those shapes as jigsaw pieces, lying flat on a table—but *don't mentally flip any of the shapes over.* Leave them flat on the imaginary table.

6. **Watch out for mirror images.** Shapes that are reversed—mirror images—will never be able to be rotated into place, no matter how smart you are. Whether it's a unique-looking shape or a fairly plain one, don't get in so much of a hurry that you get fooled by this trick on your eyes.

LINE-CONNECTOR ASSEMBLY PROBLEMS

In the second (line-connector assembly) type of problem, you will be shown two shapes and a connector line. One point on each of the shapes will be labeled with a letter (for instance, "A" on the first shape and "B" on the second shape). The ends of the connector line will be labeled with the same letters—in this case, one end with "A" and the other end with the letter "B." You will be asked which of the four figures best shows how the two shapes and a connector line in the first group will touch if the letters for each object are matched, as in the example below.

EXAMPLE

Which figure best shows how the objects in the group of objects on the left will touch if the letters for each object are matched?

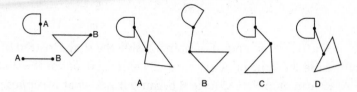

In this example, the correct answer is "C."
Again, here are some general principles that will help you with this kind of problem.

1. **Check the placement of the points.** In the example above, there are two shapes: a kind of half-oval and a rotated right triangle. Point A is midway along the flat side of the half-oval, and Point B is at one of the non-right-angle corners of the triangle. Look at the placement of the dot on first one shape and then the other to see if you can eliminate any choices. (Proper placement may be as simple to see as it is in this problem, or it may involve determining its relationship to a landmark on an irregular shape. Either way, this principle will help you figure it out.) By doing this in the example above, you can quickly eliminate Choice B from the running because the dot (Point A) on the half-oval is on the corner instead of in the middle of the flat side. Likewise, in this example, if you check the choices for the proper placement of Point B, you can eliminate Choices A and D because the dot on the triangle is in the middle of a side instead of at an angle. The only remaining choice is Choice C.

Hey, wait, we just solved the whole problem! See how checking the placement of the points on both shapes eliminated all the incorrect choices? Just like Sherlock Holmes said: "When you have eliminated the impossible, whatever remains, no matter how improbable, must be the truth."

Not all of this type of problem will be this easy, though. Here's another example that's not as easy.

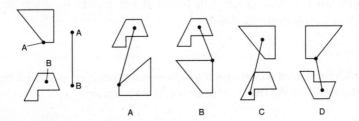

A   B   C   D

Here, we will look at a point or points inside the shape instead of on the edge. If we use the same principle we used before and look at the shape with Point A, we can eliminate Choice B because it has what is supposed to be Point A on the wrong side of the shape (the longer side instead of the short-est side). We can also eliminate Choice C because it has the point placed incorrectly on both shapes. This leaves us only Choices A and D to consider, doubling the chance that we'll get this one right.

To get the final (correct) answer, let's look at one more tip.

2. **Watch out for mirrored shapes.** Just as in the jigsaw puzzle-piece assembly problem, this can be tricky, but you can figure it out if you take a systematic approach and take the few seconds necessary to get this right. Just look at first one shape and then the other to see if they can be rotated into the same position as the shapes in the initial drawing. If you have to, imagine the shape is a paper cutout and you have just stuck a straight pin through the middle of the shape into the cork bulletin board behind it. This leaves the shape free to spin around its axis (the pin). By doing this, you can see that the shapes in Choice A are OK—one of them is already in the same position as the shape in the initial drawing. The shapes in Choice D, though, are a different matter—by mentally spinning them around that straight pin through their middles, you can see that both these shapes are mirror images—just tricksters and very much not correct. That leaves only Choice A as the correct choice.

The exact format of the Assembling Objects subtest is still evolving, so the types of shapes and illustrations you see here may change, but these suggestions will still help you. None of the ASVAB subtests, however, exist to give you a free ride—you will have to put some effort into deducing the correct answer to each question. This means that more than one of the choices may be plausible at first glance. However, if you follow these steps—and especially if you use them to practice this skill of assembling objects in each of the four practice tests in this book—you should do well on the actual ASVAB.

Practice Questions

1.

   (A)   (B)   (C)   (D)

2.

   (A)   (B)   (C)   (D)

3.

   (A)   (B)   (C)   (D)

4.

   (A)   (B)   (C)   (D)

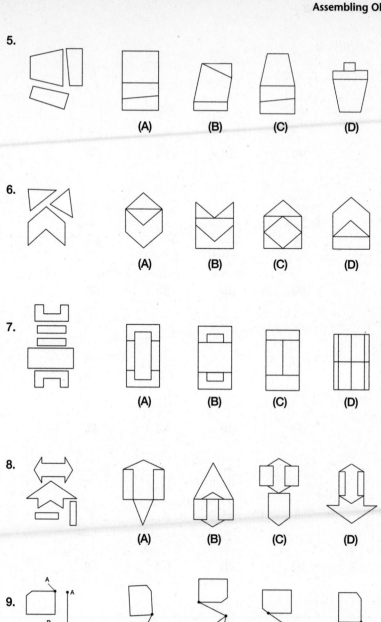

5.

(A)　(B)　(C)　(D)

6.

(A)　(B)　(C)　(D)

7.

(A)　(B)　(C)　(D)

8.

(A)　(B)　(C)　(D)

9.

(A)　(B)　(C)　(D)

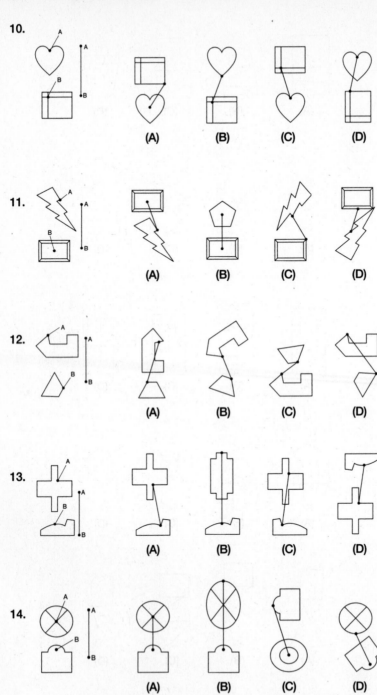

15.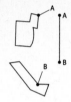

(A)　　(B)　　(C)　　(D)

16.

(A)　　(B)　　(C)　　(D)

Answer Key

1. **B**	5. **C**	9. **B**	13. **D**
2. **C**	6. **A**	10. **C**	14. **A**
3. **D**	7. **A**	11. **A**	15. **B**
4. **B**	8. **D**	12. **C**	16. **C**

PART FOUR
TEST YOURSELF
(AFQT)

The two Model Exams that follow include the Arithmetic Reasoning, the Word Knowledge, the Paragraph Comprehension, and the Mathematics Knowledge subtests of the ASVAB—the four sections that comprise the Armed Forces Qualification Test (AFQT).

Extra practice in these areas will improve your chances of doing well in these subject areas, and thus increase the degree of your eligibility for joining the branch of the service of your choice.

ANSWER SHEET—EXAMINATION ONE

Arithmetic Reasoning	Word Knowledge	Paragraph Comprehension	Mathematics Knowledge
1. Ⓐ Ⓑ Ⓒ Ⓓ	1. Ⓐ Ⓑ Ⓒ Ⓓ	1. Ⓐ Ⓑ Ⓒ Ⓓ	1. Ⓐ Ⓑ Ⓒ Ⓓ
2. Ⓐ Ⓑ Ⓒ Ⓓ	2. Ⓐ Ⓑ Ⓒ Ⓓ	2. Ⓐ Ⓑ Ⓒ Ⓓ	2. Ⓐ Ⓑ Ⓒ Ⓓ
3. Ⓐ Ⓑ Ⓒ Ⓓ	3. Ⓐ Ⓑ Ⓒ Ⓓ	3. Ⓐ Ⓑ Ⓒ Ⓓ	3. Ⓐ Ⓑ Ⓒ Ⓓ
4. Ⓐ Ⓑ Ⓒ Ⓓ	4. Ⓐ Ⓑ Ⓒ Ⓓ	4. Ⓐ Ⓑ Ⓒ Ⓓ	4. Ⓐ Ⓑ Ⓒ Ⓓ
5. Ⓐ Ⓑ Ⓒ Ⓓ	5. Ⓐ Ⓑ Ⓒ Ⓓ	5. Ⓐ Ⓑ Ⓒ Ⓓ	5. Ⓐ Ⓑ Ⓒ Ⓓ
6. Ⓐ Ⓑ Ⓒ Ⓓ	6. Ⓐ Ⓑ Ⓒ Ⓓ	6. Ⓐ Ⓑ Ⓒ Ⓓ	6. Ⓐ Ⓑ Ⓒ Ⓓ
7. Ⓐ Ⓑ Ⓒ Ⓓ	7. Ⓐ Ⓑ Ⓒ Ⓓ	7. Ⓐ Ⓑ Ⓒ Ⓓ	7. Ⓐ Ⓑ Ⓒ Ⓓ
8. Ⓐ Ⓑ Ⓒ Ⓓ	8. Ⓐ Ⓑ Ⓒ Ⓓ	8. Ⓐ Ⓑ Ⓒ Ⓓ	8. Ⓐ Ⓑ Ⓒ Ⓓ
9. Ⓐ Ⓑ Ⓒ Ⓓ	9. Ⓐ Ⓑ Ⓒ Ⓓ	9. Ⓐ Ⓑ Ⓒ Ⓓ	9. Ⓐ Ⓑ Ⓒ Ⓓ
10. Ⓐ Ⓑ Ⓒ Ⓓ	10. Ⓐ Ⓑ Ⓒ Ⓓ	10. Ⓐ Ⓑ Ⓒ Ⓓ	10. Ⓐ Ⓑ Ⓒ Ⓓ
11. Ⓐ Ⓑ Ⓒ Ⓓ	11. Ⓐ Ⓑ Ⓒ Ⓓ	11. Ⓐ Ⓑ Ⓒ Ⓓ	11. Ⓐ Ⓑ Ⓒ Ⓓ
12. Ⓐ Ⓑ Ⓒ Ⓓ	12. Ⓐ Ⓑ Ⓒ Ⓓ	12. Ⓐ Ⓑ Ⓒ Ⓓ	12. Ⓐ Ⓑ Ⓒ Ⓓ
13. Ⓐ Ⓑ Ⓒ Ⓓ	13. Ⓐ Ⓑ Ⓒ Ⓓ	13. Ⓐ Ⓑ Ⓒ Ⓓ	13. Ⓐ Ⓑ Ⓒ Ⓓ
14. Ⓐ Ⓑ Ⓒ Ⓓ	14. Ⓐ Ⓑ Ⓒ Ⓓ	14. Ⓐ Ⓑ Ⓒ Ⓓ	14. Ⓐ Ⓑ Ⓒ Ⓓ
15. Ⓐ Ⓑ Ⓒ Ⓓ	15. Ⓐ Ⓑ Ⓒ Ⓓ	15. Ⓐ Ⓑ Ⓒ Ⓓ	15. Ⓐ Ⓑ Ⓒ Ⓓ
16. Ⓐ Ⓑ Ⓒ Ⓓ	16. Ⓐ Ⓑ Ⓒ Ⓓ		16. Ⓐ Ⓑ Ⓒ Ⓓ
17. Ⓐ Ⓑ Ⓒ Ⓓ	17. Ⓐ Ⓑ Ⓒ Ⓓ		17. Ⓐ Ⓑ Ⓒ Ⓓ
18. Ⓐ Ⓑ Ⓒ Ⓓ	18. Ⓐ Ⓑ Ⓒ Ⓓ		18. Ⓐ Ⓑ Ⓒ Ⓓ
19. Ⓐ Ⓑ Ⓒ Ⓓ	19. Ⓐ Ⓑ Ⓒ Ⓓ		19. Ⓐ Ⓑ Ⓒ Ⓓ
20. Ⓐ Ⓑ Ⓒ Ⓓ	20. Ⓐ Ⓑ Ⓒ Ⓓ		20. Ⓐ Ⓑ Ⓒ Ⓓ
21. Ⓐ Ⓑ Ⓒ Ⓓ	21. Ⓐ Ⓑ Ⓒ Ⓓ		21. Ⓐ Ⓑ Ⓒ Ⓓ
22. Ⓐ Ⓑ Ⓒ Ⓓ	22. Ⓐ Ⓑ Ⓒ Ⓓ		22. Ⓐ Ⓑ Ⓒ Ⓓ
23. Ⓐ Ⓑ Ⓒ Ⓓ	23. Ⓐ Ⓑ Ⓒ Ⓓ		23. Ⓐ Ⓑ Ⓒ Ⓓ
24. Ⓐ Ⓑ Ⓒ Ⓓ	24. Ⓐ Ⓑ Ⓒ Ⓓ		24. Ⓐ Ⓑ Ⓒ Ⓓ
25. Ⓐ Ⓑ Ⓒ Ⓓ	25. Ⓐ Ⓑ Ⓒ Ⓓ		25. Ⓐ Ⓑ Ⓒ Ⓓ
26. Ⓐ Ⓑ Ⓒ Ⓓ	26. Ⓐ Ⓑ Ⓒ Ⓓ		
27. Ⓐ Ⓑ Ⓒ Ⓓ	27. Ⓐ Ⓑ Ⓒ Ⓓ		
28. Ⓐ Ⓑ Ⓒ Ⓓ	28. Ⓐ Ⓑ Ⓒ Ⓓ		
29. Ⓐ Ⓑ Ⓒ Ⓓ	29. Ⓐ Ⓑ Ⓒ Ⓓ		
30. Ⓐ Ⓑ Ⓒ Ⓓ	30. Ⓐ Ⓑ Ⓒ Ⓓ		
	31. Ⓐ Ⓑ Ⓒ Ⓓ		
	32. Ⓐ Ⓑ Ⓒ Ⓓ		
	33. Ⓐ Ⓑ Ⓒ Ⓓ		
	34. Ⓐ Ⓑ Ⓒ Ⓓ		
	35. Ⓐ Ⓑ Ⓒ Ⓓ		

ARITHMETIC REASONING

Directions: This test has questions about arithmetic. Each question is followed by four possible answers. Decide which answer is correct. Then, on your answer form, blacken the space which has the same number and letter as your choice. Use your scratch paper for any figuring you wish to do.

SAMPLE QUESTION

1. If 1 quart of milk costs $0.80, what is the cost of 2 quarts?

    (A) $2.00
    (B) $1.60
    (C) $1.20
    (D) $1.00

The cost of 2 quarts is $1.60; therefore, answer B is correct.

Your score on this test will be based on the number of questions you answer correctly. You should try to answer every question. Do not spend too much time on any one question.

The actual test will say:
Do not turn this page until told to do so.

Arithmetic Reasoning

Time —36 minutes
30 Questions

1. The Parkers bought a table that was marked $400. On the installment plan, they made a down payment equal to 25% of the marked price, plus 12 monthly payments of $30 each. How much more than the marked price did they pay by buying it this way?

(A) $25
(B) $50
(C) $60
(D) $460

2. A scientist planted 120 seeds, of which 90 sprouted. What percent of the seeds failed to sprout?

(A) 25%
(B) 24%
(C) 30%
(D) 75%

3. An airplane traveled 1,000 miles in 2 hours and 30 minutes. What was the average rate or speed, in miles per hour, for the trip?

(A) 200 miles per hour
(B) 300 miles per hour
(C) 400 miles per hour
(D) 500 miles per hour

4. What is the value of this expression?

$$\frac{0.05 \times 4}{0.1}$$

(A) 20
(B) 2
(C) 0.2
(D) 0.02

5. Joan Smith's bank balance was $2,674. Her bank balance changed as follows over the next four-month period:

$$-\$348, +\$765, +\$802, -\$518$$

What was her bank balance at the end of the four-month period?

(A) $5,107
(B) $4,241
(C) $3,475
(D) $3,375

6. If 1 gallon of milk costs $3.84, what is the cost of 3 pints?

   (A) $1.44
   (B) $2.82
   (C) $2.04
   (D) $1.96

7. A square measures 9 feet on a side. If each side of the square is increased by 3 feet, how many square feet are added to the area?

   (A) 144
   (B) 81
   (C) 60
   (D) 63

8. What is the average of $\frac{1}{4}$ and $\frac{1}{6}$?

   (A) $\frac{5}{24}$

   (B) $\frac{7}{24}$

   (C) $\frac{5}{12}$

   (D) $\frac{1}{5}$

9. Joe Gray's salary was increased from $260 per week to $290 per week. What was the increase in his salary, to the nearest percent?

   (A) 12%
   (B) 11%
   (C) 10%
   (D) 9%

10. If 1 pound, 12 ounces of fish costs $2.24, what is the cost of the fish per pound?

   (A) $1.20
   (B) $1.28
   (C) $1.24
   (D) $1.40

11. A front lawn measures 25 feet in length, and 15 feet in width. The back lawn of the same house measures 50 feet in length and 30 feet in width. What is the ratio of the area of the front lawn to the area of the back lawn?

   (A) 1:2
   (B) 2:3
   (C) 3:4
   (D) 1:4

12. The price of a car was increased from $6,400 to $7,200. What was the percent of increase?

(A) 10%

(B) $11\frac{1}{9}$%

(C) $12\frac{1}{2}$%

(D) 15%

13. What is the next term in this series: $3\frac{1}{2}$; $2\frac{1}{4}$; $13\frac{1}{4}$; 12; _____?

(A) $1\frac{1}{4}$

(B) $10\frac{3}{4}$

(C) 23

(D) $14\frac{1}{2}$

14. A movie house opens at 10:00 A.M. and closes at 11:30 P.M. If a complete showing of a movie takes 2 hours and 15 minutes, how many complete showings are given at the movie house each day?

(A) 5
(B) 6
(C) 7
(D) 8

15. At a concert, orchestra seats sell for $20 each, and balcony seats sell for $10 each. If 324 orchestra seats were occupied, and the box office collected $10,000, how many balcony seats were sold?

(A) 375
(B) 352
(C) 330
(D) 310

16. In a certain city, taxicab fare is $0.80 for the first $\frac{1}{4}$ mile, and $0.20 for each additional $\frac{1}{4}$ mile. How far, in miles, can a passenger travel for $5.00?

(A) 5 miles

(B) $4\frac{1}{4}$ miles

(C) $5\frac{1}{2}$ miles

(D) $5\frac{3}{4}$ miles

17. A scale drawing of a building plot has a scale of 1 inch to 40 feet. How many inches on the drawing represent a distance of 175 feet on the plot?

(A) $4\frac{1}{8}$ inches

(B) $4\frac{3}{8}$ inches

(C) $4\frac{1}{2}$ inches

(D) $4\frac{3}{4}$ inches

18. The wholesale list price of a watch was $50. A dealer bought a shipment of watches at a discount of 20% and sold the watches at 10% above the wholesale list price. What was her profit on each watch?

(A) $8
(B) $10
(C) $12
(D) $15

19. The minute hand of the clock is missing, but the hour hand is on the 11-minute mark. What time was it when the clock broke?

(A) 5 minutes after 11
(B) 11 minutes after 12
(C) 12 minutes after 2
(D) 20 minutes after 1

20. During a season a professional basketball player tried 320 shots and made 272 of them. What percent of the shots tried were successful?

(A) 85%
(B) 80%
(C) 75%
(D) 70%

21. A painter and a helper spend 3 days painting a house. The painter receives twice as much as the helper. If the two men receive $375 for the job, how much does the painter receive?

(A) $175
(B) $200
(C) $225
(D) $250

22. What is the difference between 50% discount and a discount of $33\frac{1}{3}$%?

   (A) 0.17
   (B) $\frac{1}{3}$
   (C) 0.25
   (D) $\frac{1}{6}$

23. What is the value of $3a^2 - 2a + 5$, when $a = 4$?

   (A) 43
   (B) 45
   (C) 61
   (D) 21

24. This table gives the annual premiums for a life insurance policy, based on the age of the holder when the policy is taken out.

Age in Years	Premium per $1,000
22	$18
30	$22
38	$28
46	$38

   Over 20 years, how much is saved by taking out a $1,000 policy at age 30, rather than at age 46?

   (A) $16
   (B) $32
   (C) $320
   (D) $400

25. A chair was marked for sale at $240. This sale price was 25% less than the original price. What was the original price?

   (A) $300
   (B) $280
   (C) $320
   (D) $60

26. What is the quotient when 0.675 is divided by 0.9?

   (A) 7.5
   (B) 0.075
   (C) 75
   (D) 0.75

27. On May 15, an electric meter read 5,472 kilowatt hours. The following month, on June 15, the meter read 5,687 kilowatt hours. The utility charges the following rates for electric service.

    First 10 kilowatt hours—$2.48
    Next 45 kilowatt hours—$0.16 per kilowatt hour
    Next 55 kilowatt hours—$0.12 per kilowatt hour
    Over 110 kilowatt hours—$0.07 per kilowatt hour

    What was the total charge for the kilowatt hours consumed during the month from May 15 to June 15?

    (A) $22.53
    (B) $23.63
    (C) $22.63
    (D) $24.43

28. What is the difference between the square of 49 and the square of 31?

    (A) 18
    (B) $1\frac{1}{2}$
    (C) 1,440
    (D) 2,056

29. An auditorium contains x rows, with y seats in each row. What is the number of seats in the auditorium?

    (A) xy
    (B) $x + y$
    (C) $x - y$
    (D) $y - x$

30. When a certain number is divided by 15, the quotient is 8, and the remainder is 7. What is the number?

    (A) 127
    (B) $8\frac{1}{2}$
    (C) $3\frac{3}{5}$
    (D) 77

WORD KNOWLEDGE

Directions: This test has questions about the meanings of words. Each question has an underlined boldface word. You are to decide which one of the four words in the choices most nearly means the same as the underlined boldface word; then, mark the space on your answer form which has the same number and letter as your choice.

SAMPLE QUESTION

1. It was a **small** table.

    (A) sturdy
    (B) round
    (C) cheap
    (D) little

The question asks which of the four words means the same as the boldface word, **small**.

Little means the same as **small**. Answer D is the best one.

Your score on this test will be based on the number of questions you answer correctly. You should try to answer every question. Do not spend too much time on any one question.

The actual test will say:
Do not turn this page until told to do so.

Word Knowledge

1. <u>Subsume</u> most nearly means

   (A) understate
   (B) absorb
   (C) include
   (D) belong

2. Our committee reached <u>consensus</u>.

   (A) accord
   (B) abridgment
   (C) presumption
   (D) quota

3. <u>Altercation</u> most nearly means

   (A) defeat
   (B) concurrence
   (C) controversy
   (D) vexation

4. Don't accuse him of being <u>irresolute</u>.

   (A) wavering
   (B) insubordinate
   (C) impudent
   (D) unobservant

5. <u>Laconic</u> most nearly means

   (A) slothful
   (B) concise
   (C) punctual
   (D) melancholy

6. <u>Audition</u> most nearly means

   (A) reception
   (B) contest
   (C) hearing
   (D) display

7. The job was filled by a(n) **novice**.

   (A) volunteer
   (B) expert
   (C) beginner
   (D) amateur

8. A(n) **conciliatory** attitude sometimes helps.

   (A) pacific
   (B) contentious
   (C) obligatory
   (D) offensive

9. The drug will **counteract** any effect.

   (A) undermine
   (B) censure
   (C) preserve
   (D) neutralize

10. **Precedent** most nearly means

    (A) example
    (B) theory
    (C) law
    (D) conformity

11. **Diaphanous** most nearly means

    (A) transparent
    (B) opaque
    (C) diaphragmatic
    (D) diffusive

12. We **deferred** our judgment.

    (A) reversed
    (B) accelerated
    (C) rejected
    (D) delayed

13. To **accentuate** most nearly means

    (A) to modify
    (B) to hasten
    (C) to sustain
    (D) to intensify

14. <u>Authentic</u> most nearly means

    (A) detailed
    (B) reliable
    (C) valuable
    (D) practical

15. <u>Unanimity</u> most nearly means

    (A) emphasis
    (B) namelessness
    (C) disagreement
    (D) concurrence

16. Their actions made them <u>notorious</u>.

    (A) condemned
    (B) unpleasant
    (C) vexatious
    (D) well-known

17. <u>Previous</u> most nearly means

    (A) abandoned
    (B) former
    (C) timely
    (D) younger

18. Use a <u>flexible</u> metal.

    (A) breakable
    (B) flammable
    (C) pliable
    (D) weak

19. <u>Option</u> most nearly means

    (A) use
    (B) choice
    (C) value
    (D) preference

20. You should <u>verify</u> the facts.

    (A) examine
    (B) explain
    (C) confirm
    (D) guarantee

21. **Pert** most nearly means

   (A) ill
   (B) lazy
   (C) slow
   (D) saucy

22. **Aesthetic** most nearly means

   (A) sentient
   (B) sensitive
   (C) tasteful
   (D) inartistic

23. **Decimation** most nearly means

   (A) killing
   (B) annihilation
   (C) armistice
   (D) brawl

24. She made an **indignant** response.

   (A) angry
   (B) poor
   (C) indigent
   (D) lazy

25. **Cliché** most nearly means

   (A) commonplace
   (B) banality
   (C) hackney
   (D) platitude

26. **Harmony** most nearly means

   (A) rhythm
   (B) pleasure
   (C) discord
   (D) agreement

27. **Indolent** most nearly means

    (A) moderate
    (B) hopeless
    (C) lazy
    (D) idle

28. His **respiration** was impaired.

    (A) recovery
    (B) breathing
    (C) pulsation
    (D) sweating

29. The job requires a **vigilant** attitude.

    (A) sensible
    (B) watchful
    (C) suspicious
    (D) restless

30. **Incidental** most nearly means

    (A) independent
    (B) needless
    (C) infrequent
    (D) casual

31. To **succumb** most nearly means

    (A) to aid
    (B) to oppose
    (C) to yield
    (D) to check

32. That solution is not **feasible**.

    (A) capable
    (B) harmful
    (C) beneficial
    (D) practicable

33. **Versatile** most nearly means

    (A) well-known
    (B) up-to-date
    (C) many-sided
    (D) ambidextrous

34. His **imperturbability** helps in a crisis.

    (A) obstinacy
    (B) serenity
    (C) sagacity
    (D) confusion

35. **Strident** most nearly means

    (A) swaggering
    (B) domineering
    (C) angry
    (D) harsh

PARAGRAPH COMPREHENSION

Directions: This is a test of your ability to understand what you read. In this section you will find one or more paragraphs of reading material followed by incomplete statements or questions. You are to read the paragraph and select one of four lettered choices which best completes the statement or answers the question. When you have selected your answer, blacken in the correct numbered letter on your answer sheet.

SAMPLE QUESTION

In certain areas water is so scarce that every attempt is made to conserve it. For instance, on one oasis in the Sahara Desert the amount of water necessary for each date palm tree has been carefully determined.

1. How much water is each tree given?

    (A) no water at all
    (B) exactly the amount required
    (C) water only if it is healthy
    (D) water on alternate days

The amount of water each tree requires has been carefully determined, so answer B is correct.

Your score on this test will be based on the number of questions you answer correctly. You should try to answer every question. Do not spend too much time on any one question.

The actual test will say:
Do not turn this page until told to do so.

Paragraph Comprehension

Time —13 minutes
15 Questions

1. Twenty-five percent of all household burglaries can be attributed to unlocked windows or doors. Crime is the result of opportunity plus desire. To prevent crime, it is each individual's responsibility to

   (A) provide the opportunity.
   (B) provide the desire.
   (C) prevent the opportunity.
   (D) prevent the desire.

2. From a building designer's standpoint, three things that make a home livable are the client, the building site, and the amount of money the client has to spend. According to the passage, to make a home livable

   (A) the prospective piece of land makes little difference.
   (B) it can be built on any piece of land.
   (C) the design must fit the owner's income and site.
   (D) the design must fit the designer's income.

3. Family camping has been described as the "biggest single growth industry in the booming travel/leisure market." Camping ranges from backpacking to living in motor homes with complete creature comforts. It is both an end in itself and a magic carpet to a wide variety of other forms of outdoor recreation.

   It can be inferred from the passage that the LEAST luxurious form of camping is

   (A) backpacking
   (B) travel trailers
   (C) truck campers
   (D) motor homes

4. Most drivers try to drive safely. A major part of safe driving is the right speed. But what is the "right" speed? Is it 20 miles per hour, or 35, or 60? That question is hard to answer. On some city streets and in heavy traffic, twenty miles per hour could be too fast. On a superhighway, 35 miles per hour could be too slow. Of course, a good driver must follow the speed limit, but he must also use good judgment. The "right" speed will vary by the number of cars, surface of the road, and the visibility.

   The general theme of this passage is that a good driver:

   (A) drives at 35 miles an hour.
   (B) adjusts to different driving conditions.
   (C) always drives at the same speed.
   (D) always follows the speed limit.

5. Gardening can be an easygoing hobby, a scientific pursuit, an opportunity for exercise and fresh air, a serious source of food to help balance the family budget, a means of expression in art and beauty, an applied experiment in green plant growth, or all of these things together.

All of the following are made possible by gardening according to the passage EXCEPT

(A) relaxation.
(B) exercise.
(C) experimentation.
(D) hard work.

6. About three fourths of the surface of the earth is water. Of the 336 million cubic miles of water, most (97.2%) is found in the oceans and is salty. Glaciers hold another two percent of the total. Less than one percent (.8%) is available as fresh water for people to use. And much of that is not near people who need it.

The amount of fresh water available for people to use is:

(A) 97.2%
(B) .8%
(C) 2%
(D) 75%

7. Early settlers in the United States made the most of the herring fishing season. When spring came the fish arrived in great numbers in the rivers. No nets or hooks were needed. Men used what was called a *pinfold*. This was a large circular pen built in shallow water. It was made by driving stakes closely together in the floor of the river.

A *pinfold* was made with:

(A) hooks and nets.
(B) only nets.
(C) stakes driven into the river bottom.
(D) fishing rods.

8. The powers of the United States government are divided. One part of government, the Congress, makes the laws. Another part, the President and the different heads of departments, put the laws into effect. The third part, the courts, must try cases when laws are broken. The idea behind this is to prevent one part or branch of government from getting all the power.

As a result of the divided powers of government

(A) Congress rules the United States.
(B) the President rules the United States.
(C) power is shared.
(D) no branch has power.

9. A narcotic is a drug which, in proper doses, relieves pain and induces profound sleep, but which, in poisonous doses, induces stupor, coma, or convulsions. Narcotics tend to be habit-forming and, in many instances, repeated doses lead to addiction.

A proper dose of narcotic induces

(A) coma.
(B) convulsions.
(C) deep sleep.
(D) stupor.

10. Because nitrogen, phosphorus, and potassium are used by plants in large amounts, these nutrients are likely to be deficient in the soil. When you buy a fertilizer, therefore, you generally buy it for its content of these materials.

Unfertilized soil naturally deficient in nitrogen, phosphoric oxide, and potash probably lacks these nutrients because

(A) they are not soluble.
(B) manufacturers do not recommend them to gardeners.
(C) they are rare elements never found in the earth.
(D) plants use them up in large quantities.

11. Where does pollution come from? It comes from a wide variety of sources, including furnaces, smokestacks, incinerators, power-generating stations, industrial plants, dirt and dust caused by tearing down old buildings and putting up new ones, ordinary street dirt, restaurants that emit smoke and odors, cars, buses, trucks, planes, and steamships. Sixty percent of pollution is caused by motor vehicle exhausts, while another thirty percent is due to industry.

Most air pollution in that city is caused by

(A) industry and incinerators.
(B) cars, trucks, and buses.
(C) airplanes.
(D) smokestacks of buildings.

12. The use of sunglasses as an aid to vision is important. For the most part, the eye is a "daytime" instrument. It requires light to work properly. However, too much bright light and glare can create discomfort. As a result the eyes blink, squint, get tears, or have trouble seeing well. Sunglasses help by keeping much of this bright light and glare from reaching the eyes.

The main purpose of sunglasses is to

(A) hide the eyes.
(B) screen out harmful rays of the sun.
(C) remove the need for regular glasses.
(D) protect the eyes from dirt.

13. Would you like to be good at a trade? Would you like to know a skill that pays well? One sure way to skill, good pay, and regular work is to train on the job. This is called apprentice training. While it is not the only way to learn, apprentice training has good points. You can earn while you learn. You know the skill "from the ground up." You can advance on the job.

Apprentice training is described by discussing:

(A) both sides.
(B) the good side.
(C) the bad side.
(D) a specific trade.

14. When you work at a job covered by Social Security, you and your employer contribute equal amounts. Your portion of the tax is taken from your wages or pay check before you receive it. This is called a *deduction*.

    (A) Total tax rate is retirement rate plus insurance rate.
    (B) Insurance rates are higher than retirement rates.
    (C) Money taken from your pay is called a deduction.
    (D) Only your employer contributes to Social Security.

15. Nucleic acids are found in all living organisms from viruses to man. They received their name because of their discovery in the nuclei of white blood cells and fish sperm by Miescher in 1869. However, it is now well established that nucleic acids occur outside of the cell nucleus as well.

    Nucleic acids are found

    (A) only in cells of man.
    (B) only in viruses.
    (C) in all living cells.
    (D) only in white blood cells.

MATHEMATICS KNOWLEDGE

Directions: This is a test of your ability to solve general mathematical problems. Each problem is followed by four answer choices. Select the correct response from the choices given. Then mark the space on your answer form that has the same number and letter as your choice. Use scratch paper to do any figuring that you wish.

SAMPLE PROBLEM

1. If $x + 8 = 9$, then x is equal to

    (A) 0
    (B) 1
    (C) –1
    (D) $\frac{9}{8}$

The correct answer is 1, so B is the correct response.

Your score on this test will be based on the number of questions you answer correctly. You should try to answer every question. Do not spend too much time on any one question.

The actual test will say:
Do not turn this page until told to do so.

Mathematics Knowledge

Time —24 minutes

25 Questions

1. Which of the following is the smallest prime number greater than 200?

    (A) 201
    (B) 205
    (C) 211
    (D) 214

2. If 40% is equal to the fraction $\frac{x}{30}$, what is the value of x?

    (A) 0.4
    (B) 15
    (C) 1,200
    (D) 12

3. The expression "5 factorial" equals

    (A) 125
    (B) 120
    (C) 25
    (D) 10

4. What is the result of subtracting $3x^2 - 5x - 1$ from $8x^2 + 2x - 9$?

    (A) $5x^2 - 3x - 10$
    (B) $-5x^2 - 3x - 10$
    (C) $5x^2 + 7x - 8$
    (D) $-5x^2 - 7x + 8$

5. What is the meaning of the statement $-30 < -5$?

    (A) 30 is greater than 5
    (B) 30 is less than minus 5
    (C) minus 30 is less than minus 5
    (D) minus 30 is greater than minus 5

6. Solve for x: $8x - 2 - 5x = 8$

(A) $x = 1.3$

(B) $x = 2\dfrac{1}{2}$

(C) $x = 3\dfrac{1}{3}$

(D) $x = -7$

7. A woman has $500 in a bank account. Every week, she writes out a check for $50. If she doesn't make any new deposits, what will her bank account hold x weeks from now?

(A) $500 + 50x$

(B) $500 - 50x$

(C) $550 - x$

(D) $500 + $50 + x$

8. When the temperature is 20 degrees Celsius (C), what is it on the Fahrenheit (F) scale? (Use the following formula).

$$F = \left(\frac{9}{5} \times C\right) + 32$$

(A) $93\dfrac{3}{5}$ degrees

(B) 78 degrees

(C) $62\dfrac{3}{5}$ degrees

(D) 68 degrees

9. The perimeter of a rectangle is 38". If the length is 3" more than the width, find the width.

(A) $17\dfrac{1}{2}$"

(B) 8"

(C) 11"

(D) $14\dfrac{1}{2}$"

10. Find the square root of 85 correct to the nearest tenth.

(A) 9.1

(B) 9.2

(C) 9.3

(D) 9.4

11. If $5x = 30$, then x is equal to

(A) 150
(B) 25
(C) 6
(D) 0.6

12. What is the product of $(a - 5)$ and $(a + 3)$?

(A) $a^2 - 15$
(B) $a^2 + 2a - 15$
(C) $a^2 - 2a - 15$
(D) $a^2 - 2$

13. Solve for z: $3z - 5 + 2z = 25 - 5z$

(A) $z = 0$
(B) $z = 3$
(C) $z = -3$
(D) no solution

14. A park commissioner designs a new playground in the shape of a pentagon. If he plans to have a fountain at every corner of the park, how many fountains will there be?

(A) 4
(B) 5
(C) 6
(D) 7

15. If one of the angles of a right triangle is 30 degrees, what are the other two angles?

(A) 30 degrees, 120 degrees
(B) 60 degrees, 45 degrees
(C) 60 degrees, 90 degrees
(D) 45 degrees, 90 degrees

16. What is the value of x in the equation $\frac{x}{2} = 7$?

   (A) $x = 14$
   (B) $x = 3\frac{1}{2}$
   (C) $x = 9$
   (D) $x = 5$

17. Divide $15a^3b^2c$ by $5abc$.

   (A) $10abc$
   (B) $3abc$
   (C) $5a^2b^2$
   (D) $3a^2b$

18. Two circles have the same center. If their radii are 7" and 10", find the area that is part of the larger circle, but not the smaller one.

   (A) 3 square inches
   (B) 17 square inches
   (C) 51 pi square inches
   (D) 70 pi square inches

19. My average grade on a set of five tests was 88%. I can remember only that the first four grades were 78%, 86%, 96%, and 94%. What was my fifth grade?

   (A) 88
   (B) 86
   (C) 84
   (D) 82

20. How many cubic yards of concrete are needed to make a cement floor that is 9' by 12' by 6" thick?

   (A) 2
   (B) 18
   (C) 54
   (D) 648

21. A wildlife preserve is laid out in the shape of a perfect circle, whose radius is 14 miles. The lions' territory in this preserve is shaped like a wedge and has a fence around it. Two inner sides of a fence meet at a 90-degree angle in the center of the preserve. How much territory do the lions have?

    (A) 140 square miles
    (B) $3\frac{1}{2}$ square miles
    (C) 210 square miles
    (D) 154 square miles

22. Find the value of $(-3)^4 + (-2)^4 + (-1)^4$

    (A) 98
    (B) -98
    (C) -21
    (D) 21

23. A cylindrical can has a radius of 7" and a height of 15". How many gallons of milk can it hold? (There are 231 cubic inches in a gallon.)

    (A) 15 gallons
    (B) 14 gallons
    (C) 140 gallons
    (D) 10 gallons

24. A 10-foot-high ladder is resting against an 8-foot-high wall in a tennis court. If the top of the ladder is exactly even with the top of the wall, how far is the base of the ladder from the wall?

    (A) 18 feet
    (B) 6 feet
    (C) 12 feet
    (D) 9 feet

25. Ten ounces of liquid contain 20% fruit juice and 80% water. The mixture is diluted by adding 40 additional ounces of water. What is the percent of fruit juice in the new solution?

    (A) 4%
    (B) 10%
    (C) 20%
    (D) 40%

ANSWER KEYS AND ANSWER EXPLANATIONS

Arithmetic Reasoning

Answer Key

1. **C**	6. **A**	11. **D**	16. **C**	21. **D**	26. **D**
2. **A**	7. **D**	12. **C**	17. **B**	22. **D**	27. **B**
3. **C**	8. **A**	13. **C**	18. **D**	23. **B**	28. **C**
4. **B**	9. **A**	14. **B**	19. **C**	24. **C**	29. **A**
5. **D**	10. **B**	15. **B**	20. **A**	25. **C**	30. **A**

Answer Explanations

1. **(C)** The down payment was 25% (or $\frac{1}{4}$) of the total payment.

    $400 \times \frac{1}{4} = \$100$

    $30 \times 12 = \$360$ (sum of monthly payments)

    $360 + \$100 = \$460$ (cost on installment plan)

    $460 - \$400 = \$60$ (extra cost on installment)

2. **(A)** The number of seeds that failed to sprout was
    $$120 - 90 = 30$$
    The percentage of seeds that failed to sprout was
    $$\frac{30}{120} = \frac{1}{4} = 25\%$$

3. **(C)** To find the average rate of speed, divide the distance covered (1,000 miles) by the time spent traveling ($2\frac{1}{2}$ or 2.5 hours). Clear the decimal in the divisor.
    $$\frac{1,000}{2.5} = \frac{10,000}{25} = 400 \text{ miles per hour}$$

4. **(B)** Solve by multiplying first, and then dividing. Clear the decimal in the divisor.
    $$\frac{0.05 \times 4}{0.1} = \frac{0.20}{0.1} = \frac{0.2}{0.1} = \frac{2}{1} = 2$$

5. **(D)** Find the sum of the deposits and the sum of the withdrawals.

    $765 + \$802 = \$1,567$ (deposits)

    $348 + \$518 = \$866$ (withdrawals)

    Find the difference between deposits and withdrawals.

    $1,567 - \$866 = \$701$ (overall gain)

    Add this gain to the original balance.

    $701 + \$2,674 = \$3,375$ (new balance)

6. **(A)** Find the cost of 1 pint. (There are 8 pints in 1 gallon.)

$$\$3.84 \div 8 = \$0.48$$

Find the cost of 3 pints.

$$\$0.48 \times 3 = \$1.44$$

7. **(D)** Multiply one side of a square by itself to find the area. Thus
$9' \times 9' = 81$ square feet
By adding 3 feet to each side of the 9-foot square, you produce a
12-foot square. Thus $12' \times 12' = 144$ square feet
Find the difference between the areas of the two squares
$144 - 81 = 63$ square feet

8. **(A)** First, change both fractions to a common denominator (12) and
add them.

$$\frac{1}{4} = \frac{3}{12} \qquad \frac{1}{6} = \frac{2}{12} \qquad \frac{3}{12} + \frac{2}{12} = \frac{5}{12}$$

To get the average, divide the sum by 2.

$$\frac{5}{12} \div 2 = \frac{5}{12} \times \frac{1}{2} = \frac{5}{24}$$

9. **(A)** First find the salary increase.
$\$290 - \$260 = \$30$ (amount of increase)
To find the percent of increase, use the original salary as the base and
carry the division out of three decimal places.

$$\frac{\text{(increase)}}{\text{(original salary)}} = \frac{\$30}{\$260} = \frac{3.000}{26} = 0.115$$

Rounded to the nearest hundredth, 0.115 is 0.12.
$0.12 = 12\%$

10. **(B)** Express the total weight of the fish in ounces.
1 pound = 16 ounces
16 ounces + 12 ounces = 28 ounces
Find the cost of one ounce, and multiply it by 16 to find the cost of
1 pound.

$$\$2.24 \div 28 = \$0.08$$
$$\$0.08 \times 16 = \$1.28$$

11. **(D)** Find the area of each lawn.
$25' \times 25' = 375$ square feet (front lawn)
$50' \times 30' = 1,500$ square feet (back lawn)
To find the ratio, divide one area by the other.

$$\frac{\text{(front lawn)}}{\text{(back lawn)}} = \frac{375}{1,500} = \frac{1}{4}$$

The ratio of the front lawn to the back lawn is 1:4.

12. **(C)** Find the amount of price increase.
$$\$7,200 - \$6,400 = \$800$$
To find the rate of increase, use the original price as your base.
$$\frac{\text{(increase)}}{\text{(original price)}} = \frac{\$800}{\$6,400} = \frac{1}{8}$$
$$\frac{1}{8} = 12\frac{1}{2}\% \text{ (rate of increase)}$$

13. **(C)** Find the relationship between each pair of numbers in the series. Thus

$$(3\frac{1}{2}; 2\frac{1}{4}) \quad 3\frac{1}{2} - 1\frac{1}{4} = 2\frac{1}{4}$$

$$(2\frac{1}{4}; 13\frac{1}{4}) \quad 2\frac{1}{4} + 11 = 13\frac{1}{4}$$

$$(13\frac{1}{4}; 12) \quad 13\frac{1}{4} - 1\frac{1}{4} = 12$$

The pattern so far is: $-1\frac{1}{4}$, $+11$, $-1\frac{1}{4}$
To continue the series, add 11 to the fourth number in the series:
$$12 + 11 = 23$$

14. **(B)** Find the number of hours the movie house is open.
From 10:00 A.M. to 10:00 P.M. is 12 hours

From 10:00 P.M. to 11:30 P.M. is $1\frac{1}{2}$ hours

$$12 + 1\frac{1}{2} = 13\frac{1}{2} \text{ (hours)}$$

Divide this total by the length of time for a complete showing of the

movie (2 hours and 15 minutes, or $2\frac{1}{4}$ hours).

$$13\frac{1}{2} \div 2\frac{1}{4} = \frac{27}{2} \div \frac{9}{4} = \frac{27}{2} \times \frac{4}{9} = 6 \text{ (showings)}$$

15. **(B)** Find the amount taken in for orchestra seats.
$$324 \times \$20 = \$6,480$$
Out of \$10,000, the remaining amount came from balcony seats.
$$\$10,000 - \$6,480 = \$3,520$$
Divide this amount by \$10 to find the number of balcony seat tickets that were sold.
$$\$3,520 \div \$10 = 352 \text{ (balcony seats)}$$

16. **(C)** Since the first $\frac{1}{4}$ mile costs $0.80, this leaves $4.20 for the balance

of the trip. At $0.20 for each additional $\frac{1}{4}$ mile, find the number of $\frac{1}{4}$

miles that $4.20 will cover. (Clear the decimal in the divisor.)

$4.20 ÷ $0.20 =

4.2 ÷ 0.2 =

42 ÷ 2 = 21 (additional $\frac{1}{4}$ miles)

Add the first $\frac{1}{4}$ mile (at $0.80) to this total.

21 + 1 = 22 ($\frac{1}{4}$ miles)

Change the $\frac{1}{4}$ miles to miles.

$22 ÷ 4 = 5\frac{1}{2}$ (miles for $5)

17. **(B)** Divide the distance by the number of feet (40) to an inch.

$$175' ÷ 40' = 4\frac{15}{40} = 4\frac{3}{8} \text{ (inches)}$$

18. **(D)** Find the discounted price paid by the dealer.

$50 × 20% =

$50 × 0.2 = $10 (discount)

$50 − $10 = $40 (price paid by dealer)

Then find the dealer's selling price, based on an increase over the original wholesale list price.

$50 × 10% =

$50 × 0.1 = $5 (increase over list price)

$50 + $5 = $55 (dealer's selling price)

Finally, find the dealer's profit.

$55 − $40 = $15 (dealer's profit)

19. **(C)** When the hour hand is on the 10-minute mark, it is actually on the number 2 (for 2 o'clock). The hour hand advances to a new minute mark every 12 minutes of actual time. Thus, when the hour hand stopped at the 11-minute mark, it was 12 minutes after 2.

20. **(A)** Divide the number of successful shots by the total number of shots the player tried. Change your answer to percent.

$$\frac{272}{320} = \frac{34}{40} = \frac{17}{20}$$

$$\frac{17}{20} = 0.85 = 85\%$$

21. **(D)** Let x equal the amount the helper receives. Let $2x$ equal the amount the painter receives. Write an equation to show that, together, they receive $375 for painting the house.

$$2x + x = \$375$$

Combine the similar terms, and then divide both sides of the equation by the number with x. (This is to undo the multiplication.)

$$3x = \$375$$
$$x = \$125 \text{ (the helper's wages)}$$
$$2x = \$250 \text{ (what the painter receives)}$$

22. **(D)** Find the difference between the two percents.

$$50\% \qquad\qquad 48\%$$
$$-33\tfrac{1}{3}\% \text{ (or)} \qquad -33\tfrac{1}{3}\%$$

$$16\tfrac{2}{3}\%$$

Divide the answer by 100% to change it to a simple fraction.

$$16\tfrac{2}{3}\% \div 100\% = \frac{50}{3} \div \frac{100}{1}$$

$$= \frac{50}{3} \times \frac{1}{100}$$

$$= \frac{50}{300} = \frac{1}{6}$$

23. **(B)** To solve, substitute the number value for the letter and do the arithmetic operations.

$$3a^2 - 2a + 5 =$$
$$(3 \times a^2) - (2 \times a) + 5 =$$
$$(3 \times 4^2) - (2 \times 4) + 5 =$$
$$(3 \times 16) - (2 \times 4) + 5 =$$
$$48 - 8 + 5 =$$
$$40 + 5 = 45$$

24. **(C)** Find the annual difference between the premium paid by someone who is 30 and the premium paid by someone who is 46.

$$\$38 - \$22 = \$16$$

Multiply the answer by 20 to find the total amount saved over 20 years by taking out a policy at an early age.

$$\$16 \times 20 = \$320 \text{ (saved)}$$

25. **(C)** On sale, the chair is 25% less than the original price. In other words, the sale price is a fraction of the original price.

$$100\% - 25\% = 75\% \text{ (or } \tfrac{3}{4}\text{) of the original price}$$

If x equals the original price, then the sale price can be written as an equation.

$$\tfrac{3}{4}x = \$240$$

To solve for x, divide each side of the equation by $\tfrac{3}{4}$. (This is to undo the multiplication.)

$$\tfrac{3}{4}x \div \tfrac{3}{4} = \$240 \div \tfrac{3}{4}$$

$$\tfrac{3}{4}x \times \tfrac{4}{3} = \$240 \times \tfrac{4}{3}$$

$$x = \$320 \text{ (original price)}$$

26. **(D)** The quotient is the answer in division. (Clear the decimal in the divisor before doing the arithmetic.)

$$\frac{0.675}{0.9} = \frac{6.75}{9} = 0.75 \text{ (quotient)}$$

27. **(B)** For the month between May 15 and June 15, the meter showed that the electric usage was

$$5{,}687 - 5{,}472 = 215 \text{ (kilowatt hours)}$$

The first 10 kilowatt hours cost	$2.48
The next 45 kilowatt hours cost $0.16 per kilowatt hour	$7.20
The next 55 kilowatt hours cost $0.12 per kilowatt hour	$6.60
All usage over the first 110 kilowatt hours was charged at a lower rate.	
Thus, 215 – 110, or 105 kilowatt hours cost $0.07 per kilowatt hour	$ 7.35
TOTAL bill for the month	$23.63

28. **(C)** To square a number, multiply it by itself.

$$49^2 = 49 \times 49 = 2,401$$
$$31^2 = 39 \times 39 = -\underline{961}$$
$$1,440 \text{ (difference)}$$

29. **(A)** To find the number of seats in the auditorium, multiply the number of rows (x) by the number of seats in each row (y). This is expressed as xy.

30. **(A)** One way of checking a division example is to multiply the quotient (the answer) by the divisor. After multiplying, add the remainder (if there was one in the division answer). Thus

$$\begin{array}{r} 15 \text{ (divisor)} \\ \underline{\times 8} \text{ (quotient)} \\ 120 \\ \underline{+\ 7} \text{ (remainder, after division)} \\ 127 \text{ (original number)} \end{array}$$

Word Knowledge

Answer Key

1. **C**	6. **C**	11. **A**	16. **D**	21. **D**	26. **D**	31. **C**
2. **A**	7. **C**	12. **D**	17. **B**	22. **C**	27. **D**	32. **D**
3. **C**	8. **A**	13. **D**	18. **C**	23. **A**	28. **B**	33. **C**
4. **A**	9. **D**	14. **B**	19. **B**	24. **A**	29. **B**	34. **B**
5. **B**	10. **A**	15. **D**	20. **C**	25. **D**	30. **D**	35. **D**

Answer Explanations

1. **(C)** To **subsume** means to include within a larger class or order.
2. **(A)** **Consensus**, like *accord*, means agreement.
3. **(C)** **Altercation**, like *controversy*, means a disagreement.
4. **(A)** **Irresolute**, like *wavering*, means to hesitate between choices.
5. **(B)** **Laconic**, like *concise*, means to express much in a few words.
6. **(C)** **Audition**, like *hearing*, means an opportunity to be heard.
7. **(C)** **Novice** designates one who has no training or experience in a specific field or activity and is hence a beginner.
8. **(A)** **Pacific**, like *conciliatory*, implies trying to preserve or obtain peace.
9. **(D)** To **neutralize**, like to *counteract*, means to render ineffective.
10. **(A)** **Precedent**, like *example*, refers to an individual instance (e.g., act, statement, case) taken as representative of a type.

11. **(A) Diaphanous** ("dia-" is a Greek prefix meaning "through, across"), like *transparent*, describes material that light rays can pass through.

12. **(D) Deferred**, like *delayed*, means postponed.

13. **(D)** To **accentuate**, like *intensify*, means to emphasize or increase in degree.

14. **(B) Authentic** (from the Greek, "warranted"), like *reliable*, means entitled to acceptance or belief.

15. **(D) Unanimity**, like *concurrence*, means complete accord.

16. **(D) Notorious** and *well-known* are almost synonymous in meaning: being or constituting something commonly known.

17. **(B)** *Former* means preceding in time and is synonymous with **previous**.

18. **(C)** Both *pliable* and **flexible** mean to be easily bent or yielding, usually without breaking.

19. **(B)** *The opportunity to choose* is equivalent to freedom to select or exercise an **option**.

20. **(C)** To **confirm**, like *verify*, means to make certain, to corroborate or authenticate.

21. **(D) Saucy**, like *pert*, means bold or impudent.

22. **(C) Tasteful**, similar to *aesthetic* (from the Greek, "perceptive"), means having the ability to appreciate what is beautiful.

23. **(A) Decimation** means to kill a large part of.

24. **(A) Angry**, like *indignant* (from the Latin, "deeming unworthy"), implies deep and strong feelings aroused by injury, injustice, or wrong.

25. **(D) Platitude**, like *cliché* (originally, to pattern in clay), refers to a remark or an idea that has become trite–lost its original freshness and impressive force.

26. **(D) Agreement** means *harmony* among people, thoughts, or ideas.

27. **(D) Lazy**, like *indolent*, applies to one who is not active.

28. **(B) Breathing**, like *respiration*, means inhalation and exhalation of air.

29. **(B) Watchful**, like *vigilant*, means alert.

30. **(D) Casual**, similar to *incidental*, means happening by chance or without definite intention.

31. **(C)** To **succumb** is to cease to resist or contend before a superior force, hence to yield.

32. **(D) Feasible** describes that which is likely to come about, and is hence practicable.

33. **(C) Many-sided**, like *versatile* (from the Latin, "turning about"), means capable of turning with ease from one task to another.

34. **(B) <u>Imperturbability</u>** or calmness is almost synonymous with *serenity*.

35. **(D) <u>Strident</u>** (from the Latin, "creaking") means having an irritating or unpleasant, hence *harsh, sound*.

Paragraph Comprehension

Answer Key

1. **C**	6. **B**	11. **B**
2. **C**	7. **C**	12. **B**
3. **A**	8. **C**	13. **B**
4. **B**	9. **C**	14. **C**
5. **D**	10. **D**	15. **C**

Answer Explanations

1. **(C)** Each individual must prevent the opportunity for crime to occur to prevent crimes.

2. **(C)** The design must fit the owner's income and building site.

3. **(A)** The selection describes a range of camping styles from backpacking to motor homes with complete creature comforts, so backpacking can be inferred to be the least luxurious.

4. **(B)** According to the selection, the "right" speed varies depending on the number of cars, the road surface, and the visibility, so a driver should adjust to different driving conditions.

5. **(D)** Hard work is the only term in the list not mentioned in the passage.

6. **(B)** The selection states that less than one percent (.8%) is available as fresh water for people to use.

7. **(C)** A *pinfold* is described in the passage as a large circular pen made by driving stakes closely together in the floor of the river.

8. **(C)** The division of powers prevents one part or branch of government from getting all the power; therefore, power is shared.

9. **(C)** The passage states that a proper dose of narcotic relieves pain and induces profound sleep.

10. **(D)** The passage mentions that nitrogen, phosphorus, and potassium are used by plants in large amounts.

11. **(B)** The passage mentions that 60 percent of pollution is caused by motor vehicle exhausts, so the choice is B—cars, trucks, and buses.

12. **(B)** Since too much bright light can create discomfort for the eyes and create difficulties for seeing well, the main purpose of sunglasses is to screen out harmful rays.

13. **(B)** The selection mentions only the good points of apprentice training, none of the negative points.

14. **(C)** The selection does not deal with insurance rates, tax rates, or retirement rates. It defines what a deduction from your paycheck is.

15. **(C)** The first sentence states that nucleic acids are found in the simplest living things to the most complex.

Mathematics Knowledge

Answer Key

1. **C**	6. **C**	11. **C**	16. **A**	21. **D**
2. **D**	7. **B**	12. **C**	17. **D**	22. **A**
3. **B**	8. **D**	13. **B**	18. **C**	23. **D**
4. **C**	9. **B**	14. **B**	19. **B**	24. **B**
5. **C**	10. **B**	15. **C**	20. **A**	25. **A**

Answer Explanations

1. **(C)** A prime number is a number larger than 1 that has only itself and 1 as factors. (It can be evenly divided only by itself and 1.) 201 is divisible by 3. 205 is divisible 5. 211, however, is a prime number.

2. **(D)** Change 40% to a decimal, and write an equation to solve for x.

$$0.4 = \frac{x}{30}$$

Multiply both sides by 30. You are undoing the division.

$$0.4 \times 30 = \frac{x}{30} \times 30$$

$$0.4 \times 30 = x \text{ (Be careful with the decimal.)}$$

$$12.0 = x$$

$$x = 12$$

3. **(B)** The product of all integers from 1 to x is called the "x factorial." The product of all numbers from 1 to 5 is "5 factorial." Thus

$$(5)(4)(3)(2)(1) =$$
$$20\,(3)(2)(1) =$$
$$60\,(2)(1) =$$
$$120\,(1) = 120$$

The expression "5 factorial" is equal to 120.

4. **(C)** To subtract one polynomial from another, you change the signs of the terms in the subtrahend. First write the example as a subtraction in arithmetic.

$$\text{(From)} \quad 8x^2 + 2x - 9$$
$$\text{(Take)} \quad 3x^2 - 5x - 1$$

Then change the signs of the terms in the bottom row (the subtrahend), and combine terms that are alike.

$$8x^2 + 2x - 9$$
$$\underline{-3x^2 + 5x + 1}$$
$$5x^2 + 7x - 8$$

5. **(C)** In deciding whether a number is greater or less than another, it helps to use a number line.

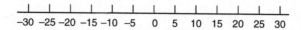

On the number line above, –5 is to the left of 0 and is, therefore, less than 0. But –30 is to the left of –5. This makes –30 less than –5. The (<) sign is a symbol of inequality, meaning "less than." The statement (–30 < –5) means "minus 30 is less than minus 5."

6. **(C)** To solve for x, combine all similar terms, and set the equation equal to zero.

$$(8x - 5x) + (-2 - 8) = 0$$

Do the operations inside the parentheses.

$$3x - 10 = 0$$

Next, add 10 to each side. You are undoing the subtraction.

$$3x - 10 + 10 = 0 + 10$$
$$3x = 10$$

Finally, divide each side by 3 to find the value of x. You are undoing the multiplication.

$$\frac{3x}{3} = \frac{10}{3}$$

$$x = 3\frac{1}{3}$$

7. **(B)** In x weeks, she will make out checks for x times $50, or $50x$. To find out how much she still has after writing those checks, she would subtract $50x$ from $500. Thus her bank account will hold

$$\$500 - \$50x.$$

8. **(D)** Use the formula

$$F = \left(\frac{9}{5} \times C\right) + 32$$

Substitute 20 degrees for C.

$$F = \left(\frac{9}{5} \times 20\right) + 32$$

$$F = 36 + 32 = 68 \text{ degrees}$$

9. **(B)** The perimeter of a rectangle is the sum of its four sides. If x equals its width, then $x + 3$ equals the length. (The length is 3 inches more than the width.) From this, you can write an equation to find the perimeter. (Use the formula $2w + 2l = P$.)

$$x + x + (x + 3) + (x + 3) = 38$$

To solve for x, combine similar terms.

$$4x + 6 = 38$$
$$4x = 38 - 6$$
$$4x = 32$$
$$x = 8 \text{ (inches)}$$

10. **(B)** One way to solve this is to square each of the suggested answers, to see which is close to 85. Thus

9.1	9.2	9.3	9.4
$\times 9.1$	$\times 9.2$	$\times 9.3$	$\times 9.4$
91	184	279	376
819	828	837	846
82.81	84.64	86.49	88.36

The squares of 9.2 and 9.3 are near 85. Find the difference between the square of each of these numbers and 85.

(9.2)	85.00	(9.3)	86.49
	−84.64		−85.00
	0.36		1.49

The square of 9.2 is closer to 85 than the square of 9.3. Therefore, the square root of 85, to the nearest tenth, is 9.2.

11. **(C)** The statement $5x = 30$ means "5 times a certain number is equal to 30." To find the number, divide each side by 5. This is to undo the multiplication.

$$\frac{5x}{5} = \frac{30}{5}$$
$$x = 6$$

12. **(C)** Set this up as a multiplication example in arithmetic. Remember that when you multiply terms with unlike signs, the product has a minus sign.

$$a - 5$$
$$\underline{\times\ a + 3}$$
$$3a - 15$$
$$a^2 - 5a$$
$$\overline{a^2 - 2a - 15}$$

13. **(B)** Begin by combining like terms.

$$3z - 5 + 2z = 25 - 5z$$
$$5z - 5 = 25 - 5z$$

Next add $5z$ to each side, to eliminate the $-5z$ from the right side.

$$5z - 5 + 5z = 25 - 5z + 5z$$
$$10z - 5 = 25$$

Now add 5 to each side to undo the remaining subtraction.

$$10z - 5 + 5 = 25 + 5$$
$$10z = 30$$
$$z = 3$$

14. **(B)** A pentagon is a five-sided figure. If the park commissioner places a fountain at every corner of the park, there will be 5 fountains.

15. **(C)** Every right triangle contains an angle of 90 degrees. This particular right triangle also has an angle of 30 degrees. To find the third angle, subtract the sum of these two angles from 180 degrees.

$$180 - (30 + 90) =$$
$$180 - 120 =$$
$$60 = \text{degrees in third angle}$$

The other two angles are 60 and 90 degrees.

16. **(A)** To solve for x in this equation, multiply both sides by 2. This is to undo the division.

$$2 \times \frac{x}{2} = 2 \times 7$$
$$x = 14$$

17. **(D)** Divide only similar terms. First divide numbers, then letters. When dividing powers of a letter, just subtract the exponents.

$$\frac{15a^3b^2c}{5abc} = \frac{15}{5} \times \frac{a^3}{a} \times \frac{b^2}{b} \times \frac{c}{c} = 3a^2b$$

18. **(C)** The formula for the area of a circle is Pi $\times$ R^2. Find the area of the larger circle first.

$$\text{Pi} \times 10^2 = 100 \text{ Pi square inches}$$

Then find the area of the smaller circle.

$$Pi \times 7^2 = 49 \; Pi \text{ square inches}$$

To find the part of the larger circle that the smaller one doesn't touch, subtract the two areas.

$$100 - 49 = 51 \; Pi \text{ square inches}$$

19. **(B)** The easiest way to solve this is to form an equation, using x as the unknown grade.

$$\frac{78 + 86 + 96 + 94 + x}{5} = 88$$

$$354 + \frac{x}{5} = 88$$

Multiply both sides by 5. This is to undo the division.

$$5 \times \frac{354 + x}{5} = 88 \times 5$$

Simplify both sides of the equation.

$$354 + x = 440$$
$$x = 440 - 354$$
$$x = 86 \text{ (grade)}$$

20. **(A)** First change all measurements to yards

$$9' = 3 \text{ yds} \quad 12' = 4 \text{ yds} \quad 6'' = \frac{1}{6} \text{ yd}$$

To find the volume of the concrete, multiply the length times the width times the height.

$$3 \times 4 \times \frac{1}{6} =$$

$$12 \times \frac{1}{6} = 2 \text{ cubic yards}$$

21. **(D)** First find the area of the entire wildlife preserve. Since it is a circle, use the formula for the area of a circle. (Area equals Pi times the square of the radius.)

$$A = pi \times R^2$$

$$= \frac{22}{7} \times (14)^2 = \frac{22}{7} \times 196$$

$$= 22 \times 28$$

$$= 616 \text{ square feet}$$

The lions' territory is a wedge formed by a 90-degree angle at the center of the circle. Since a circle has 360 degrees, we can find the part of the preserve inhabited by lions.

$$\frac{90}{360} = \frac{1}{4}$$

Next find what this equals in square miles.

$$\frac{1}{4} \times \frac{616}{1} = 154 \text{ sqare miles}$$

22. **(A)** Solve by doing each arithmetic operation and combining answers. Remember that the product of 2 negative or 2 positive numbers is a positive number. The product of a negative and a positive number is negative.

$$(-3)^4 = (-3)(-3)(-3)(-3) = 81$$
$$(-2)^4 = (-2)(-2)(-2)(-2) = 16$$
$$(-1)^4 = (-1)(-1)(-1)(-1) = \underline{1}$$
$$98$$

23. **(D)** To find the volume (V) of a cylinder, multiply Pi times the square of the radius (r) times the height (h).

$$V = Pi \times r^2 \times h$$

$$V = \frac{22}{7} \times \frac{7}{1} \times \frac{7}{1} \times \frac{15}{1}$$

$$V = 154 \times 15$$

$$V = 2{,}310 \text{ cubic inches (volume)}$$

To find the number of gallons this cylinder will hold, divide its volume by 231.

$$2{,}310 \div 231 = 10 \text{ gallons}$$

24. **(B)** The wall, the ladder, and the ground in the tennis court form a right triangle. The ladder is on a slant, and is opposite the right angle formed by the wall and the ground. In this position, the ladder is the "hypotenuse" of the right triangle. In geometry, the Pythagorean Theorem states that the square of the hypotenuse (c^2) equals the sum of the squares of the other two sides ($a^2 + b^2$).

Thus, $a^2 + b^2 = c^2$

$$8^2 + x^2 = 10^2$$

Solve by doing the arithmetic operations, and by clearing one side of the equation for x^2.

$$64 + x^2 = 100$$
$$x^2 = 100 - 64$$
$$x^2 = 36$$

Then find the square root of x^2 and of 36.

$$x = 6$$

The base of the ladder is 6 feet from the wall.

25. **(A)** First find how many ounces of the original mixture were fruit juice.

$$10 \times 20\% = 10 \times .2 = 2 \text{ ounces}$$

Next find the total number of ounces in the new mixture.

$$10 + 40 = 50 \text{ ounces}$$

Then find what part of the new mixture is fruit juice, and convert it to a percent.

$$\frac{2}{50} = \frac{1}{25} = \frac{4}{100} = 4\%$$

ANSWER SHEET—EXAMINATION TWO

Arithmetic Reasoning	Word Knowledge	Paragraph Comprehension	Mathematics Knowledge
1. Ⓐ Ⓑ Ⓒ Ⓓ	1. Ⓐ Ⓑ Ⓒ Ⓓ	1. Ⓐ Ⓑ Ⓒ Ⓓ	1. Ⓐ Ⓑ Ⓒ Ⓓ
2. Ⓐ Ⓑ Ⓒ Ⓓ	2. Ⓐ Ⓑ Ⓒ Ⓓ	2. Ⓐ Ⓑ Ⓒ Ⓓ	2. Ⓐ Ⓑ Ⓒ Ⓓ
3. Ⓐ Ⓑ Ⓒ Ⓓ	3. Ⓐ Ⓑ Ⓒ Ⓓ	3. Ⓐ Ⓑ Ⓒ Ⓓ	3. Ⓐ Ⓑ Ⓒ Ⓓ
4. Ⓐ Ⓑ Ⓒ Ⓓ	4. Ⓐ Ⓑ Ⓒ Ⓓ	4. Ⓐ Ⓑ Ⓒ Ⓓ	4. Ⓐ Ⓑ Ⓒ Ⓓ
5. Ⓐ Ⓑ Ⓒ Ⓓ	5. Ⓐ Ⓑ Ⓒ Ⓓ	5. Ⓐ Ⓑ Ⓒ Ⓓ	5. Ⓐ Ⓑ Ⓒ Ⓓ
6. Ⓐ Ⓑ Ⓒ Ⓓ	6. Ⓐ Ⓑ Ⓒ Ⓓ	6. Ⓐ Ⓑ Ⓒ Ⓓ	6. Ⓐ Ⓑ Ⓒ Ⓓ
7. Ⓐ Ⓑ Ⓒ Ⓓ	7. Ⓐ Ⓑ Ⓒ Ⓓ	7. Ⓐ Ⓑ Ⓒ Ⓓ	7. Ⓐ Ⓑ Ⓒ Ⓓ
8. Ⓐ Ⓑ Ⓒ Ⓓ	8. Ⓐ Ⓑ Ⓒ Ⓓ	8. Ⓐ Ⓑ Ⓒ Ⓓ	8. Ⓐ Ⓑ Ⓒ Ⓓ
9. Ⓐ Ⓑ Ⓒ Ⓓ	9. Ⓐ Ⓑ Ⓒ Ⓓ	9. Ⓐ Ⓑ Ⓒ Ⓓ	9. Ⓐ Ⓑ Ⓒ Ⓓ
10. Ⓐ Ⓑ Ⓒ Ⓓ	10. Ⓐ Ⓑ Ⓒ Ⓓ	10. Ⓐ Ⓑ Ⓒ Ⓓ	10. Ⓐ Ⓑ Ⓒ Ⓓ
11. Ⓐ Ⓑ Ⓒ Ⓓ	11. Ⓐ Ⓑ Ⓒ Ⓓ	11. Ⓐ Ⓑ Ⓒ Ⓓ	11. Ⓐ Ⓑ Ⓒ Ⓓ
12. Ⓐ Ⓑ Ⓒ Ⓓ	12. Ⓐ Ⓑ Ⓒ Ⓓ	12. Ⓐ Ⓑ Ⓒ Ⓓ	12. Ⓐ Ⓑ Ⓒ Ⓓ
13. Ⓐ Ⓑ Ⓒ Ⓓ	13. Ⓐ Ⓑ Ⓒ Ⓓ	13. Ⓐ Ⓑ Ⓒ Ⓓ	13. Ⓐ Ⓑ Ⓒ Ⓓ
14. Ⓐ Ⓑ Ⓒ Ⓓ	14. Ⓐ Ⓑ Ⓒ Ⓓ	14. Ⓐ Ⓑ Ⓒ Ⓓ	14. Ⓐ Ⓑ Ⓒ Ⓓ
15. Ⓐ Ⓑ Ⓒ Ⓓ	15. Ⓐ Ⓑ Ⓒ Ⓓ	15. Ⓐ Ⓑ Ⓒ Ⓓ	15. Ⓐ Ⓑ Ⓒ Ⓓ
16. Ⓐ Ⓑ Ⓒ Ⓓ	16. Ⓐ Ⓑ Ⓒ Ⓓ		16. Ⓐ Ⓑ Ⓒ Ⓓ
17. Ⓐ Ⓑ Ⓒ Ⓓ	17. Ⓐ Ⓑ Ⓒ Ⓓ		17. Ⓐ Ⓑ Ⓒ Ⓓ
18. Ⓐ Ⓑ Ⓒ Ⓓ	18. Ⓐ Ⓑ Ⓒ Ⓓ		18. Ⓐ Ⓑ Ⓒ Ⓓ
19. Ⓐ Ⓑ Ⓒ Ⓓ	19. Ⓐ Ⓑ Ⓒ Ⓓ		19. Ⓐ Ⓑ Ⓒ Ⓓ
20. Ⓐ Ⓑ Ⓒ Ⓓ	20. Ⓐ Ⓑ Ⓒ Ⓓ		20. Ⓐ Ⓑ Ⓒ Ⓓ
21. Ⓐ Ⓑ Ⓒ Ⓓ	21. Ⓐ Ⓑ Ⓒ Ⓓ		21. Ⓐ Ⓑ Ⓒ Ⓓ
22. Ⓐ Ⓑ Ⓒ Ⓓ	22. Ⓐ Ⓑ Ⓒ Ⓓ		22. Ⓐ Ⓑ Ⓒ Ⓓ
23. Ⓐ Ⓑ Ⓒ Ⓓ	23. Ⓐ Ⓑ Ⓒ Ⓓ		23. Ⓐ Ⓑ Ⓒ Ⓓ
24. Ⓐ Ⓑ Ⓒ Ⓓ	24. Ⓐ Ⓑ Ⓒ Ⓓ		24. Ⓐ Ⓑ Ⓒ Ⓓ
25. Ⓐ Ⓑ Ⓒ Ⓓ	25. Ⓐ Ⓑ Ⓒ Ⓓ		25. Ⓐ Ⓑ Ⓒ Ⓓ
26. Ⓐ Ⓑ Ⓒ Ⓓ	26. Ⓐ Ⓑ Ⓒ Ⓓ		
27. Ⓐ Ⓑ Ⓒ Ⓓ	27. Ⓐ Ⓑ Ⓒ Ⓓ		
28. Ⓐ Ⓑ Ⓒ Ⓓ	28. Ⓐ Ⓑ Ⓒ Ⓓ		
29. Ⓐ Ⓑ Ⓒ Ⓓ	29. Ⓐ Ⓑ Ⓒ Ⓓ		
30. Ⓐ Ⓑ Ⓒ Ⓓ	30. Ⓐ Ⓑ Ⓒ Ⓓ		
	31. Ⓐ Ⓑ Ⓒ Ⓓ		
	32. Ⓐ Ⓑ Ⓒ Ⓓ		
	33. Ⓐ Ⓑ Ⓒ Ⓓ		
	34. Ⓐ Ⓑ Ⓒ Ⓓ		
	35. Ⓐ Ⓑ Ⓒ Ⓓ		

Model AFQT Examination Two

Model AFQT Examination Two

13

ARITHMETIC REASONING

Directions: This test has questions about arithmetic. Each question is followed by four possible answers. Decide which answer is correct. Then, on your answer form, blacken the space which has the same number and letter as your choice. Use your scratch paper for any figuring you wish to do.

SAMPLE QUESTION

1. If 10 pounds of sugar cost $2.00, what is the cost of one pound?

   (A) 90 cents
   (B) 80 cents
   (C) 50 cents
   (D) 20 cents

The cost of one pound is 20 cents; therefore, the answer D is correct.

Your score on this test will be based on the number of questions you answer correctly. You should try to answer every question. Do not spend too much time on any one question.

The actual test will say:
Do not turn this page until told to do so.

Arithmetic Reasoning

Time —36 minutes
30 Questions

1. You need 8 barrels of water to sprinkle $\frac{1}{2}$ mile of roadway. How many barrels of water do you need to sprinkle $3\frac{1}{2}$ miles of roadway?
   (A) 7
   (B) 15
   (C) 50
   (D) 56

2. A snapshot 8 inches long and 6 inches wide is to be enlarged so that its length will be 12 inches. How many inches wide will the enlarged snapshot be?
   (A) 8
   (B) 6
   (C) 9
   (D) 10

3. Lee Robinson has an ordinary life insurance policy with a face value of $10,000. At her age, the annual premium is $24.00 per thousand. What is the total premium paid for this policy every six months?
   (A) $100
   (B) $120
   (C) $240
   (D) $400

4. If two pounds of cottage cheese cost $3.20, what is the cost of a 3-ounce portion of cottage cheese?
   (A) $0.30
   (B) $0.20
   (C) $0.25
   (D) $0.15

5. Mr. Green drove for 12 hours at a speed of 55 miles per hour. If his car covered 22 miles for each gallon of gas used, how many gallons of gas did he use?
   (A) 32 gallons
   (B) 34 gallons
   (C) 36 gallons
   (D) 30 gallons

6. Matty Smith earns $7.50 per hour. If he works from 8:45 A.M. until 5:15 P.M., with one hour off for lunch, how much does he earn in one day?
   (A) $58.50
   (B) $56.25
   (C) $55.00
   (D) $53.75

7. If 5 shirts and 3 ties cost $52 and each tie costs $4, what is the cost of a shirt?

(A) $6
(B) $8
(C) $10
(D) $7.50

8. What is the fifth term in the series: 5; 2; 9; 6; ____?

(A) 16
(B) 15
(C) 14
(D) 13

9. In a theater audience of 500 people, 80% were adults. How many children were in the audience?

(A) 20
(B) 50
(C) 100
(D) 125

10. A table usually sells for $240, but because it is slightly shopworn, the store manager lets it go for $210. What is the percent of reduction?

(A) $12\frac{1}{2}\%$

(B) $14\frac{2}{7}\%$

(C) $16\frac{2}{3}\%$

(D) $18\frac{3}{4}\%$

11. Mr. and Mrs. Turner bought a home for $55,000. It was assessed at 80% of the purchase price. If the real estate tax was $4.74 per $100, how much realty tax did the Turners pay?

(A) $2,085.60
(B) $1,985.60
(C) $2,607
(D) $285.60

12. A scale on a map is 1 inch to 50 miles. On the map, two cities are $2\frac{1}{2}$ inches apart. What is the actual distance between the two cities?

(A) 75 miles
(B) 100 miles
(C) 225 miles
(D) 125 miles

13. A shipment of 2,200 pounds of fertilizer is packed in 40-ounce bags. How many bags are needed for the shipment?

(A) 800
(B) 880
(C) 780
(D) 640

14. A television set priced at $400 was reduced 25% during a weekend sale. In addition, there was a 10% discount for cash. What was the cash price of the set during the sale?

(A) $130
(B) $260
(C) $270
(D) $320

15. In a store, four clerks each receive $255 per week, while two part-timers each earn $120. What is the average weekly salary paid these six workers?

(A) $200
(B) $210
(C) $187.50
(D) $190

16. The perimeter of a rectangle is 40 feet. If the length is 15 feet, 6 inches, what is the width of the rectangle?

(A) 4 feet, 6 inches
(B) 9 feet, 6 inches
(C) 5 feet, 6 inches
(D) 5 feet

17. What is the result of dividing 0.675 by 0.9?

(A) 7.5
(B) 0.075
(C) 75
(D) 0.75

18. Two planes leave the same airport, traveling in opposite directions. One is flying at the rate of 340 miles per hour, the other at 260 miles per hour. In how many hours will the two planes be 3,000 miles apart?

(A) 5
(B) 4
(C) 6
(D) 10

19. What is the cost of 5 feet, 3 inches of plastic slipcover material that sells for $8 per foot?

    (A) $14
    (B) $42
    (C) $23
    (D) $21.12

20. If one gallon of milk costs $3.84, what is the cost of 3 pints?

    (A) $1.44
    (B) $2.82
    (C) $2.04
    (D) $1.96

21. A man left $72,000 to his wife and son. The ratio of the wife's share to the son's share was 5:3. How much did his wife receive?

    (A) $27,000
    (B) $14,000
    (C) $45,000
    (D) $54,000

22. A recipe calls for $2\frac{1}{2}$ ounces of chocolate and $\frac{1}{2}$ cup of corn syrup. If only 2 ounces of chocolate are available, how much corn syrup should be used?

    (A) $\frac{1}{2}$ cup

    (B) $\frac{1}{3}$ cup

    (C) $\frac{2}{5}$ cup

    (D) $\frac{3}{10}$ cup

23. A ship sails x miles the first day, y miles the second day, and z miles the third day. What was the average distance covered per day?

    (A) $\frac{xyz}{3}$

    (B) $\frac{x+y+z}{3}$

    (C) $3xyz$
    (D) none of these

24. A man invests $6,000 at 5% annual interest. How much more must he invest at 6% annual interest so that his annual income from both investments is $900?

    (A) $3,000
    (B) $5,000
    (C) $8,000
    (D) $10,000

25. Which of these is an example of similar figures?

   (A) a plane and a scale model of that plane
   (B) a pen and a pencil
   (C) a motorcycle and a car
   (D) an equilateral triangle and a right triangle

26. Find the numerical value of $5a^2b - 3ab^2$ if $a = 7$ and $b = 4$.

   (A) 846
   (B) 644
   (C) 488
   (D) 224

27. If the circumference of a circle is divided by the length of its diameter, what is the result?

   (A) 2
   (B) 27
   (C) Pi
   (D) 7

28. A businesswoman spends $\frac{1}{5}$ of her income for rent, and $\frac{3}{8}$ of the remainder of her income for salaries. What part of her income does she spend for salaries?

   (A) $\frac{23}{40}$

   (B) $\frac{3}{10}$

   (C) $\frac{1}{2}$

   (D) $\frac{3}{4}$

29. Using the following formula, find the value of C when $F = 50$.

$$C = \frac{5}{9} (F - 32)$$

   (A) 10
   (B) 18
   (C) 90
   (D) 40

30. What is the average of these temperature readings, taken on a cold day last winter?

6:00 A.M.	−12 degrees
7:00 A.M.	−7 degrees
8:00 A.M.	−2 degrees
9:00 A.M.	0 degrees
10:00 A.M.	+6 degrees

   (A) 0 degrees
   (B) 2 degrees
   (C) −1 degree
   (D) −3 degrees

WORD KNOWLEDGE

Directions: This test has questions about the meanings of words. Each question has an underlined boldface word. You are to decide which one of the four words in the choices most nearly means the same as the underlined boldface word; then, mark the space on your answer form which has the same number and letter as your choice.

SAMPLE QUESTION

1. It was a **small** table.

   (A) sturdy
   (B) round
   (C) cheap
   (D) little

The question asks which of the four words means the same as the boldface word, **small**.

Little means the same as **small**. Answer D is the best one.

Your score on this test will be based on the number of questions you answer correctly. You should try to answer every question. Do not spend too much time on any one question.

The actual test will say:
Do not turn this page until told to do so.

Model AFQT Examination Two

Word Knowledge

Time —11 minutes
35 Questions

1. <u>Opulence</u> most nearly means

    (A) affluence.
    (B) generosity.
    (C) poverty.
    (D) luxury.

2. <u>Mimesis</u> most nearly means

    (A) impersonation.
    (B) pretense.
    (C) cartoon.
    (D) imitation.

3. Her <u>languid</u> appearance was revealing.

    (A) sad
    (B) energetic
    (C) healthy
    (D) listless

4. <u>Inherence</u> most nearly means

    (A) essential.
    (B) intrinsic.
    (C) accidental.
    (D) necessity.

5. <u>Anomie</u> most nearly means

    (A) essential.
    (B) vacuum.
    (C) control.
    (D) anonym.

6. <u>Tenuous</u> most nearly means

    (A) tensile.
    (B) tentative.
    (C) ethereal.
    (D) substantial.

7. Most letters require a <u>salutation</u>.

    (A) offering
    (B) greeting
    (C) discussion
    (D) appeasement

8. **Mesmerize** most nearly means

    (A) hypnotize.
    (B) hypostatize.
    (C) metabolize.
    (D) change.

9. A **panoply** of flowers covered the shelf.

    (A) pansophy
    (B) display
    (C) resistance
    (D) parry

10. **Syntactic** most nearly means

    (A) morphological.
    (B) grammatical.
    (C) standard.
    (D) inflexional.

11. **Umbrage** most nearly means

    (A) resentment.
    (B) umbo.
    (C) impertinence.
    (D) pleasure.

12. **Raucous** most nearly means

    (A) ravenous.
    (B) harsh.
    (C) pleasing.
    (D) rankling.

13. **Prosecution** most nearly means

    (A) protection.
    (B) imprisonment.
    (C) trial.
    (D) punishment.

14. The **miasma** of modern cities causes discomfort.

    (A) pollution
    (B) fumes
    (C) exhalations
    (D) stench

Model AFQT Examination Two

15. **Paragon** most nearly means

    (A) paradox.
    (B) model.
    (C) prototype.
    (D) ideal.

16. She has **innate** talent.

    (A) eternal
    (B) well-developed
    (C) temporary
    (D) native

17. **Urbanity** most nearly means

    (A) loyalty.
    (B) refinement.
    (C) weakness.
    (D) barbarism.

18. We all **encounter** difficulties.

    (A) recall
    (B) overcome
    (C) retreat from
    (D) meet

19. **Banal** most nearly means

    (A) commonplace.
    (B) forceful.
    (C) tranquil.
    (D) indifferent.

20. **Small** most nearly means

    (A) sturdy.
    (B) round.
    (C) cheap.
    (D) little.

21. The accountant **discovered** an error.

    (A) searched
    (B) found
    (C) enlarged
    (D) entered

22. You must **inform** us.

    (A) ask
    (B) turn
    (C) tell
    (D) ignore

23. The wind is **variable** today.

    (A) shifting
    (B) chilling
    (C) steady
    (D) mild

24. **Cease** most nearly means

    (A) start.
    (B) change.
    (C) continue.
    (D) stop.

25. Drinking can **impair** your judgment.

    (A) direct
    (B) improve
    (C) weaken
    (D) stimulate

26. We knew the **rudiments** of the program.

    (A) basic methods and procedures
    (B) politics
    (C) promotion opportunities
    (D) minute details

27. **Imprudent** most nearly means

    (A) reckless.
    (B) unexcitable.
    (C) poor.
    (D) domineering.

28. **Dissension** stimulated the discussion.

    (A) friction
    (B) analysis
    (C) injury
    (D) slyness

29. <u>Disconnect</u> most nearly means

    (A) separate.
    (B) cripple.
    (C) lesson.
    (D) dismiss.

30. <u>Rudimentary</u> most nearly means

    (A) discourteous.
    (B) brutal.
    (C) displeasing.
    (D) elementary.

31. The commission made <u>autonomous</u> decisions.

    (A) self-improvement
    (B) self-educated
    (C) self-explanatory
    (D) self-governing

32. <u>Meander</u> most nearly means

    (A) grumble.
    (B) wander aimlessly.
    (C) come between.
    (D) weigh carefully.

33. <u>Destitution</u> most nearly means

    (A) fate.
    (B) lack of practice.
    (C) extreme poverty.
    (D) recovery.

34. Do not <u>malign</u> his name.

    (A) slander
    (B) prophesy
    (C) entreat
    (D) praise

35. <u>Impotent</u> most nearly means

    (A) unwise.
    (B) lacking strength.
    (C) free of sin.
    (D) commanding.

PARAGRAPH COMPREHENSION

> **_Directions:_** This is a test of your ability to understand what you read. In this section you will find one or more paragraphs of reading material followed by incomplete statements or questions. You are to read the paragraph and select one of four lettered choices which best completes the statement or answers the question. When you have selected your answer, blacken in the correct numbered letter on your answer sheet.

SAMPLE QUESTION

In certain areas water is so scarce that every attempt is made to conserve it. For instance, on one oasis in the Sahara Desert the amount of water necessary for each date palm tree has been carefully determined.

1. How much water is each tree given?

   (A) no water at all
   (B) exactly the amount required
   (C) water only if it is healthy
   (D) water on alternate days

The amount of water each tree requires has been carefully determined, so answer B is correct.

Your score on this test will be based on the number of questions you answer correctly. You should try to answer every question. Do not spend too much time on any one question.

The actual test will say:
Do not turn this page until told to do so.

Paragraph Comprehension

1. The duty of the lighthouse keeper is to keep the light burning no matter what happens, so that ships will be warned of the presence of dangerous rocks. If a shipwreck should occur near the lighthouse, even though he would like to aid in the rescue of its crew and passengers, the lighthouse keeper must

   (A) stay at his light.
   (B) rush to their aid.
   (C) turn out the light.
   (D) quickly sound the siren.

2. In certain areas water is so scarce that every attempt is made to conserve it. For instance, on one oasis in the Sahara Desert the amount of water necessary for each date palm tree has been carefully determined.

   How much water is each tree given?

   (A) no water at all
   (B) exactly the amount required
   (C) water only if it is healthy
   (D) water on alternate days

3. Plants should be gradually "hardened," or toughened for 2 weeks before being moved outdoors. This is done by withholding water and lowering the temperature. Hardening slows down the plants' rate of growth to prepare them to withstand such conditions as chilling, drying winds, or high temperatures.

   You toughen a seedling

   (A) by putting it in a cooler environment.
   (B) by putting it in a six-inch pot.
   (C) by watering it thoroughly.
   (D) by using ready-made peat pellets.

4. At depths of several miles inside the earth, the weight of rocks causes great pressure. This rock pressure, as well as other forces, sometimes causes rocks to break and slip. Faults (great cracks) form. When slippage occurs, shock waves are felt and can be detected with seismographs thousands of miles away.

   The most frequent cause of major earthquakes is

   (A) faulting
   (B) folding
   (C) landslides
   (D) submarine currents

5. The leaf can catch sunlight and turn this energy into food which is stored in the tree or plant. To run this factory the leaf must have air, water, and sunlight. By a chemical process called *photosynthesis,* the leaf combines the air and water with the energy of the sun.

The process of *photosynthesis:*

(A) combines air, water, and sun to make food
(B) makes leaves grow in fancy shapes
(C) causes water to form in clouds
(D) is a physical process

6. Most telephone sales are made by *reputable* persons, who try to sell in an honest manner. These persons use the telephone as an aid to business and they know they depend upon being fair and reasonable. The opposite of the reputable salesmen are the *over-aggressive* talkers who try to force you to make up your mind quickly.

The word *reputable* is closest in meaning to:

(A) reasonable
(B) trusted
(C) friendly
(D) aggressive

7. When someone in your family suffers a minor burn, reach for an ice cube fast. Place it directly over the burn until the sting is gone when the cube is removed. Ice is a great first aid for burns and kills the pain. Afterwards you'll be amazed to discover there is very little swelling, blisters probably won't appear, and healing will be much faster.

The topic sentence or key idea in this paragraph is that

(A) ice prevents burn blisters.
(B) ice cubes remove the pain.
(C) ice is great first aid for burns.
(D) ice reduces swelling.

8. A stranger meets you and shows you some cash he has just "found." He wants to divide it with you. He says that you must show your "good faith" and put up some of your own money. When you agree to give your money, the stranger finds some reason to leave for a while. Do you see him again? Not likely; you have just been cheated or swindled.

The main theme of this passage is:

(A) Do not speak to strangers
(B) Be careful of "get-rich-quick" plans
(C) How to make money
(D) Do not believe strangers

9. Statistically, by far the most common types of home accidents are falls. Each year over 10,500 Americans meet death in this way, within the four walls of their home, or in yards around the house. Nine out of 10 of the victims are over 65, but people of all ages experience serious injuries as a result of home falls.

Falls most frequently result in death for

(A) children
(B) adults under 35
(C) all age groups
(D) adults over 65

10. "Gray water" is slightly used water—the water you have collected at the bottom of the tub after you have showered or the rinse water from the washing machine. It is still useful, and we cannot afford to let it go down the drain.

Which of the following is an example of gray water?

(A) carbonated water
(B) rain water
(C) soapy water
(D) tap water

11. Glaciers are frozen masses of snow and ice. As the weight of snow increases each year, the lower layers become hard-packed like ice. The weight also causes the glacier to move slowly downhill. Speeds of glaciers are usually figured in inches per day rather than miles per hour.

The glacier moves as a result of its

(A) speed.
(B) weight.
(C) temperature.
(D) layers.

12. It is time to get this country moving again. No American wants to stand by and see this country go the other way. The men who have been elected are no longer in touch. A fresh point of view, new ideas, and more action are needed. The voters should finally wake up and give power to those who will make changes.

This passage tries to make you believe that

(A) changes are needed.
(B) no changes are needed.
(C) changes will never happen.
(D) no action is needed.

13. Up until a few years ago most parents, teachers, baby doctors, and coaches felt that right was right. There was even an old wives' tale that left-handed people did not learn as well. But, I'm happy to report, this right-thinking is gone. Today parents and teachers understand left-handedness, and our number is rising.

The main idea of this passage is that the feelings about left-handedness

(A) have not changed at all.
(B) have completely changed.
(C) have changed partly.
(D) will not change.

14. According to Newton's Third Law, to each action there is an equal and opposite reaction. You can illustrate the principle by blowing up a rubber balloon, and then allowing the air to escape. Notice that the balloon moves forward as the air escapes in the opposite direction.

Which of the following describes Newton's Third Law?

(A) an object at rest
(B) gravitational force
(C) falling bodies
(D) action equals reaction

15. Water is a good conductor of sound waves. If you were swimming underwater while someone struck two rocks together underwater ten feet away, you would be surprised at how loud the sound was. The U.S. Navy makes use of this knowledge in detecting enemy submarines.

Of the following, which is the best restatement of the main idea?

(A) Fish cannot hear ordinary sounds.
(B) Sound waves become compressed in very deep water.
(C) Water is a good conductor of sound waves.
(D) Submarines cannot detect sound waves.

MATHEMATICS KNOWLEDGE

Directions: This is a test of your ability to solve general mathematical problems. Each problem is followed by four answer choices. Select the correct response from the choices given. Then mark the space on your answer form that has the same number and letter as your choice. Use scratch paper to do any figuring that you wish.

SAMPLE PROBLEM

1. If $x + 8 = 9$, then x is equal to

    (A) 0
    (B) 1
    (C) −1
    (D) $\dfrac{9}{8}$

The correct answer is 1, so B is the correct response.

Your score on this test will be based on the number of questions you answer correctly. You should try to answer every question. Do not spend too much time on any one question.

The actual test will say:
Do not turn this page until told to do so.

Mathematics Knowledge

Time —24 minutes
25 Questions

1. If $b - 3 = 7$, then b is equal to

   (A) 10
   (B) 4
   (C) 21
   (D) 8

2. What is the product of $(z + 2)(2z - 3)$?

   (A) $3z - 6$
   (B) $z + 4z - 3$
   (C) $z^2 + 4z - 6$
   (D) $2z^2 + z - 6$

3. Smith Township has a public pool in the shape of a quadrilateral. If the town wants to put a lifeguard on each side of the pool, how many lifeguards are needed?

   (A) 8
   (B) 6
   (C) 4
   (D) 3

4. If the largest possible circular tabletop is cut from a square whose side is 2 feet, how much wood is wasted? (Use 3.14 for Pi.)

   (A) 1 square foot
   (B) 1.86 square feet
   (C) 5.86 square feet
   (D) 0.86 square feet

5. Solve for x: $3x + 2 = -13$

   (A) $x = 13$
   (B) $x = -4\frac{1}{3}$
   (C) $x = 8$
   (D) $x = -5$

6. An artist sold 4 of his paintings. These represented 0.05 of all the artwork he had done. How many paintings had he made?

   (A) 100
   (B) 80
   (C) 50
   (D) 20

Model AFQT Examination Two

7. One of the equal angles of an isosceles triangle is 40 degrees. What is the angle opposite to unequal side?

   (A) 40 degrees
   (B) 90 degrees
   (C) 100 degrees
   (D) 140 degrees

8. If you divide $24x^3 + 16x^2 - 8x$ by $8x$, how many x's will be there in the quotient?

   (A) 0
   (B) 5
   (C) 2
   (D) −1

9. A room is 19 feet long, 10 feet wide, and 8 feet high. If you want to paint the walls and ceiling, how many square feet of surface would you cover with paint?

   (A) 232 square feet
   (B) 422 square feet
   (C) 464 square feet
   (D) 654 square feet

10. If a car traveled 200 miles at an average rate of speed of r miles per hour, the time it took for the trip could be written as

   (A) $\dfrac{200}{r}$

   (B) $\dfrac{r}{200}$

   (C) $200r$

   (D) $\dfrac{r}{60}$

11. An equilateral triangle has the same perimeter as a square whose side is 12". What is the length of a side of the triangle?

   (A) 9"
   (B) 12"
   (C) 18"
   (D) 16"

12. What is the value of (0.1)3 ?

   (A) 0.3
   (B) 0.003
   (C) 0.1
   (D) 0.001

13. How many inches are contained in *f* feet and *i* inches?

   (A) $f \times i$
   (B) $f + i$
   (C) $f + 12i$
   (D) $12f + i$

14. A good rule of thumb is that a house should cost no more than $2\frac{1}{2}$ times its owner's income. How much should you be earning to afford a $64,000 home?

   (A) $20,500
   (B) $25,000
   (C) $32,000
   (D) $160,000

15. What is the value of $(+2)(-5)(+3)(-3)$?

   (A) +90
   (B) +60
   (C) –13
   (D) –3

16. Solve for x: $x^2 = 3x + 10$

   (A) $x = 3, x = 10$
   (B) $x = -3, x = -10$
   (C) $x = -2, x = 5$
   (D) $x = 2, x = -5$

17. Which of these is a cylinder?

   (A) a stick of butter
   (B) an orange
   (C) inflated parachute
   (D) a frozen-juice can

18. Solve the following formula for *R*.
   $$N = \frac{CR}{C+R}$$

   (A) $R = \frac{C}{C+N}$

   (B) $R = \frac{NC}{C-N}$

   (C) $R = \frac{N}{C-R}$

   (D) $R = \frac{C-N}{R}$

19. What is the reciprocal of $\frac{5}{3}$?

    (A) 0.6
    (B) $1\frac{2}{3}$
    (C) 2
    (D) 1

20. What is the value of $(\sqrt{13})^2$?

    (A) 26
    (B) 13
    (C) 87
    (D) 169

21. Mr. Larson drove his car steadily at 40 mph for 120 miles. He then increased his speed and drove the next 120 miles at 60 mph. What was his average speed?

    (A) 48 miles per hour
    (B) 52 miles per hour
    (C) 50 miles per hour
    (D) 46 miles per hour

22. An architect designs two walls of a museum to meet at an angle of 120 degrees. What is an angle of this size called?

    (A) acute
    (B) obtuse
    (C) right
    (D) straight

23. Solve the following equations for x.

$$5x + 4y = 27$$
$$x - 2y = 11$$

    (A) $x = 3$
    (B) $x = 9$
    (C) $x = 4.5$
    (D) $x = 7$

24. If a is a negative number, and ab is a positive number, then which of the following must be true?

    (A) b is positive.
    (B) a is greater than b.
    (C) b is negative.
    (D) b is greater than a.

25. Solve the following inequality.

    $x + 5 > 7$

    (A) $x = 2$
    (B) $x > 2$
    (C) $x - 7 > 5$
    (D) $x - 5 > 7$

ANSWER KEYS AND ANSWER EXPLANATIONS

Arithmetic Reasoning

Answer Key

1. **D**	6. **B**	11. **A**	16. **A**	21. **C**	26. **B**
2. **C**	7. **B**	12. **D**	17. **D**	22. **C**	27. **C**
3. **B**	8. **D**	13. **B**	18. **A**	23. **B**	28. **B**
4. **A**	9. **C**	14. **C**	19. **B**	24. **D**	29. **A**
5. **D**	10. **A**	15. **B**	20. **A**	25. **A**	30. **D**

Answer Explanations

1. **(D)** You need 8 barrels of water to sprinkle $\frac{1}{2}$ mile.

    You need 16 barrels of water to sprinkle 1 mile.

    You need 3 × 16 (or 48) barrels to sprinkle 3 miles.

    You need 48 + 8 (or 56) barrels to sprinkle $3\frac{1}{2}$ miles.

2. **(C)** Since the picture and its enlargement are similar, the lengths have the same ratio as the widths.

    $$\frac{\text{length of picture}}{\text{length of enlargement}} = \frac{\text{width of picture}}{\text{width of enlargement}}$$

    $$\frac{8}{12} = \frac{6}{\text{width of enlargement } (x)}$$

    To solve this, cross-multiply the measurements, using x for the one you don't know.

    $$8 \times x = 12 \times 6 = 72$$

    $$x = \frac{72}{8} = 9 \text{ (width)}$$

3. **(B)** There are ten units of $1,000 in $10,000. Thus, Lee Robinson pays 10 × $24 (or $240) each year in premiums. That means that every 6 months, Lee Robinson pays $\frac{1}{2}$ of $240, or $120.

4. **(A)** There are 16 ounces in 1 pound. Therefore, if 2 pounds of cottage cheese costs $3.20, then 1 pound of cottage cheese costs $1.60.
    1 ounce costs $1.60 ÷ 16 (or $0.10)
    3 ounces cost 3 × $0.10 (or $0.30)

5. **(D)** To find the distance Mr. Green drove, multiply the hours by the miles per hour. Thus,

    $$12 \times 55 = 660 \text{ (distance covered)}$$

To find the number of gallons he used, divide the distance by the miles for each gallon. Thus,

$$660 \div 22 = 30 \text{ (gallons used)}$$

6. **(B)** From 8:45 A.M. to 4:45 P.M. is 8 hours.

From 4:45 P.M. to 5:15 P.M. is $\frac{1}{2}$ hour.

Subtract Matty's lunch hour.

$$8\frac{1}{2} - 1 = 7\frac{1}{2} \text{ (or 7.5 hours)}$$

Multiply his work hours by his hourly rate.

$$7.5 \times \$7.50 = \$56.25 \text{ (day's salary)}$$

7. **(B)** Find the cost of 3 ties: $3 \times \$4 = \$12$

Find the cost of the shirts alone: $\$52 - \$12 = \$40$

Find the cost of 1 shirt: $\$40 \div 5 = \$8$

8. **(D)** Find the relationship between each pair of numbers in the series. Thus,

$$(5; 2)\ 5 - 3 = 2$$
$$(2; 9)\ 2 + 7 = 9$$
$$(9; 6)\ 9 - 3 = 6$$

The pattern so far is: $-3, +7, -3$

To continue the series, add 7 to the fourth number in the series:

$$6 + 7 = 13$$

9. **(C)** If 80% of the audience were adults, then the percentage of children was

$$100\% - 80\% = 20\% \ (0.2)$$

To find the number of children, multiply

$$500 \times 0.2 = 100.0 = 100 \text{ children}$$

10. **(A)** Find the amount of reduction by subtracting.

$$\$240 - \$210 = \$30$$

To find the percentage of reduction, divide it by the original price.

$$\frac{\text{(reduction) }\$30}{\text{(original price) }\$240} = \frac{1}{8} = 12\frac{1}{2}\%$$

11. **(A)** Multiply the cost of the home by the assessment rate.

$$\$55,000 \times 80\% =$$
$$\$55,000 \times 0.8 = \$44,000$$

The realty tax is $4.74 for each $100 in $44,000.

$$\$44,000 \div 100 = 440 \text{ (hundreds)}$$
$$\$4.74 \times 440 = \$2,085.60 \text{ (tax)}$$

12. **(D)** If 1 inch equals 50 miles, then $2\frac{1}{2}$ inches equal $2\frac{1}{2}$ times 50.

$$\frac{50}{1} \times \frac{5}{2} = 125 \text{ (miles)}$$

13. **(B)** One pound equals 16 ounces. Find the number of ounces in 2,200 pounds by multiplying.

$$2,200 \times 16 = 35,200 \text{ (ounces)}$$

Find the number of 40-ounce bags needed to pack 35,200 ounces by dividing.

$$35,200 \div 40 = 880 \text{ (bags)}$$

14. **(C)** Find the first reduction and the weekend sale price. $(25\% = \frac{1}{4})$

$\$400 \times \dfrac{1}{4} = \$100$ (first reduction)

$\$400 - \$100 = \$300$ (weekend sale price)

Use this weekend sale price to find the reduction for paying cash and the final price. $(10\% = 0.1)$

$$\$300 \times 0.1 = \$30 \text{ (second reduction)}$$
$$\$300 - \$30 = \$270 \text{ (cash price)}$$

15. **(B)** Find the combined salaries of the 4 clerks.

$$\$255 \times 4 = \$1,020$$

Find the combined salaries of the part-timers.

$$\$120 \times 2 = \$240$$

Add both totals and divide by 6 for the average.

$$\$1,020 + \$240 = \$1,260$$
$$\$1,260 \div 6 = \$210 \text{ (average salary)}$$

16. **(A)** The perimeter of a rectangle is equal to the sum of two lengths and two widths. If 15 feet, 6 inches ($15\frac{1}{2}$ feet) equal 1 length, then

$$2 \times 15\frac{1}{2} = 31 \text{ feet (2 lengths)}$$
$$40 - 31 = 9 \text{ feet (both widths)}$$
$$9 \div 2 = 4\frac{1}{2} \text{ feet (1 width)}$$

17. **(D)** Before dividing by a decimal, clear the decimal point in both the divisor and the dividend.

$$\frac{0.675}{0.9} = \frac{6.75}{9} = 0.75$$

18. **(A)** In the first hour, the two planes will be a combined distance of 340 plus 260 miles apart. Thus,

$$340 + 260 = 600 \text{ miles apart in 1 hour}$$

Find how many hours it will take them to be 3,000 miles apart by dividing.

$$3,000 \div 600 = 5 \text{ (hours)}$$

19. **(B)** Multiply the cost per foot by the length of the material.

12 inches equal 1 foot

3 inches equal $\frac{1}{4}$ foot

5 feet, 3 inches equal $5\frac{1}{4}$ feet (or 5.25 feet)

$$\$8 \times 5.25 = \$42$$

20. **(A)** Find the cost of 1 pint. (There are 8 pints in 1 gallon.)

$$\$3.84 \div 8 = \$0.48$$

Find the cost of 3 pints.

$$\$0.48 \times 3 = \$1.44$$

21. **(C)** Begin by letting x equal 1 share of the inheritance. According to the ratio, the widow received 5 shares ($5x$), and the son received 3 shares ($3x$). Together, they inherited \$72,000. This can be written as an equation.

$$5x + 3x = \$72,000$$

Solve for x by combining similar terms.

$$8x = \$72,000$$
$$x = \$9,000 \text{ (one share)}$$

Multiply the value of 1 share by the number of shares the mother received.

$$5x = \$45,000 \text{ (mother's share)}$$

22. **(C)** Begin by setting up a statement of proportion.

$$\frac{\text{chocolate}}{\text{chocolate}} = \frac{\text{corn syrup (recipe)}}{\text{corn syrup (amount available)}}$$

$$\frac{2\frac{1}{2}}{2} = \frac{\frac{1}{2}}{x} \text{ (or) } \frac{\frac{5}{2}}{2} = \frac{\frac{1}{2}}{x}$$

Simplify each side of the proportion.

(a) $\dfrac{5}{2} \div \dfrac{2}{1} = \dfrac{5}{2} \times \dfrac{1}{2} = \dfrac{5}{4}$

(b) $\dfrac{1}{2} \div \dfrac{x}{1} = \dfrac{1}{2} \times \dfrac{1}{x} = \dfrac{1}{2x}$

Then solve the proportion by cross-multiplying

$$\frac{5}{4} = \frac{1}{2x} \text{ (or) } 10x = 4$$

Divide each side of the equation by 10, to find the value of x.

$$10x = 4$$

$$x = \frac{4}{10}$$

$$x = \frac{2}{5} \text{ cup of corn syrup}$$

23. **(B)** To find the average of three numbers, divide their sum by 3.

$x + y + z$ (sum of three numbers)

$\dfrac{x + y + z}{3}$ (sum of numbers, divided by 3)

24. **(D)** First find the income he gets on the $6,000 at 5% annual interest.

$$\$6,000 \times 0.05 = \$300.00 \text{ (income)}$$

Next find how much more interest he wants to earn in a year.

$$\$900 - \$300 = \$600 \text{ (additional interest)}$$

This $600 will equal 6% of the amount (x) he has to invest. Write this as an equation.

$$\$600 = 0.06 \text{ times } x$$
$$\$600 = 0.06x$$

To solve for x, divide each side of the equation by 0.06. (Clear the decimal in the divisor.)

$$\frac{\$600.00}{0.06} = \left(\frac{0.06}{0.06}\right)x$$
$$\$10,000 = x \text{ (new amount needed)}$$

$x = \$10,000$

25. **(A)** Two figures are similar if they have the same shape. They may or may not have the same size. A plane and a scale model of that plane have the same shape and are therefore similar.

26. **(B)** Solve by substituting number values for letters and then doing the arithmetic operations.

$$5a^2b - 3ab^2 =$$
$$(5 \times a^2 \times b) - (3 \times a \times b^2) =$$
$$(5 \times 7^2 \times 4) - (3 \times 7 \times 4^2) =$$
$$(5 \times 49 \times 4) - (3 \times 7 \times 16) =$$
$$980 - 336 = 644$$

27. **(C)** The formula for the circumference (C) of a circle can be written in terms of its radius (R) or its diameter (D).

$$C = 2 \times R \times Pi \text{ (or) } C = D \times Pi$$

Thus, if you divide the circumference of a circle by its diameter, you are left with Pi.

$$\frac{C}{D} = \frac{C \times Pi}{D}$$

$$\frac{C}{D} = Pi$$

28. **(B)** If the businesswoman spends $\frac{1}{5}$ of her income for rent, she has $\frac{4}{5}$ of her income left.

$$\frac{5}{5} - \frac{1}{5} = \frac{4}{5} \text{ (remainder)}$$

She then spends $\frac{3}{8}$ of the remainder on salaries.

$$\frac{4}{5} \times \frac{3}{8} = \frac{12}{40} = \frac{3}{10} \text{ (salaries)}$$

29. **(A)** Solve by substituting the number value for F, and then doing the arithmetic operations.

$$C = \frac{5}{9}(F - 32)$$

$$C = \frac{5}{9}(50 - 32)$$

$$C = \frac{5}{9} \times (18)$$

$$C = 10$$

30. **(D)** To obtain the average, add the five temperatures and divide the total by 5.

Add: $-12 + (-7) + (-2) + 0 + 6 = -21 + 6 = -15$

Divide: $\frac{-15}{5} = -3$ (average temperature)

Word Knowledge

Answer Key

1. **A**	6. **C**	11. **A**	16. **D**	21. **B**	26. **A**	31. **D**
2. **D**	7. **B**	12. **B**	17. **B**	22. **C**	27. **A**	32. **B**
3. **D**	8. **A**	13. **C**	18. **D**	23. **A**	28. **A**	33. **C**
4. **B**	9. **B**	14. **A**	19. **A**	24. **D**	29. **A**	34. **A**
5. **B**	10. **B**	15. **B**	20. **D**	25. **C**	30. **D**	35. **B**

Answer Explanations

1. **(A) Luxury**, like *opulence* (from the Latin, "rich, wealthy"), is conducive to sumptuous living.

2. **(D) Mimesis** (from the Greek, "imitation") means reproduction of the supposed words of another, usually in order to represent his or her character.

3. **(D) Languid** means weak, indifferent, weary, or exhausted, implying a languid person.

4. **(B) Inherence** (from the Latin, "sticking in or to") means the state of existing in something as a permanent and inseparable element, quality, or attribute, and thus, like intrinsic, implies belonging to the nature of a thing itself.

5. **(B) Anomie** (from the Greek, "lawlessness") describes a social condition marked by the absence of social norms or values, and therefore, like vacuum, implies the absence of components from an area.

6. **(C)** Ethereal describes something which is light and airy, and thus may be *unsubstantial*, as implied by **tenuous** (from the Latin, "thin").

7. **(B)** Like **salutation**, *greeting* means to address with some expression of pleasure.

8. **(A) Hypnotize**, like *mesmerize*, means to put in the condition or state allied to sleep.

9. **(B) Display**, similar to *panoply*, means an impressive array of assembled persons or things.

10. **(B)** Like **syntactic** (from the Greek, "arrangement"), which pertains to patterns of formation of sentences and phrases in a particular language, grammatical pertains to sounds, words, formation, and arrangement of words.

11. **(A) Resentment**, like *umbrage*, describes the feeling of indignation at something regarded as an injury or insult.

12. **(B)** Harsh means rough to any of the senses, while **raucous** denotes hoarse, or harsh, of voice or sound.

13. **(C) Trial**, like *prosecution*, means determining a person's guilt or innocence by due process of law.

14. **(A)** Pollution, which means defiling, rendering impure, making foul, unclean, dirty, is closely related to **miasma** (from the Greek, "pollution").

15. **(B) Model**, like *paragon*, is a pattern of excellence for exact imitation.

16. **(D) Innate**, like *native*, means belonging by birth.

17. **(B) Urbanity** indicates elegant courtesy or politeness, hence *refinement*.

18. **(D)** To **encounter** means to come upon, hence *to meet*.

19. **(A) Banal**, like *commonplace*, characterizes as lifeless and uninteresting.
20. **(D) Little**, like *small*, means not much in comparison to other things.
21. **(B) Found**, like *discover*, means to unearth something hidden or lost.
22. **(C) Tell**, like *inform*, means to communicate knowledge or give information.
23. **(A) Shifting**, like *variable*, means subject to change.
24. **(D) Stop**, like *cease*, means to end.
25. **(C) Weaken**, like *impair*, means to worsen or to damage.
26. **(A) Rudiments** are fundamental skills or basic principles, like *basic methods* and *procedures*.
27. **(A) Reckless**, like *imprudent*, means lacking discretion.
28. **(A) Friction**, like *dissension*, both refer to quarreling.
29. **(A) Separate**, like *disconnect*, means to become detached.
30. **(D) Elementary**, like *rudimentary*, refers to something fundamental or imperfectly developed.
31. **(D) Self-governing**, like *autonomous*, means governing without control.
32. **(B) Wander aimlessly**, like *meander*, means to follow a winding course without a definite destination.
33. **(C) Extreme poverty**, like *destitution*, characterizes the state of lacking resources and possessions.
34. **(A) Slander**, like *malign*, means to speak misleading or false reports about someone.
35. **(B) Lacking strength**, like *impotent*, means lacking power or vigor.

Paragraph Comprehension

Answer Key

1. **A**	6. **B**	11. **B**
2. **B**	7. **C**	12. **A**
3. **A**	8. **B**	13. **C**
4. **A**	9. **D**	14. **D**
5. **A**	10. **C**	15. **C**

Answer Explanations

1. **(A)** The first sentence states that the duty of the lighthouse keeper is to keep the light burning no matter what happens.
2. **(B)** The second sentence mentions that the exact amount of water needed has been carefully determined.
3. **(A)** "Hardening" or toughening seedlings is done by reducing the water the seedlings obtain and lowering the temperature.

4. **(A)** Earthquakes occur when rock layers break and slip, forming cracks or faults.

5. **(A)** Photosynthesis combines air, water, and energy from the sun to make food.

6. **(B)** In this selection reputable means honest, or trusted.

7. **(C)** The main idea of the selection is that ice can relieve many of the effects of a burn and is therefore great first aid.

8. **(B)** The main idea of the selection is to warn you to be careful of "get-rich-quick" plans.

9. **(D)** The third sentence mentions that 9 out of 10 victims of fatal falls are over 65.

10. **(C)** "Gray water" is defined as slightly used water. The only choice which represents used water is soapy water.

11. **(B)** The third sentence specifies that a glacier moves because of its weight.

12. **(A)** Every sentence of the selection expresses disapproval of the present state of things and implies that changes are needed.

13. **(C)** The selection states that some categories of people have changed, but the fact that the "number is rising" implies that not everyone has changed.

14. **(D)** According to the first sentence, Newton's Third Law is that to each action there is an equal and opposite reaction, or action equals reaction.

15. **(C)** The first sentence, and main idea of the paragraph, states that water is a good conductor of sound waves.

Mathematics Knowledge

Answer Key

1. **A**	6. **B**	11. **D**	16. **C**	21. **A**
2. **D**	7. **C**	12. **D**	17. **D**	22. **B**
3. **C**	8. **C**	13. **D**	18. **B**	23. **D**
4. **D**	9. **D**	14. **B**	19. **A**	24. **C**
5. **D**	10. **A**	15. **A**	20. **B**	25. **B**

Answer Explanations

1. **(A)** This equation means "a number, decreased by 3, is equal to 7."

    $$b - 3 = 7$$

    To arrive at a true statement for b, we want to eliminate -3 on the left side of the equation. We do this by adding 3. (This is undoing the subtraction.) We then add 3 to the other side, so that the statement remains an equation.

$$(b - 3) + 3 = 7 + 3$$

By simplifying both sides, we isolate b, and thus find the solution.

$$b = 10$$

2. **(D)** An easy way to perform the multiplication is to do four separate multiplications. Then the procedure looks like ordinary multiplication in arithmetic.

$$
\begin{array}{ll}
2z - 3 & \\
\underline{z + 2} & \\
4z - 6 & \text{Multiply } (2z - 3) \text{ by 2} \\
\underline{2z^2 - 3z} & \text{Multiply } (2z - 3) \text{ by } z \\
2z^2 + z - 6 & \text{Add the partial products as you do in arithmetic.}
\end{array}
$$

3. **(C)** Since a quadrilateral is a four-sided figure, the township will need four lifeguards. (If the sides of a quadrilateral are parallel, it is also called a parallelogram. If all four sides are equal and all four angles are right angles, it is called a square.)

4. **(D)** Step 1. Find the area of the square.

$$2' \times 2' = 4 \text{ square feet}$$

Step 2. Find the area of the circle, using the formula $A = Pi \times R^2$. (The radius equals half the diameter; the diameter of this circle is 2 feet—the same length as one side of the square.)

$$3.14 \times 1^2 = 3.14 \text{ square feet}$$

Step 3. Subtract 3.14 square feet from 4 square feet to find the wood that is wasted, 0.86 square feet.

5. **(D)** Step 1. Subtract 2 from each side of the equation in order to eliminate + 2 from the left side. (You are undoing the addition.)

$$3x + 2 - 2 = -13 - 2$$
$$3x = -15$$

Step 2. Now divide each side by 3 to find x. (You are undoing the multiplication.)

$$\frac{3x}{3} = \frac{-15}{3}$$
$$x = -5$$

6. **(B)** Let p stand for the number of paintings the artist made. The 4 paintings he sold are equal to 0.05 of all his paintings. This can be expressed as an equation.

$$0.05p = 4$$

To solve for p, divide both sides by 0.05. You are undoing the multiplication of 0.05 and p.

$$\frac{0.05p}{0.05} = \frac{4}{0.05} \text{ (Clear the decimal in the divisor).}$$

$$\frac{1p}{1} = \frac{400}{5}$$

$$p = 80 \text{ (paintings made)}$$

7. **(C)** In an isosceles triangle, two of the sides are equal. This means that the angles opposite them are equal, too. If one is 40 degrees, then so is the other. To find the angle opposite the unequal side, begin by adding the equal angles.

$$40 + 40 = 80 \text{ degrees}$$

To find the third angle, subtract this amount from 180 (the number of degrees in any triangle).

$$180 - 80 = 100 \text{ degrees (third angle)}$$

8. **(C)** An easy way to do this example is to break it into three examples, dividing each term by $8x$. Divide the numbers first, and then the letters. However, to divide the exponents of x, just find the difference between them. (Thus, $x^3 \div x = x^{(3-1)} = x^2$.)

$$\frac{25x^3}{8x} + \frac{16x^2}{8x} - \frac{8x}{8x} = 3x^2 + 2x - 1$$

Since the question asks only how many x's there are in the quotient (not how many x^2's), the answer is 2.

9. **(D)** First, find the area (surface) of the ceiling. Since it is opposite the floor, it has the same length and width ($A = \ell \times w$).

$$19' \times 10' = 190 \text{ square feet (ceiling)}$$

Next find the combined area of two matching (opposite) walls. Start with the walls formed by the length and height of the room.

$$19' \times 8' = 152 \text{ square feet (first wall)}$$

$$152' \times 2' = 304 \text{ square feet (matching walls)}$$

Then find the area of the walls formed by the width and height of the room.

$$10' \times 8' = 80 \text{ square feet (second wall)}$$

$$80' \times 2' = 160 \text{ square feet (matching walls)}$$

Finally, combine all surfaces to be painted.

$$190 + 304 + 160 = 654 \text{ square feet}$$

10. **(A)** The basic formula for travel is "distance equals rate multiplied by time," or $D = rt$. The car traveled 200 miles (D); therefore $200 = rt$. To solve for t (time), divide both sides of the equation by r. (You are undoing the multiplication.)

$$\frac{200}{r} = \frac{rt}{r}$$

$$\frac{200}{r} = t \text{ (time it took for trip)}$$

11. **(D)** The perimeter of a square is 4 times a side. Therefore, the perimeter of this square is 4 × 12' or 48'. The equilateral triangle has the same perimeter as the square. Since the 3 sides of an equilateral triangle are equal, divide by 3 to find the length of one side.

$$48' \div 3' = 16' \text{ (length of one side)}$$

12. **(D)** The exponent in $(0.1)^3$ means you use 0.1 as a multiplier three times.

$$(0.1)^3 = (0.1)(0.1)(0.1) = 0.001$$

When multiplying decimals, count off one decimal place in the answer for each decimal place in the numbers you multiply.

13. **(D)** In 1 foot, there are 12 inches (12 × 1). In 2 feet, there are 24 inches (12 × 2). Therefore, in f feet, there are 12 × f or $12f$ inches. Add $12f$ inches to i inches to obtain the total of $12f + i$.

14. **(B)** Use m as the owner's income. According to the rule of thumb, a house costing \$64,000 should be no more than $2\frac{1}{2}$ times an owner's income, or $2\frac{1}{2}m$ (2.5m). This can be stated as an equation.

$$2.5m = \$64,000$$

To solve for m, divide both sides by 2.5. You are undoing the multiplication.

$$\frac{2.4m}{2.5} = \frac{\$640,000}{2.5m} \text{ (Clear the decimal in the divisor.)}$$

$$m = \frac{\$640,000}{25} = 25,600 \text{ (owner's income)}$$

15. **(A)** To find the product of more than two numbers, work on only two numbers at a time. If both of these numbers have plus signs (+), their product has a plus sign. If both have minus signs (–), their product has a plus (not a minus) sign. But if their signs are different, the product has a minus sign.

$$(+2)(-5)(+3)(-3)$$
$$= (-10)(+3)(-3)$$
$$= (-30)(-3)$$
$$= +90$$

16. **(C)** To solve the equation $x^2 = 3x + 10$, turn it into an equation equal to 0, find the two factors of the new equation, and then set each factor equal to 0, to solve for x.

Step 1. Move all expressions to one side of the equal sign. Change the signs of terms that are moved.

$$x^2 - 3x - 10 = 0$$

Step 2. Find the two factors that you would multiply to produce this polynomial. Do this one expression at a time. What gives you x^2?
The answer is x times x. Therefore place an x at the beginning of each factor.

$$(x \quad) (x \quad)$$

Next find the two numbers you would multiply to get 10. They could be 10 and 1, or 5 and 2, but remember that the two numbers also have to produce 3, the middle term in the polynomial. The difference between 5 and 2 is 3. Therefore 5 and 2 are the numbers that complete the factors.

$$(x \quad 5) (x \quad 2)$$

Now decide the signs that belong in each factor. The appearance of –10 in the polynomial means that 5 and 2 have different signs. The $-3x$ in the polynomial indicates that 5 (the larger number) has the minus sign, and that 2 has a plus sign. Thus

$$(x - 5) (x + 2)$$

Step 3. Set each factor equal to zero and solve the equations.

$$x - 5 = 0 \qquad\qquad x + 2 = 0$$
$$x = 5 \qquad\qquad x = -2$$

CHECK. Substitute each answer in the original equation.

$$x^2 = 3x + 10 \qquad\qquad x^2 = 3x + 10$$
$$(-2)^2 = 3(-2) + 1 \qquad\qquad (5)^2 = 3(5) + 10$$
$$4 = -6 + 10 \qquad\qquad 25 = 15 + 10$$
$$4 = 4 \qquad\qquad 25 = 25$$

This proves that x is equal to –2 and 5.

17. **(D)** A cylinder is a solid figure, whose upper and lower bases are circles. A small can of frozen-juice concentrate is an example of a cylinder. (An orange is a sphere. A stick of butter is a rectangular solid. An inflated (round) parachute is a hemisphere.)

18. **(B)** Your goal is to find the value of R in terms of the other letters in the equation.

$$N = \frac{CR}{C + R}$$

Begin by multiplying both sides of the equation by $(C + R)$. You are undoing the division.

$$N(C + R) = \frac{CR}{(C + R)} \times (C + R)$$

$$N(C + R) = CR$$

$$NC + NR = CR \text{ (isolate terms with } R)$$

Next, gather all terms with R on one side of the equation. To do this, subtract NR from both sides. You are undoing the addition.

$$NC + NR - NR = CR - NR$$

$$NC = CR - NR$$

$$NC = R(C - N) \text{ (simplify for } R)$$

Finally, divide both sides of the equation by $(C - N)$. You are undoing the multiplication.

$$\frac{NC}{(C - N)} = \frac{R(C - N)}{(C - N)}$$

$$\frac{NC}{(C - N)} = R \text{ (transpose the statement)}$$

$$R = \frac{NC}{(C - N)}$$

19. **(A)** When the product of two numbers is 1, each number is the reciprocal of the other. In the following equation, r is the reciprocal you want to find.

$$r \times \frac{5}{3} = 1$$

To isolate r, divide each side by $\frac{5}{3}$. This is undoing the multiplication.

$$r \times \frac{5}{3} \div \frac{5}{3} = 1 \div \frac{5}{3}$$

$$r \times \frac{5}{3} \times \frac{3}{5} = 1 \div \frac{3}{5}$$

$$r = \frac{3}{5} \text{ (reciprocal of } \frac{5}{3})$$

Written as a decimal, $\frac{3}{5}$ equals 0.6.

20. **(B)** This prolem does not have to be computed, because the two symbols cancel each other. The radical sign ($\sqrt{\ }$) in $(\sqrt{13})^2$ tells you to find the square root of 13. But the exponent (^{2}) tells you to square the answer—that is, to multiply the square root of 13 by itself. This would get you back to 13.

21. **(A)** To find the average rate of speed (mph), divide the distance he covered by the time he spent traveling ($R = D/T$). In this example, begin by finding the distance traveled.

$$120 + 120 = 240 \text{ miles (distance)}$$

Next find the length of time he traveled. At the beginning of his trip, he drove 120 miles at 40 mph.

$$\frac{120}{40} = 3 \text{ hours (first part of trip)}$$

Later, he increased his speed.

$$\frac{120}{60} = 2 \text{ hours (second part of trip)}$$

Altogether, he traveled for 5 hours. Now apply the formula for finding his average rate of speed.

$$\frac{D}{T} = \frac{240}{5} = 48 \text{ mph (rate of speed)}$$

22. **(B)** An angle of 180 degrees is a straight angle.
An angle of 90 degrees is a right angle.
An angle greater than 90 degrees but less than 180 degrees is an obtuse angle.
An angle less than 90 degrees is an acute angle.

23. **(D)** To solve these equations for x, begin by finding a way to eliminate y. Multiply both sides of the second equation by 2.

$$2(x - 2y) = 2 \times 11$$
$$2x - 4y = 22$$

Add the new form of the second equation to the first equation, and solve for x.

$$5x + 4y = 27$$
$$2x - 4y = 22 \text{ (+4 cancels −4)}$$
$$7x \quad = 49$$
$$x = 7$$

24. **(C)** The product of a negative number and a positive number is always negative. The product of two negative numbers is always a positive number. Since ab is positive, and a is negative, b must be negative, too.

25. **(B)** The expression $(x + 5 > 7)$ is a statement of inequality. It means that x plus 5 is greater than 7—not equal to it. To solve this inequality, subtract 5 from both sides of the statement.

$$x + 5 > 7$$
$$x + 5 - 5 > 7 - 5$$
$$x > 2$$

Thus the statement of inequality is true for any value of x that is greater than 2. Try it with 3, for example.

$$3 + 5 > 7$$
$$8 > 7, \text{ a true statement}$$

PART FIVE
COMPLETE
ASVAB PRACTICE
EXAMINATION

ANSWER SHEET—PRACTICE EXAMINATION

General Science—Subtest 1

1. Ⓐ Ⓑ Ⓒ Ⓓ 6. Ⓐ Ⓑ Ⓒ Ⓓ 11. Ⓐ Ⓑ Ⓒ Ⓓ 16. Ⓐ Ⓑ Ⓒ Ⓓ 21. Ⓐ Ⓑ Ⓒ Ⓓ
2. Ⓐ Ⓑ Ⓒ Ⓓ 7. Ⓐ Ⓑ Ⓒ Ⓓ 12. Ⓐ Ⓑ Ⓒ Ⓓ 17. Ⓐ Ⓑ Ⓒ Ⓓ 22. Ⓐ Ⓑ Ⓒ Ⓓ
3. Ⓐ Ⓑ Ⓒ Ⓓ 8. Ⓐ Ⓑ Ⓒ Ⓓ 13. Ⓐ Ⓑ Ⓒ Ⓓ 18. Ⓐ Ⓑ Ⓒ Ⓓ 23. Ⓐ Ⓑ Ⓒ Ⓓ
4. Ⓐ Ⓑ Ⓒ Ⓓ 9. Ⓐ Ⓑ Ⓒ Ⓓ 14. Ⓐ Ⓑ Ⓒ Ⓓ 19. Ⓐ Ⓑ Ⓒ Ⓓ 24. Ⓐ Ⓑ Ⓒ Ⓓ
5. Ⓐ Ⓑ Ⓒ Ⓓ 10. Ⓐ Ⓑ Ⓒ Ⓓ 15. Ⓐ Ⓑ Ⓒ Ⓓ 20. Ⓐ Ⓑ Ⓒ Ⓓ 25. Ⓐ Ⓑ Ⓒ Ⓓ

Arithmetic Reasoning—Subtest 2

1. Ⓐ Ⓑ Ⓒ Ⓓ 7. Ⓐ Ⓑ Ⓒ Ⓓ 13. Ⓐ Ⓑ Ⓒ Ⓓ 19. Ⓐ Ⓑ Ⓒ Ⓓ 25. Ⓐ Ⓑ Ⓒ Ⓓ
2. Ⓐ Ⓑ Ⓒ Ⓓ 8. Ⓐ Ⓑ Ⓒ Ⓓ 14. Ⓐ Ⓑ Ⓒ Ⓓ 20. Ⓐ Ⓑ Ⓒ Ⓓ 26. Ⓐ Ⓑ Ⓒ Ⓓ
3. Ⓐ Ⓑ Ⓒ Ⓓ 9. Ⓐ Ⓑ Ⓒ Ⓓ 15. Ⓐ Ⓑ Ⓒ Ⓓ 21. Ⓐ Ⓑ Ⓒ Ⓓ 27. Ⓐ Ⓑ Ⓒ Ⓓ
4. Ⓐ Ⓑ Ⓒ Ⓓ 10. Ⓐ Ⓑ Ⓒ Ⓓ 16. Ⓐ Ⓑ Ⓒ Ⓓ 22. Ⓐ Ⓑ Ⓒ Ⓓ 28. Ⓐ Ⓑ Ⓒ Ⓓ
5. Ⓐ Ⓑ Ⓒ Ⓓ 11. Ⓐ Ⓑ Ⓒ Ⓓ 17. Ⓐ Ⓑ Ⓒ Ⓓ 23. Ⓐ Ⓑ Ⓒ Ⓓ 29. Ⓐ Ⓑ Ⓒ Ⓓ
6. Ⓐ Ⓑ Ⓒ Ⓓ 12. Ⓐ Ⓑ Ⓒ Ⓓ 18. Ⓐ Ⓑ Ⓒ Ⓓ 24. Ⓐ Ⓑ Ⓒ Ⓓ 30. Ⓐ Ⓑ Ⓒ Ⓓ

Word Knowledge—Subtest 3

1. Ⓐ Ⓑ Ⓒ Ⓓ 8. Ⓐ Ⓑ Ⓒ Ⓓ 15. Ⓐ Ⓑ Ⓒ Ⓓ 22. Ⓐ Ⓑ Ⓒ Ⓓ 29. Ⓐ Ⓑ Ⓒ Ⓓ
2. Ⓐ Ⓑ Ⓒ Ⓓ 9. Ⓐ Ⓑ Ⓒ Ⓓ 16. Ⓐ Ⓑ Ⓒ Ⓓ 23. Ⓐ Ⓑ Ⓒ Ⓓ 30. Ⓐ Ⓑ Ⓒ Ⓓ
3. Ⓐ Ⓑ Ⓒ Ⓓ 10. Ⓐ Ⓑ Ⓒ Ⓓ 17. Ⓐ Ⓑ Ⓒ Ⓓ 24. Ⓐ Ⓑ Ⓒ Ⓓ 31. Ⓐ Ⓑ Ⓒ Ⓓ
4. Ⓐ Ⓑ Ⓒ Ⓓ 11. Ⓐ Ⓑ Ⓒ Ⓓ 18. Ⓐ Ⓑ Ⓒ Ⓓ 25. Ⓐ Ⓑ Ⓒ Ⓓ 32. Ⓐ Ⓑ Ⓒ Ⓓ
5. Ⓐ Ⓑ Ⓒ Ⓓ 12. Ⓐ Ⓑ Ⓒ Ⓓ 19. Ⓐ Ⓑ Ⓒ Ⓓ 26. Ⓐ Ⓑ Ⓒ Ⓓ 33. Ⓐ Ⓑ Ⓒ Ⓓ
6. Ⓐ Ⓑ Ⓒ Ⓓ 13. Ⓐ Ⓑ Ⓒ Ⓓ 20. Ⓐ Ⓑ Ⓒ Ⓓ 27. Ⓐ Ⓑ Ⓒ Ⓓ 34. Ⓐ Ⓑ Ⓒ Ⓓ
7. Ⓐ Ⓑ Ⓒ Ⓓ 14. Ⓐ Ⓑ Ⓒ Ⓓ 21. Ⓐ Ⓑ Ⓒ Ⓓ 28. Ⓐ Ⓑ Ⓒ Ⓓ 35. Ⓐ Ⓑ Ⓒ Ⓓ

Paragraph Comprehension—Subtest 4

1. Ⓐ Ⓑ Ⓒ Ⓓ 4. Ⓐ Ⓑ Ⓒ Ⓓ 7. Ⓐ Ⓑ Ⓒ Ⓓ 10. Ⓐ Ⓑ Ⓒ Ⓓ 13. Ⓐ Ⓑ Ⓒ Ⓓ
2. Ⓐ Ⓑ Ⓒ Ⓓ 5. Ⓐ Ⓑ Ⓒ Ⓓ 8. Ⓐ Ⓑ Ⓒ Ⓓ 11. Ⓐ Ⓑ Ⓒ Ⓓ 14. Ⓐ Ⓑ Ⓒ Ⓓ
3. Ⓐ Ⓑ Ⓒ Ⓓ 6. Ⓐ Ⓑ Ⓒ Ⓓ 9. Ⓐ Ⓑ Ⓒ Ⓓ 12. Ⓐ Ⓑ Ⓒ Ⓓ 15. Ⓐ Ⓑ Ⓒ Ⓓ

ASVAB Practice Examination

Mathematics Knowledge—Subtest 5

1. Ⓐ Ⓑ Ⓒ Ⓓ   6. Ⓐ Ⓑ Ⓒ Ⓓ   11. Ⓐ Ⓑ Ⓒ Ⓓ   16. Ⓐ Ⓑ Ⓒ Ⓓ   21. Ⓐ Ⓑ Ⓒ Ⓓ
2. Ⓐ Ⓑ Ⓒ Ⓓ   7. Ⓐ Ⓑ Ⓒ Ⓓ   12. Ⓐ Ⓑ Ⓒ Ⓓ   17. Ⓐ Ⓑ Ⓒ Ⓓ   22. Ⓐ Ⓑ Ⓒ Ⓓ
3. Ⓐ Ⓑ Ⓒ Ⓓ   8. Ⓐ Ⓑ Ⓒ Ⓓ   13. Ⓐ Ⓑ Ⓒ Ⓓ   18. Ⓐ Ⓑ Ⓒ Ⓓ   23. Ⓐ Ⓑ Ⓒ Ⓓ
4. Ⓐ Ⓑ Ⓒ Ⓓ   9. Ⓐ Ⓑ Ⓒ Ⓓ   14. Ⓐ Ⓑ Ⓒ Ⓓ   19. Ⓐ Ⓑ Ⓒ Ⓓ   24. Ⓐ Ⓑ Ⓒ Ⓓ
5. Ⓐ Ⓑ Ⓒ Ⓓ   10. Ⓐ Ⓑ Ⓒ Ⓓ   15. Ⓐ Ⓑ Ⓒ Ⓓ   20. Ⓐ Ⓑ Ⓒ Ⓓ   25. Ⓐ Ⓑ Ⓒ Ⓓ

Electronics Information—Subtest 6

1. Ⓐ Ⓑ Ⓒ Ⓓ   5. Ⓐ Ⓑ Ⓒ Ⓓ   9. Ⓐ Ⓑ Ⓒ Ⓓ   13. Ⓐ Ⓑ Ⓒ Ⓓ   17. Ⓐ Ⓑ Ⓒ Ⓓ
2. Ⓐ Ⓑ Ⓒ Ⓓ   6. Ⓐ Ⓑ Ⓒ Ⓓ   10. Ⓐ Ⓑ Ⓒ Ⓓ   14. Ⓐ Ⓑ Ⓒ Ⓓ   18. Ⓐ Ⓑ Ⓒ Ⓓ
3. Ⓐ Ⓑ Ⓒ Ⓓ   7. Ⓐ Ⓑ Ⓒ Ⓓ   11. Ⓐ Ⓑ Ⓒ Ⓓ   15. Ⓐ Ⓑ Ⓒ Ⓓ   19. Ⓐ Ⓑ Ⓒ Ⓓ
4. Ⓐ Ⓑ Ⓒ Ⓓ   8. Ⓐ Ⓑ Ⓒ Ⓓ   12. Ⓐ Ⓑ Ⓒ Ⓓ   16. Ⓐ Ⓑ Ⓒ Ⓓ   20. Ⓐ Ⓑ Ⓒ Ⓓ

Automotive & Shop Information—Subtest 7

1. Ⓐ Ⓑ Ⓒ Ⓓ   6. Ⓐ Ⓑ Ⓒ Ⓓ   11. Ⓐ Ⓑ Ⓒ Ⓓ   16. Ⓐ Ⓑ Ⓒ Ⓓ   21. Ⓐ Ⓑ Ⓒ Ⓓ
2. Ⓐ Ⓑ Ⓒ Ⓓ   7. Ⓐ Ⓑ Ⓒ Ⓓ   12. Ⓐ Ⓑ Ⓒ Ⓓ   17. Ⓐ Ⓑ Ⓒ Ⓓ   22. Ⓐ Ⓑ Ⓒ Ⓓ
3. Ⓐ Ⓑ Ⓒ Ⓓ   8. Ⓐ Ⓑ Ⓒ Ⓓ   13. Ⓐ Ⓑ Ⓒ Ⓓ   18. Ⓐ Ⓑ Ⓒ Ⓓ   23. Ⓐ Ⓑ Ⓒ Ⓓ
4. Ⓐ Ⓑ Ⓒ Ⓓ   9. Ⓐ Ⓑ Ⓒ Ⓓ   14. Ⓐ Ⓑ Ⓒ Ⓓ   19. Ⓐ Ⓑ Ⓒ Ⓓ   24. Ⓐ Ⓑ Ⓒ Ⓓ
5. Ⓐ Ⓑ Ⓒ Ⓓ   10. Ⓐ Ⓑ Ⓒ Ⓓ   15. Ⓐ Ⓑ Ⓒ Ⓓ   20. Ⓐ Ⓑ Ⓒ Ⓓ   25. Ⓐ Ⓑ Ⓒ Ⓓ

Mechanical Comprehension—Subtest 8

1. Ⓐ Ⓑ Ⓒ Ⓓ   6. Ⓐ Ⓑ Ⓒ Ⓓ   11. Ⓐ Ⓑ Ⓒ Ⓓ   16. Ⓐ Ⓑ Ⓒ Ⓓ   21. Ⓐ Ⓑ Ⓒ Ⓓ
2. Ⓐ Ⓑ Ⓒ Ⓓ   7. Ⓐ Ⓑ Ⓒ Ⓓ   12. Ⓐ Ⓑ Ⓒ Ⓓ   17. Ⓐ Ⓑ Ⓒ Ⓓ   22. Ⓐ Ⓑ Ⓒ Ⓓ
3. Ⓐ Ⓑ Ⓒ Ⓓ   8. Ⓐ Ⓑ Ⓒ Ⓓ   13. Ⓐ Ⓑ Ⓒ Ⓓ   18. Ⓐ Ⓑ Ⓒ Ⓓ   23. Ⓐ Ⓑ Ⓒ Ⓓ
4. Ⓐ Ⓑ Ⓒ Ⓓ   9. Ⓐ Ⓑ Ⓒ Ⓓ   14. Ⓐ Ⓑ Ⓒ Ⓓ   19. Ⓐ Ⓑ Ⓒ Ⓓ   24. Ⓐ Ⓑ Ⓒ Ⓓ
5. Ⓐ Ⓑ Ⓒ Ⓓ   10. Ⓐ Ⓑ Ⓒ Ⓓ   15. Ⓐ Ⓑ Ⓒ Ⓓ   20. Ⓐ Ⓑ Ⓒ Ⓓ   25. Ⓐ Ⓑ Ⓒ Ⓓ

Assembling Objects—Subtest 9

1. Ⓐ Ⓑ Ⓒ Ⓓ   5. Ⓐ Ⓑ Ⓒ Ⓓ   9. Ⓐ Ⓑ Ⓒ Ⓓ   13. Ⓐ Ⓑ Ⓒ Ⓓ
2. Ⓐ Ⓑ Ⓒ Ⓓ   6. Ⓐ Ⓑ Ⓒ Ⓓ   10. Ⓐ Ⓑ Ⓒ Ⓓ   14. Ⓐ Ⓑ Ⓒ Ⓓ
3. Ⓐ Ⓑ Ⓒ Ⓓ   7. Ⓐ Ⓑ Ⓒ Ⓓ   11. Ⓐ Ⓑ Ⓒ Ⓓ   15. Ⓐ Ⓑ Ⓒ Ⓓ
4. Ⓐ Ⓑ Ⓒ Ⓓ   8. Ⓐ Ⓑ Ⓒ Ⓓ   12. Ⓐ Ⓑ Ⓒ Ⓓ   16. Ⓐ Ⓑ Ⓒ Ⓓ

Complete ASVAB Practice Examination

14

GENERAL SCIENCE—SUBTEST 1

Directions: This test has questions about science. Pick the best answer for each question, then blacken the space on your separate answer form which has the same number and letter as your choice.

SAMPLE QUESTION

1. An example of a chemical change is

    (A) melting ice.
    (B) breaking glass.
    (C) rusting metal.
    (D) making sawdust from wood.

The correct answer is rusting metal, so you would blacken the space for C on your answer form.

Your score on this test will be based on the number of questions you answer correctly. You should try to answer every question. Do not spend too much time on any one question.

The actual test will say:
Do not turn this page until told to do so.

General Science

Time —11 minutes
25 Questions

1. Which of the following determines the sex of a human offspring?

   (A) egg cell
   (B) polar body
   (C) egg nucleus
   (D) sperm

2. Rocks are frequently split apart by

   (A) running water
   (B) wind
   (C) sudden changes in temperature
   (D) meteorites

3. Sand is made up of colorless crystals of

   (A) iron
   (B) mica
   (C) shale
   (D) quartz

4. Which material is an acid?

   (A) ammonia water
   (B) baking soda
   (C) vinegar
   (D) rain water

5. Isotopes of the same element have the same number of

   (A) protons only
   (B) electrons and protons only
   (C) neutrons only
   (D) neutrons and protons only

6. As heat is applied to boiling water, the temperature remains the same. The best explanation for this is that

   (A) convection increases at the boiling point of water
   (B) radiation increases at the boiling point of water
   (C) escaping vapor is taking away energy
   (D) the applied heat is absorbed quickly by the surroundings

7. Which of the following is outside the solar system?

    (A) Mars
    (B) nebulae
    (C) satellites
    (D) asteroids

8. Solar energy is transmitted through space by

    (A) convection
    (B) radiation
    (C) reflection
    (D) absorption

9. Which is an example of a sex-linked trait?

    (A) eye color
    (B) anemia
    (C) height
    (D) hemophilia

10. The fact that supports the position that viruses are living is that viruses

    (A) are made of common chemicals
    (B) cause disease
    (C) duplicate themselves
    (D) are protein molecules

11. A thermometer which indicates the freezing point of water at zero degrees and the boiling point of water at 100 degrees is called the

    (A) Centigrade thermometer
    (B) Fahrenheit thermometer
    (C) Kelvin thermometer
    (D) Reaumur thermometer

12. Vegetation should be kept on slopes because

    (A) plants aid weathering
    (B) runoff increases
    (C) plant roots hold the soil
    (D) plants enrich the soil

13. A 25-pound force has two components which are at right angles to each other. If one component is 15 pounds, the other component is

   (A) 10 pounds
   (B) 20 pounds
   (C) 40 pounds
   (D) 25 pounds

14. What device is used to test the solution in a storage battery?

   (A) voltameter
   (B) hydrometer
   (C) ammeter
   (D) anemometer

15. Fluorides are added to drinking water in order to

   (A) improve taste
   (B) increase metabolism
   (C) prevent caries
   (D) prevent typhoid fever

16. Blinking in response to bright light is an example of a(n)

   (A) phototropism
   (B) habit
   (C) reflex
   (D) instinct

17. The Rh factor is important in the study of

   (A) fingerprinting
   (B) the blood
   (C) the acidity of a solution
   (D) the determination of sex

18. What mineral element is part of hemoglobin?

   (A) calcium
   (B) fluorine
   (C) carbon
   (D) iron

19. In the winter the coldest areas are usually

   (A) island coasts
   (B) continental interiors
   (C) oceans
   (D) hilltops

20. If the mass of an object were doubled, its acceleration due to gravity would be

(A) halved
(B) doubled
(C) unchanged
(D) quadrupled

21. Respiration in plants takes place

(A) only during the day
(B) only in the presence of carbon dioxide
(C) both day and night
(D) only at night

22. Wind is mainly the result of

(A) clouds
(B) storms
(C) high humidity
(D) unequal heating of air

23. Which appeared most recently on the earth?

(A) reptiles
(B) mammals
(C) amphibians
(D) insects

24. When all the colors of the spectrum are mixed, the light is

(A) yellow
(B) black
(C) white
(D) blue

25. A solution that has a high ratio of solute to solvent is said to be

(A) unsaturated
(B) saturated
(C) dilute
(D) concentrated

ARITHMETIC REASONING—SUBTEST 2

> *Directions:* This test has questions about arithmetic. Each question is followed by four possible answers. Decide which answer is correct. Then, on your answer form, blacken the space which has the same number and letter as your choice. Use your scratch paper for any figuring you wish to do.

SAMPLE QUESTION

1. If 1 quart of milk costs $0.80, what is the cost of 2 quarts?

   (A) $2.00
   (B) $1.60
   (C) $1.20
   (D) $1.00

The cost of 2 quarts is $1.60; therefore, answer B is correct.

Your score on this test will be based on the number of questions you answer correctly. You should try to answer every question. Do not spend too much time on any one question.

The actual test will say:
Do not turn this page until told to do so.

Arithmetic Reasoning

Time —36 minutes
30 Questions

1. Mr. Winter bought a $500 TV set that was marked at a 15% discount. He made a down payment of $65 and agreed to pay the balance in 12 equal monthly install-ments. How much was each installment?

   (A) $25
   (B) $30
   (C) $42.50
   (D) $360

2. A farmer uses 2 gallons of insecticide concentrate to spray each $\frac{1}{4}$ acre of his land. How many gallons of the concentrate will he need to spray $10\frac{1}{2}$ acres?

   (A) 80
   (B) $80\frac{1}{4}$
   (C) 82
   (D) 84

3. An engineering drawing on a sheet of paper that measures 12 inches by 18 inches is to be enlarged so that the length is 45 inches. How many inches wide will the enlarged drawing be?

   (A) 30
   (B) 39
   (C) 66
   (D) 33

4. In a quality control test at a factory, of 280 products inspected at random, 266 were found to be acceptable. What percent of the items inspected were found acceptable?

   (A) 66%
   (B) 95%
   (C) 5%
   (D) 86%

5. A candy store sells 3 pounds of a candy mix for $4.80. What is the price of a 5-ounce bag of this mix?

   (A) $1.00
   (B) $2.40
   (C) $0.25
   (D) $0.50

6. The perimeter of a square is 13 feet, 8 inches. What is the length of one side of the square?

   (A) 3 feet, 2 inches
   (B) 3 feet, 5 inches
   (C) 3 feet, 3 inches
   (D) 3 feet, 6 inches

7. A military unit has 360 members. 20% are officers. How many members of the unit are enlisted personnel?

   (A) 90
   (B) 270
   (C) 72
   (D) 288

8. Marcella Jones earns $8.50 per hour with time and a half paid for overtime in excess of 8 hours on any one day. One day she worked 10 hours. How much did she earn on that day?

   (A) $85.00
   (B) $117.50
   (C) $97.75
   (D) $93.50

9. What is the next term in the series:

   $$2\frac{1}{4}; \ 3\frac{3}{4}; \ 3\frac{1}{4}; \ 4\frac{3}{4}; \ \underline{\quad}?$$

   (A) $4\frac{1}{4}$

   (B) $6\frac{1}{4}$

   (C) $5\frac{1}{4}$

   (D) $3\frac{1}{4}$

10. Tickets for movie admissions for adults are $4.00 each, but half price is charged for children. If 265 adult tickets were sold and the box office collected $1,200, how many children's tickets were sold?

    (A) 70
    (B) 35
    (C) 280
    (D) 140

11. A woman budgets her income so that she spends $\frac{1}{4}$ of it for rent and $\frac{2}{5}$ of the remainder for food. What part of the total income does she budget for food?

(A) $\frac{1}{10}$

(B) $\frac{1}{5}$

(C) $\frac{3}{20}$

(D) $\frac{3}{10}$

12. A survey of a small group of people found that 3 of them each watched 2 hours of TV per day. 2 of them watched 1 hour per day, and 1 watched 4 hours per day. What is the average number of hours of TV watched by members of this group?

(A) $1\frac{1}{3}$

(B) $2\frac{2}{3}$

(C) 2
(D) 3

13. What is the cost of 3 yards, 2 feet of an upholstery edging material that costs $9 per yard?

(A) $30
(B) $36
(C) $29
(D) $33

14. A partnership agreement calls for the two partners to share the profits of their business in the ratio 4:5. If the profit for the year is $63,000, what is the share paid to the partner who gets the smaller portion?

(A) $28,000
(B) $7,000
(C) $35,000
(D) $15,750

15. A courier leaves an office driving at the average rate of 30 miles per hour, but forgets part of the material he was supposed to take with him. An hour later, a second courier is dispatched with the missing material and is instructed to overtake the first courier in 2 hours more. How fast must the second courier travel?

(A) 90 miles per hour
(B) 60 miles per hour
(C) 45 miles per hour
(D) 40 miles per hour

16. A merchant buys radios listed wholesale for $60 a piece at a 25% discount. He sells these radios at a 20% markup above the original wholesale price. What is his profit on each radio?

(A) $9.00
(B) $27.00
(C) $12.00
(D) $18.00

17. An airplane travels a distance x miles in y hours. What is its average rate of speed in miles per hour?

(A) $\dfrac{xy}{y}$

(B) $\dfrac{yx}{x}$

(C) $\dfrac{y}{x}$

(D) $\dfrac{x+y}{2}$

18. The cost of sending a telegram is $1.50 for the first 10 words and $0.05 for each additional word. How many words can be sent by telegram for $4.00?

(A) 51
(B) 60
(C) 81
(D) 90

19. A mapmaker is told to prepare a map with a scale of 1 inch to 40 miles. If the actual distance between two points is 110 miles, how far apart should the mapmaker show them on the map?

(A) 7 inches

(B) $3\dfrac{1}{2}$ inches

(C) $2\dfrac{1}{2}$ inches

(D) $2\dfrac{3}{4}$ inches

20. In the Town of Hampshire, houses are assessed at 75% of the purchase price. If Mr. Johnson buys a house in Hampshire for $80,000 and real estate taxes are $4.83 per $100 of assessed valuation, how much realty tax must he pay?

   (A) $2,898
   (B) $3,864
   (C) $600
   (D) $604.83

21. The ingredients in a cake recipe include $4\frac{1}{2}$ cups of flour and $\frac{3}{4}$ cup of sugar.

   It is desired to make a cake that will require only $\frac{1}{4}$ cup of sugar. How much flour should be used?

   (A) $1\frac{1}{4}$ cups

   (B) $1\frac{1}{2}$ cups

   (C) 4 cups

   (D) $1\frac{3}{4}$ cups

22. When the tolls on a bridge were increased in price, the traffic declined from 1,200 cars crossing per day to 1,044. What is the percent of the decline in traffic?

   (A) 87%
   (B) 156%
   (C) 13%
   (D) 15%

23. If a 2-gallon bucket of liquid floor polish costs $19.20, how much should a one-quart can cost?

   (A) $4.80
   (B) $2.40
   (C) $1.20
   (D) $0.60

24. A man takes a trip in which he first drives for 3 hours at 50 miles per hour. He then drives for 2 hours more at 55 miles per hour. If his car gets 20 miles per gallon, how many gallons of gas did he use for the trip?

   (A) 10
   (B) 9.5
   (C) 26
   (D) 13

25. A woman has $5,000 invested at 8% annual interest. At what rate must she invest an additional $10,000 so that her annual income from both investments is equivalent to 9% of her total investment?

(A) 10%

(B) $10\frac{1}{2}$%

(C) 9%

(D) $9\frac{1}{2}$%

26. The fuel tank of a gasoline generator contains a sufficient capacity to operate the generator for 1 hour and 20 minutes. How many times must the fuel tank be filled to run the generator from 9:15 A.M. to 3:55 P.M.?

(A) 5

(B) 6

(C) $4\frac{1}{2}$

(D) 4

27. A nurseryman mixes 10 pounds of hardy grass seed worth $1.20 per pound with 8 pounds of premium grass seed worth $3.00 per pound. At what price per pound should he sell the mixture?

(A) $2.10

(B) $2.00

(C) $1.90

(D) $2.50

28. What is the value of $\frac{0.02 \times 3}{0.001}$?

(A) 60

(B) 6

(C) 0.6

(D) 0.06

29. Find the numerical value of $1 + 5xy^2 - 3x^2y$ if $x = 3$ and $y = 2$.

(A) 25

(B) 18

(C) 739

(D) 7

30. Using the formula $I = \sqrt{\frac{P}{R}}$, find the value of I when $P = 48$ and $R = 3$.

(A) 12

(B) 8

(C) 4

(D) $\frac{4}{3}$

WORD KNOWLEDGE—SUBTEST 3

Directions: This test has questions about the meanings of words. Each question has an underlined boldface word. You are to decide which one of the four words in the choices most nearly means the same as the underlined boldface word; then, mark the space on your answer form which has the same number and letter as your choice.

SAMPLE QUESTION

1. It was a **small** table.

    (A) sturdy
    (B) round
    (C) cheap
    (D) little

The question asks which of the four words means the same as the boldface word, **small**.

Little means the same as **small**. Answer D is the best one.

Your score on this test will be based on the number of questions you answer correctly. You should try to answer every question. Do not spend too much time on any one question.

The actual test will say:
Do not turn this page until told to do so.

ASVAB Practice Examination

Word Knowledge

Time —11 minutes

35 Questions

1. **Inform** most nearly means

   (A) ask.
   (B) heed.
   (C) tell.
   (D) ignore.

2. The dress was **crimson**.

   (A) crisp
   (B) neatly pressed
   (C) reddish
   (D) colorful

3. **Caution** most nearly means

   (A) signals.
   (B) care.
   (C) traffic.
   (D) haste.

4. Rain fell **intermittently**.

   (A) constantly
   (B) annually
   (C) using intermediaries (to stay)
   (D) at irregular intervals

5. **Occurrence** most nearly means

   (A) event.
   (B) place.
   (C) occupation.
   (D) opinion.

6. The disguise was a clever **deception**.

   (A) secret
   (B) fraud
   (C) mistrust
   (D) hatred

7. **Cease** most nearly means

   (A) start.
   (B) change.
   (C) continue.
   (D) stop.

8. **Acclaim** most nearly means

   (A) amazement.
   (B) laughter.
   (C) booing.
   (D) applause.

9. The city plans to **erect** a civic center.

   (A) paint
   (B) design
   (C) destroy
   (D) construct

10. **Relish** most nearly means

    (A) care.
    (B) speed.
    (C) amusement.
    (D) enjoy.

11. **Sufficient** most nearly means

    (A) durable.
    (B) substitution.
    (C) expendable.
    (D) appropriate.

12. **Fortnight** most nearly means

    (A) two weeks.
    (B) one week.
    (C) two months.
    (D) one month.

13. That action was a **blemish** on his record.

    (A) defect
    (B) mixture
    (C) accusation
    (D) decoration

14. Rules **impose** order on the group.

    (A) disguise
    (B) escape
    (C) require
    (D) purchase

15. **Jeer** most nearly means

    (A) peek.
    (B) scoff.
    (C) turn.
    (D) judge.

16. **Alias** most nearly means

    (A) enemy.
    (B) sidekick.
    (C) hero.
    (D) other name.

17. **Impair** most nearly means

    (A) direct.
    (B) improve.
    (C) weaken.
    (D) stimulate.

18. **Itinerant** most nearly means

    (A) traveling.
    (B) shrewd.
    (C) insurance.
    (D) aggressive.

19. I don't often **abandon** a good idea.

    (A) relinquish
    (B) encompass
    (C) infiltrate
    (D) quarantine

20. The association met to **resolve** the issue.

    (A) end
    (B) understand
    (C) recall
    (D) forget

21. **Ample** most nearly means

    (A) plentiful.
    (B) enthusiastic.
    (C) well shaped.
    (D) fat.

22. The chemical spill left a **stench**.

    (A) puddle of slimy water
    (B) pile of debris
    (C) foul odor
    (D) dead animal

23. **Sullen** most nearly means

    (A) grayish yellow.
    (B) soaking wet.
    (C) very dirty.
    (D) angrily silent.

24. **Rudiments** most nearly means

    (A) basic methods and procedures.
    (B) politics.
    (C) promotion opportunities.
    (D) minute details.

25. **Clash** most nearly means

    (A) applaud.
    (B) fasten.
    (C) conflict.
    (D) punish.

26. **Camaraderie** most nearly means

    (A) interest in photography.
    (B) close friendship.
    (C) petty jealousies.
    (D) arts and crafts projects.

27. The report was **superficial**.

    (A) excellent
    (B) official
    (C) profound
    (D) cursory

28. **Tapestry** most nearly means

    (A) fabric of woven designs.
    (B) tent.
    (C) piece of elaborate jewelry.
    (D) exquisite painting.

29. The response was **terse**.

    (A) pointed
    (B) trivial
    (C) oral
    (D) lengthy

30. We had never seen such a **concoction**.

    (A) combination of ingredients
    (B) appetizer
    (C) drink made of wine and spices
    (D) relish tray

31. **Brevity** most nearly means

    (A) boldness.
    (B) shortness.
    (C) nearness.
    (D) length.

32. **Clemency** most nearly means

    (A) justice.
    (B) punishment.
    (C) mercy.
    (D) dismissal.

33. That was an act of **insubordination**.

    (A) humiliation
    (B) rejection
    (C) disobedience
    (D) carelessness

34. She advised against **preferential** treatment.

    (A) weekly
    (B) constant
    (C) unlimited
    (D) special

35. **Doldrums** most nearly means

    (A) fearful.
    (B) diseased.
    (C) low spirits.
    (D) embarrassment.

PARAGRAPH COMPREHENSION—SUBTEST 4

> _**Directions:**_ This is a test of your ability to understand what you read. In this section you will find one or more paragraphs of reading material followed by incomplete statements or questions. You are to read the paragraph and select one of four lettered choices which best completes the statement or answers the question. When you have selected your answer, blacken in the correct numbered letter on your answer sheet.

SAMPLE QUESTION

In certain areas water is so scarce that every attempt is made to conserve it. For instance, on one oasis in the Sahara Desert the amount of water necessary for each date palm tree has been carefully determined.

1. How much water is each tree given?

   (A) no water at all
   (B) exactly the amount required
   (C) water only if it is healthy
   (D) water on alternate days

The amount of water each tree requires has been carefully determined, so answer B is correct.

Your score on this test will be based on the number of questions you answer correctly. You should try to answer every question. Do not spend too much time on any one question.

The actual test will say:
Do not turn this page until told to do so.

Paragraph Comprehension

Time —13 minutes
15 Questions

1. Professional drivers, the people who drive trucks and buses for a living, have a low opinion of the average motorist. They complain that the average driver does not maintain proper speed, changes lanes without signaling, and stops without warning.

    The topic sentence or key idea in this paragraph is that

    (A) professional drivers do not think much of the average driver
    (B) people who drive trucks are professional drivers
    (C) the average driver is not a good driver
    (D) the average driver does not like professional drivers

2. The trees stood quietly under the dark gray clouds. Their bare branches shuddered as the cold wind slipped around them. Sailing along on the wind a few birds flew to shelter. No other animals were to be seen.

    In this paragraph the word *shuddered* means:

    (A) fell
    (B) shook
    (C) cracked
    (D) remained still

3. Many think of the log cabin as a New England invention. Others feel it was first made by the pioneers who crossed the Appalachian Mountains. According to one authority, the log cabin was introduced to America by the Swedes. The area around the Delaware River was settled by Swedes and Finns. These two European peoples were first to use the log cabin.

    According to this passage, the log cabin was introduced to this country by

    (A) New England colonists
    (B) Swedes and Finns
    (C) Appalachian Mountain pioneers
    (D) the English

ASVAB Practice Examination

4. Down the gently drifting stream, the boat glided softly. Soft breezes and warm sun bathed him. The fishing pole lay unused. The floppy hat shaded his half-closed eyes and much of his face. Only his lower features, framed in a pleasant smile, could be seen.

This passage describes a man who is

(A) sad
(B) active
(C) contented
(D) exhilarated

5. Would you like to be good at a trade? Would you like to know a skill that pays well? One sure way to skill, good pay, and regular work is to train on the job. This is called apprentice training. While it is not the only way to learn, apprentice training has good points. You can earn while you learn, can learn the skill "from the ground up," and can advance on the job.

Apprentice training is described in this paragraph by

(A) discussing both sides
(B) discussing the good side only
(C) discussing the bad side only
(D) comparing it to other types of training

6. Move into a house with six closets and all of them will be jammed in a short time. Move into a house with 15 closets—and the same thing will happen. In short, we never have enough closets no matter how many closets we have. But there's one thing we can do. We can make better use of the space within a closet.

The author of this paragraph suggests that we:

(A) should build more closets in houses
(B) never have enough things to fill the closets
(C) usually fill every closet in the house
(D) make the best use of space within a closet

7. There is a big difference between a liberal and a reactionary. The person who favors new ideas, tries to change, and looks for new ways is more free or liberated. On the other hand, a person may look back or want to return to the way things used to be. This person does not like progress and resents change.

The word *reactionary* can be used to describe a person who:

(A) looks ahead to the future
(B) looks back to the past
(C) favors new ideas
(D) likes change

8. This forest must be preserved. These trees have stood against natural forces for over a hundred years. Within the area wildlife flourishes and the streams are clear and sparkling. Thousands of people can find pleasure through camping or walking in a spot of unspoiled nature. The beauty and peace of this forest can renew the spirit of many a person.

This passage was probably written by a:

(A) lumber company spokesperson
(B) religious society
(C) house-building company
(D) conservation group

9. There has been enough talk. The problem has been studied from every viewpoint. The figures add up to the need for the bridge. When the bonds are approved their cost will be met by future tolls. All groups favor this and no property-owners will be hurt by it. The time for action has come.

According to this paragraph, the next logical step would be to:

(A) build the bridge
(B) pass a law to raise the money
(C) decide how to collect the tolls
(D) have a meeting of property-owners

10. Lightning is a gigantic spark, a tremendous release of energy between earth and cloud. The shorter the gap between earth and cloud, the greater the chances of discharge. Thus, lightning tends to favor objects that thrust above the surrounding terrain. This might mean you sitting in a boat or the lone tree on the golf course.

Lightning is described as:

(A) man-made energy
(B) a bolt from heaven
(C) a release of electrical energy
(D) a poorly understood phenomenon

11. Every large city has problems of traffic and people trying to use transportation. The problem is at its worst in the two hours before 9 a.m. and the two hours after 4 p.m. So many businesses, stores, and companies start work and end work at the same time. This becomes a very great problem in the downtown business centers with their many-storied skyscrapers and their thousands of workers.

The morning transportation rush starts at

(A) 9 a.m.
(B) 7 a.m.
(C) 8 a.m.
(D) 6 a.m.

12. A vision care technician assists the patient in frame selection and fitting and provides instruction in the use of contact lenses. Such a technician works with children in visual training programs and assists with testing for corneal curvature, visual acuity, and eye pressure.

The word *acuity* means:

(A) cuteness
(B) strength
(C) sharpness
(D) pressure

13. An agricultural research scientist wishes to test the germination power of a particular strain of wheat. That is, he wants to know what proportion of the seeds will grow to maturity. He picks one seed at random from a bunch of wheat and that particular grain of wheat produces a strong and healthy stalk of wheat.

We can conclude from this experiment that:

(A) the rest of the seeds are the same
(B) this seed is the only healthy one
(C) more seeds must be tested
(D) it was an accident that this seed was good

14. Most breads and cereals are well-liked, fit easily into meal plan, and cost little per serving. These foods, with whole-grain or enriched bread as examples, provide good food value. Mostly they give food energy, but they also supply vitamins and minerals. According to a recent survey, bread and cereal products provided 40% of the thiamine (a B vitamin) and 30% of the iron needed daily by a person.

What percent of the daily needs of a B vitamin come from bread and cereals?

(A) 30%
(B) more than half
(C) 40%
(D) 70%

15. In the many years before 1800 there was a great fear of plague and other illnesses. Most of the problem came from poor medical knowledge and no scientific way to fight the diseases. People knew the results of plague would be suffering and death. Naturally they tried to stay away from infection or they tried to keep the danger away from them.

The main reason for the fear of plague before 1800 was

(A) crowded cities and seaports
(B) little medical or scientific knowledge
(C) long time needed for quarantine
(D) difficulty in avoiding infection

MATHEMATICS KNOWLEDGE—SUBTEST 5

Directions: This is a test of your ability to solve general mathematical problems. Each problem is followed by four answer choices. Select the correct response from the choices given. Then mark the space on your answer form that has the same number and letter as your choice. Use scratch paper to do any figuring that you wish.

SAMPLE PROBLEM

1. If $x + 8 = 9$, then x is equal to

   (A) 0
   (B) 1
   (C) −1
   (D) $\dfrac{9}{8}$

The correct answer is 1, so B is the correct response.

Your score on this test will be based on the number of questions you answer correctly. You should try to answer every question. Do not spend too much time on any one question.

The actual test will say:
Do not turn this page until told to do so.

Mathematics Knowledge

Time —24 minutes
25 Questions

1. Solve for x: $2x + 6 = 12 - x$.

   (A) 6
   (B) 9
   (C) 2
   (D) 3

2. From $8x^2 - 7x$ subtract $2x - 3x^2$.

   (A) $11x^2 - 9x$
   (B) $5x^2 - 5x$
   (C) $6x^2 - 4x$
   (D) $10x^2 - 10x$

3. What is the product of $2x^3y$ and $(3x^2y - 4)$?

   (A) $6x^5y^2 - 4$
   (B) $6x^5y^2 - 8x^3y$
   (C) $6x^6y^2 - 8x^3y$
   (D) $6x^6y - 8x^3y$

4. A worker can do $\frac{1}{3}$ of a job by himself in one day, and his helper can do $\frac{1}{5}$ of the job by himself in one day. What portion of the job can they do if they work together for one day?

   (A) $\frac{1}{4}$

   (B) $\frac{8}{15}$

   (C) $\frac{1}{8}$

   (D) $\frac{2}{15}$

5. A length of chain is 5 feet, 3 inches long. If a piece 3 feet, 9 inches in length is cut from the chain, what is the length of the remaining piece?

   (A) 2 feet, 6 inches
   (B) 1 foot, 1 inch
   (C) 1 foot, 4 inches
   (D) 1 foot, 6 inches

6. In a regular hexagon, all the angles are equal and one of them is 120°. What is the sum of all the angles of the regular hexagon?

    (A) 240°
    (B) 480°
    (C) 720°
    (D) 360°

7. What is the product of $(3a - 2)$ and $(a + 3)$?

    (A) $4a + 1$
    (B) $3a^2 - 6$
    (C) $3a^2 - 2a - 6$
    (D) $3a^2 + 7a - 6$

8. If $x = 3$, what is the value of $|x - 7|$?

    (A) 4
    (B) – 4
    (C) 10
    (D) – 10

9. Solve the following system of equations for x:

    $$3x + y = 13$$
    $$x - 2y = 2$$

    (A) 18
    (B) 4
    (C) 3
    (D) 6

10. How many feet are there in a length of y yards and i inches?

    (A) $3y + i$
    (B) $3y + 12i$
    (C) $\dfrac{y + 12i}{3}$

    (D) $\dfrac{36y + i}{12}$

11. Solve the following formula for F: $C = \frac{5}{9}(F - 32)$.

(A) $F = \frac{9}{5}C + 32$

(B) $F = \frac{5}{9}C + 32$

(C) $F = \frac{9C + 32}{5}$

(D) $F = \frac{9}{5}C + 288$

12. A woman travels 3 miles directly east and then travels 4 miles directly north. How many miles is she from her starting point?

(A) 7
(B) 5
(C) 25
(D) $3\frac{1}{2}$

13. A line is drawn perpendicular to the base of an equilateral triangle at one of the vertices of the triangle. Find the number of degrees in the angle made by the perpendicular and the other side of the triangle that contains this vertex.

(A) 30°
(B) 45°
(C) 60°
(D) 90°

14. Solve the following inequality: $x - 6 \leq 5$

(A) $x \leq 1$
(B) $x \leq 11$
(C) $x \geq 11$
(D) $x < 11$

15. A fence which had been installed around a rectangular field 40 feet long and 36 feet wide is torn down. The entire fence is then reused to completely enclose a square field. What is the length in feet of a side of the square field?

(A) 76
(B) 19
(C) 42
(D) 38

16. A cereal manufacturer packages breakfast cereal in individual-sized boxes measuring 2 inches by 3 inches by 4 inches. The same product is also packaged in large family-sized boxes measuring 3 inches by 8 inches by 12 inches. The contents of how many of the individual-sized boxes would be required to fill one family-sized box?

    (A) 6
    (B) 12
    (C) 10
    (D) 8

17. A wheel has a diameter of 14 inches. How many inches will the wheel roll along the ground during one rotation? (Use $\frac{22}{7}$ as the value of pi.)

    (A) 44
    (B) 22
    (C) 14
    (D) 28

18. In a right triangle whose hypotenuse has a length of 21 feet, the sine of one of the angles is $\frac{3}{7}$. What is the length in feet of the side opposite this angle?

    (A) 6
    (B) 14
    (C) 9
    (D) 10

19. Find the value of $-x^4$ if $x = -0.1$.

    (A) −0.1
    (B) 0.0001
    (C) −0.0001
    (D) −0.4

20. Under the terms of a Federal subsidy, a real estate developer is required to rent at least 30% of the apartments he builds to low-income families. If he plans on having 108 low-income apartments, what is the maximum number of apartments of all types that he may build?

    (A) 360
    (B) 252
    (C) 324
    (D) 396

21. A student has grades of 60% on each of two tests and a grade of 70% on a third test. What grade must he get on a fourth test to raise his average to 75%?

    (A) 95%
    (B) 85%
    (C) 100%
    (D) He cannot achieve a 75% average.

22. A motorist travels for 3 hours at 40 miles per hour and then travels for 2 more hours at 50 miles per hour. What is her average rate of speed in miles per hour for the entire trip?

    (A) 45
    (B) 44
    (C) 43
    (D) 90

23. A radar device is capable of detecting objects within the area around it up to a radius of 10 miles. If it is used to cover a 36° angular portion of this area, how many square miles of area will it cover? (Use 3.14 as the value of pi.)

    (A) 360
    (B) 6.28
    (C) 31.4
    (D) 3.6

24. Solve for x: $x^2 + 2x = 15$.

    (A) $x = 3, x = 5$
    (B) $x = -3, x = 5$
    (C) $x = -5, x = 3$
    (D) $x = -15, x = 1$

25. 12 quarts of a radiator coolant contains 25% antifreeze and 75% water. How many quarts of water must be added to change the mixture to one containing 20% antifreeze?

    (A) 1
    (B) 2
    (C) 3
    (D) 4

ELECTRONICS INFORMATION—SUBTEST 6

Directions: This is a test of your knowledge of electrical, radio, and electronics information. You are to select the correct response from the choices given. Then mark the space on your answer form which has the same number and letter as your choice.

SAMPLE QUESTION

1. What does the abbreviation AC stand for?

   (A) additional charge
   (B) alternating coil
   (C) alternating current
   (D) ampere current

The correct answer is alternating current, so C is the correct response.

Your score on this test will be based on the number of questions you answer correctly. You should try to answer every question. Do not spend too much time on any one question.

The actual test will say:
Do not turn this page until told to do so.

Electronics Information

Time —9 minutes
20 Questions

1. Electricity is defined as

   (A) flow of electrons along a conductor.
   (B) flow of ions along a conductor.
   (C) movement of charges.
   (D) static electricity.

2. A conductor is any material that

   (A) has no free electrons.
   (B) has many free electrons.
   (C) has free ions.
   (D) has free protons.

3. Conventional current flow is from

   (A) + to +.
   (B) − to +.
   (C) + to −.
   (D) − to −.

4. Electron flow is from

   (A) + to +.
   (B) − to +.
   (C) + to −.
   (D) − to −.

5. An insulator is a material with

   (A) many free electrons.
   (B) few free electrons.
   (C) many free protons.
   (D) many free ions.

6. Opposition to current flow is measured in

   (A) ohms.
   (B) amps.
   (C) volts.
   (D) watts.

7. A watt is the power that gives rise to the production of energy at the rate of

   (A) 1 joule per minute.
   (B) 1 volt per second.
   (C) 1 amp per second.
   (D) 1 joule per second.

8. The Greek letter phi (ϕ) is used to

   (A) indicate ohms.
   (B) indicate angles or phases.
   (C) indicate volts.
   (D) indicate dielectric flux.

9. A parallel circuit with resistors of 10 ohms, 10 ohms, and 5 ohms has a total resistance of

   (A) 10 ohms.
   (B) 5 ohms.
   (C) 25 ohms.
   (D) 2.5 ohms.

10. Which of these is a symbol for a fuse?

   (A)
   (B)
   (C)
   (D)

11. The symbol for inductance is

   (A) X_L
   (B) I
   (C) L
   (D) X_C

12. Inductive reactance is found by using

   (A) $X_L = 2\pi\,FC.$
   (B) $X_L = 2\pi\,FL.$
   (C) $X_L = R.$
   (D) $X_L = Z.$

13. A capacitor of 100 microfarads has a capacity of

   (A) 100 picofarads.
   (B) 10 picofarads.
   (C) 100,000,000 picofarads.
   (D) 10,000 picofarads.

14. Impedance is represented by the symbol

    (A) X_L.
    (B) R.
    (C) X_C.
    (D) Z.

15. In electronics a CRT is a

    (A) constant radiation tube.
    (B) contrasting relief tube.
    (C) cathode ray tube.
    (D) conflicting relay tube.

16. A junction diode is used for

    (A) rectifying power-line frequencies and lower currents.
    (B) rectifying power-line frequencies and higher currents.
    (C) rectifying higher frequencies at lower currents.
    (D) rectifying higher frequencies at higher currents.

17. The SCR is a

    (A) specialized rectifier or diode.
    (B) special colored rectifier.
    (C) special controlled rectifier.
    (D) silicon-controlled relay.

18. In an FM receiver the AFC is

    (A) automatic frequency control for stabilizing the IF.
    (B) automatic frequency control for stabilizing the local oscillator.
    (C) automatic frequency control for tuning the incoming frequency.
    (D) automatic frequency control for the radio frequency amplifier.

19. Receivers with the ability to receive multiplexed signals are

    (A) FM.
    (B) FM-stereo.
    (C) AM.
    (D) AFC-FM.

20. The FM band covers

    (A) 550 to 1,600 kHz.
    (B) 88 to 108 MHz.
    (C) 100 to 200 MHz.
    (D) 550 to 1600 MHz.

AUTOMOTIVE & SHOP INFORMATION—SUBTEST 7

Directions: This test has questions about automobiles and their systems, as well as tools and common shop terminology and practices. Pick the best answer for each question, then blacken the space on your separate answer form which has the same number and letter as your choice.

SAMPLE QUESTION

1. The most commonly used fuel for running automobile engines is

   (A) kerosene.
   (B) benzine.
   (C) crude oil.
   (D) gasoline.

Gasoline is the most commonly used fuel, so D is the correct answer.

Your score on this test will be based on the number of questions you answer correctly. You should try to answer every question. Do not spend too much time on any one question.

The actual test will say:
Do not turn this page until told to do so.

Automotive & Shop Information

Time —11 minutes
25 Questions

1. The universal joint is needed to

   (A) allow the drive shaft to flex.
   (B) hold the drive shaft rigid.
   (C) make the transmission shift.
   (D) make the differential turn corners.

2. Three major pollutants emitted by a gasoline engine are

   (A) carbon dioxide, carbon monoxide, and oxygen.
   (B) hydrocarbons, nitric acid, and nitrogen.
   (C) hydrocarbons, carbon monoxide, and oxides of nitrogen.
   (D) nitrogen, oxygen, and carbon monoxide.

3. The catalytic converter

   (A) converts gasoline to the air/fuel ratio needed.
   (B) reduces the input pressure of exhaust gases to the muffler.
   (C) converts intake manifold pressure to a lower value.
   (D) converts exhaust gases to better quality emissions.

4. The differential

   (A) is located in the transmission.
   (B) is located in the clutch housing.
   (C) consists of three small bevel gears on the ends of the axle shafts.
   (D) consists of two small bevel gears on the ends of the axle shafts.

5. PCV is the abbreviation for

   (A) Pollution Control Valve.
   (B) Pollution Valve Control.
   (C) Positive Crankcase Ventilation.
   (D) Pollution Control Ventilator.

6. The formation of NO_x in an engine is minimized by

   (A) diluting the fuel/air mixture entering the combustion chamber.
   (B) burning more fuel.
   (C) using an alcohol-enriched fuel.
   (D) not using a muffler.

7. With any two gears the gear with the greater number of teeth will

   (A) turn slower than the smaller gear and produce less torque.
   (B) always turn slower and produce greater torque.
   (C) never produce much torque.
   (D) always turn faster and produce less torque.

8. The clutch is used to

   (A) change compression ratios.
   (B) stop the car.
   (C) make it possible to change gears.
   (D) drive the transmission.

9. First gear in a car is used

   (A) at high speeds.
   (B) at the start of the car from a standstill.
   (C) when the car is moving faster than 35 mph.
   (D) at speeds above 55 mph.

10. The torque converter is found in

    (A) the differential housing.
    (B) the manual transmission housing.
    (C) the engine compartment.
    (D) in an automatic transmission.

11. Disc brakes are made with

    (A) two pads and a rotating drum.
    (B) two pads and a rotating disc.
    (C) two brake shoes that slide along the inside drum mounted on the rear wheels.
    (D) all-steel pads to stop the car quickly.

12. In a front-wheel drive car the transmission

    (A) is located in the rear of the car.
    (B) is located in the engine compartment.
    (C) has a long propeller shaft.
    (D) has a short propeller shaft.

13. L_0 or L on the automatic transmission is the same as

    (A) 1st gear in the manual transmission.
    (B) 2nd gear in the manual transmission.
    (C) 3rd gear in the manual transmission.
    (D) 4th gear in the manual transmission.

14. Park (P) position on an automatic transmission indicator means the transmission

   (A) is in idle and can be towed.
   (B) is in a locked position that prevents the car from moving.
   (C) is in its highest speed position.
   (D) is ready for pulling heavy loads.

15. The internal combustion engine can be best described as

   (A) a high torque engine even at low speeds.
   (B) a low torque engine even at low speeds.
   (C) a low speed engine.
   (D) a high speed engine.

16. In concrete work, to butter a concrete block means to

   (A) put a finishing trowel to it.
   (B) put a hawk on it.
   (C) use a jointer on it.
   (D) put mortar on it.

17. Which of the following is a hardwood?

   (A) oak
   (B) spruce
   (C) pine
   (D) fir

18. Which of the following is a softwood?

   (A) poplar
   (B) maple
   (C) pine
   (D) oak

19. To prevent rapid drying, freshly cut logs are often

   (A) submerged in oil.
   (B) placed in kilns.
   (C) submerged in water.
   (D) placed in sheds to dry slowly.

20. A bumping hammer is used to smooth out dents by a(n)

   (A) sheet metal duct worker.
   (B) autobody repairman.
   (C) bumper repairman.
   (D) none of the above.

21. A groover is used to

   (A) lock seams together.
   (B) make sheet metal seams.
   (C) open a seam.
   (D) fold a seam.

22. Sheet metal is formed into round cylinders by using a

   (A) squaring shear.
   (B) slip roll.
   (C) bar folder.
   (D) punch press.

23. The tip of a soldering iron is coated with solder before it is used. This process of coating the tip is called

   (A) welding.
   (B) brazing.
   (C) soldering.
   (D) tinning.

24. Punches are used in sheet metal work to

   (A) flatten the metal.
   (B) make holes in the metal.
   (C) groove the metal.
   (D) snip the metal.

25. A squaring shear is used to

   (A) cut metal off to a straight line.
   (B) square a piece of metal.
   (C) fold a piece of sheet metal.
   (D) punch a piece of sheet metal.

MECHANICAL COMPREHENSION—SUBTEST 8

> *Directions:* This test has questions about general mechanical and physical principles. Pick the best answer to each question, then blacken the space on your separate answer form which has the same number and letter as your choice.

SAMPLE QUESTION

The follower is at its highest position between points

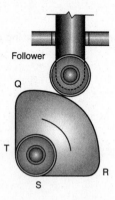

(A) Q and R.
(B) R and S.
(C) S and T.
(D) T and Q.

The correct answer is between Q and R, so you would blacken the space for A on your answer form.

Your score on this test will be based on the number of questions you answer correctly. You should try to answer every question. Do not spend too much time on any one question.

The actual test will say:
Do not turn this page until told to do so.

Mechanical Comprehension

Time —19 minutes
25 Questions

1. Force is something that can change the velocity of an object by making it

   (A) start or stop.
   (B) speed up.
   (C) slow down.
   (D) all of the above.

2. The brakes on your car use the same force that stops your car if you just let it coast. This force is called

   (A) velocity.
   (B) gravity.
   (C) friction.
   (D) newton.

3. The SI (metric) term corresponding to pounds is

   (A) gram.
   (B) newton.
   (C) kilogram.
   (D) pascal.

4. If you drop something, it falls. The force acting on it is

   (A) gravity.
   (B) friction.
   (C) elastic recoil.
   (D) equilibrium.

5. When a rope is stretched, it is said to be in a state of

   (A) equilibrium.
   (B) tension.
   (C) buoyancy.
   (D) elastic recoil.

6. When a solid moves through a liquid, there is a frictionlike force retarding the motion of the solid. This is called

   (A) gravity.
   (B) friction.
   (C) elastic recoil.
   (D) viscous drag.

7. Weight is directly proportional to the acceleration due to

    (A) friction.
    (B) elastic recoil.
    (C) viscous drag.
    (D) gravity.

8. The force that acts in an upward direction on anything submerged in a liquid or a gas is called

    (A) friction.
    (B) viscous drag.
    (C) gravity.
    (D) buoyancy.

9. Forces exist only in pairs. These forces are sometimes called

    (A) action and interaction.
    (B) reaction and interaction.
    (C) action and reaction.
    (D) friction and gravity.

10. When forces act in pairs they are

    (A) equal in magnitude and opposite in direction.
    (B) equal in magnitude and in the same direction.
    (C) equal in magnitude.
    (D) unequal in magnitude.

11. If an object is in equilibrium, it is said to be

    (A) at rest.
    (B) moving.
    (C) at rest or moving at a constant speed and in a straight line.
    (D) moving upward only.

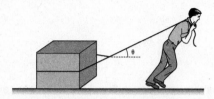

12. In the figure, the angle θ is important, since when it is

    (A) 0 degrees the entire force is dragging the box.
    (B) 90 degrees the entire force is lifting the box.
    (C) both lifting and dragging between 10 degrees and 90 degrees.
    (D) all of the above.

13. A good example of a simple machine is a

(A) manually operated pencil sharpener.
(B) doorknob.
(C) light switch.
(D) all of the above.

14. The effort times the effort distance is called

(A) the work input.
(B) the work output.
(C) the buoyancy.
(D) gravity.

15. The load times the load distance is called

(A) the work input.
(B) the work output.
(C) the buoyancy.
(D) gravity.

16. Work input is always more than work output because of

(A) gravity.
(B) buoyancy.
(C) friction.
(D) tension.

17. The ratio between work output and work input is called

(A) efficiency.
(B) work.
(C) leverage.
(D) mass.

18. The amount of magnification that a machine produces is referred to as the

(A) effort arm.
(B) work.
(C) mechanical advantage.
(D) efficiency.

19. A ramp is a device commonly used to aid in

(A) lifting.
(B) lowering weights.
(C) high-efficiency situations.
(D) loading.

20. A screw consists of a single continuous spiral wrapped around a

   (A) piston.
   (B) cylinder.
   (C) helix.
   (D) square.

21. The distance between the ridges of screw threads is called the

   (A) valley.
   (B) peak.
   (C) pitch.
   (D) count.

22. A vise is a self-locking machine because its efficiency is considered to be

   (A) near 100%.
   (B) less than 50%.
   (C) more than 50%.
   (D) less than 25%.

23. The mechanical advantage of a winch is the ratio of the radius of the crank to the radius of the

   (A) arm.
   (B) lever.
   (C) fulcrum.
   (D) shaft.

24. The ideal mechanical advantage of a gear is the ratio of the number of teeth in the load gear to the number of teeth in the

   (A) effort gear.
   (B) loaded gear.
   (C) lifting gear.
   (D) spiral gear.

25. The rate at which work is done is called

   (A) power.
   (B) effort.
   (C) watts.
   (D) horsepower.

ASSEMBLING OBJECTS—SUBTEST 9

Directions: This test measures your ability to picture how an object will look when its parts are mentally put together. Each question will show you several separate shapes; you will then pick the choice that best represents how the pieces would look if they were all fitted together correctly. There is only one best answer for each shape. Pick the best answer for each question, then blacken the space on the answer form that has the same number and letter as your choice.

SAMPLE QUESTION

Which figure best shows how the objects in the group on the left will appear if they are fitted together?

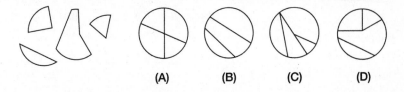

(A)   (B)   (C)   (D)

In this example, the correct answer is "D."

Your score on this test will be based on the number of questions you answer correctly. You should try to answer every question. Do not spend too much time on any one question.

The actual test will say:
Do not turn this page until told to do so.

Assembling Objects

Time —9 minutes
16 Questions

1.

(A)   (B)   (C)   (D)

2.

(A)   (B)   (C)   (D)

3.

(A)   (B)   (C)   (D)

4.

(A)   (B)   (C)   (D)

5.

    (A)   (B)   (C)   (D)

6.

    (A)   (B)   (C)   (D)

7.

    (A)   (B)   (C)   (D)

8.

    (A)   (B)   (C)   (D)

9.

    (A)   (B)   (C)   (D)

10.

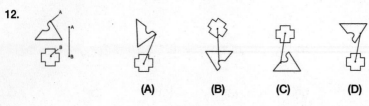

(A) (B) (C) (D)

11.

(A) (B) (C) (D)

12.

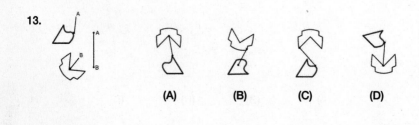

(A) (B) (C) (D)

13.

(A) (B) (C) (D)

14.

(A) (B) (C) (D)

15.

(A)   (B)   (C)   (D)

16.

(A)   (B)   (C)   (D)

ANSWER KEYS AND ANSWER EXPLANATIONS

General Science—Subtest 1

Answer Key

1. **D**	6. **C**	11. **A**	16. **C**	21. **C**
2. **C**	7. **B**	12. **C**	17. **B**	22. **D**
3. **D**	8. **B**	13. **B**	18. **D**	23. **B**
4. **C**	9. **D**	14. **B**	19. **B**	24. **C**
5. **B**	10. **C**	15. **C**	20. **C**	25. **D**

Answer Explanations

1. **(D)** The sperm carries an X or Y chromosome, while all eggs normally have one X chromosome. The union of XX results in a female, while the union of an X chromosome with a Y chromosome results in a male.

2. **(C)** Rocks do not conduct heat very quickly. If a rock becomes cold during the night but is rapidly heated during the day, the expansion and contraction may cause the outer layer to peel off. If water gets into a crack in the rock, the freezing and thawing may cause the rock to split.

3. **(D)** Sand results from the weathering of igneous rock which contains quartz crystals. Because of the relative hardness and insolubility of quartz the crystals of quartz remain after other portions of the eroded rock have been dissolved or carried away.

4. **(C)** Vinegar contains acetic acid.

5. **(B)** All atoms of the same element have the same number of protons. In the neutral atom the number of electrons is the same as the number of protons. (Protons are inside the nucleus of an atom; electrons are outside it.) Atoms of the same element may differ in the number of neutrons.

6. **(C)** When heat is applied to a liquid at its boiling point the added energy is used to separate the molecules from their neighbors, but no increase in the temperature of the liquid occurs. The molecules of vapor that leave the surface of the liquid possess increased potential energy because of the work done to overcome the forces acting on them.

7. **(B)** Nebulae are large clouds of gas and dust located between the stars. Our solar system is made up of the sun, the planets and their satellites, and asteroids.

8. **(B)** Space is a nearly perfect vacuum. The process by which solar energy (in the form of ultraviolet rays) is transmitted through space is called radiation.

9. **(D)** The gene for hemophilia lies on the X chromosome; this disorder is therefore inherited as a sex-linked disorder.

10. **(C)** Only living things can duplicate themselves.

11. **(A)** The thermometer that indicates the freezing point of water at zero and the boiling point of water at 100 degrees is known as the Centigrade, or Celsius, thermometer.

12. **(C)** A steep surface will increase runoff since the water will flow rapidly, giving it little time to be absorbed by the soil. Vegetation will make the surface more porous, decreasing the runoff and thereby decreasing the erosion of the soil.

13. **(B)** The 25-pound force is the resultant of two forces acting at right angles to each other. The resultant can be represented as the hypotenuse of a right triangle, with one side representing the 15-pound force and the other side the unknown (x) force. Then, applying the Pythagorean Theorem,

$$\text{(hypotenuse)}^2 = \text{(side)}^2 + \text{(side)}^2$$
$$(25)^2 = (15)^2 + x^2$$
$$625 = 225 + x^2$$
$$400 = x^2$$
$$20 = x$$

14. **(B)** The hydrometer is used to test the specific gravity of the acid in the storage battery. The specific gravity is an index of the extent of charge of the battery.

15. **(C)** Fluorides are added to drinking water to reduce the incidence of dental caries (cavities).

16. **(C)** A *reflex* is a simple inborn response. An *instinct* involves a series of reflexes. A *habit* is an acquired trait. *Phototropism* is a response in plants.

17. **(B)** The Rh factor is an inherited condition of the blood.

18. **(D)** Iron is part of hemoglobin, the pigment of red blood cells.

19. **(B)** Land heats up rapidly in summer and cools off rapidly in winter. The result is the climate found in continental interiors where the winters are extremely cold and the summers extremely hot.

20. **(C)** All freely falling objects, regardless of their masses near the earth, fall towards the earth with equal acceleration. Any two objects at rest that begin to fall at the same instant will have equal velocities at the end of 3 seconds or any other time interval.

21. **(C)** Living things carry on respiration at all times. Respiration in plants goes on independently of photosynthesis, which only occurs in the presence of sunlight.

22. **(D)** Where a place is heated, the warm air rises on overflows, far above the earth, toward a colder region. Meanwhile other unheated air flows in to take its place. This causes a horizontal air current which, when close to the earth's surface, is called wind.

23. **(B)** Mammals appeared most recently on earth.

24. **(C)** White light is a mixture of all of the colors of the spectrum. With the aid of a prism it may be separated into the individual colors.

25. **(D)** A solution has a high ratio of solute to solvent if there is a large amount of solute dissolved in a small amount of solvent. Such a solution, by definition, is a concentrated solution.

Arithmetic Reasoning—Subtest 2

Answer Key

1. **B**	6. **B**	11. **D**	16. **B**	21. **B**	26. **A**
2. **D**	7. **D**	12. **C**	17. **B**	22. **C**	27. **B**
3. **A**	8. **D**	13. **D**	18. **B**	23. **B**	28. **A**
4. **B**	9. **A**	14. **A**	19. **D**	24. **D**	29. **D**
5. **D**	10. **A**	15. **C**	20. **A**	25. **D**	30. **C**

Answer Explanations

1. **(B)** This discount is 15% (or 0.15) of the marked price.
$$\$500 \times .15 = \$75$$
The cost is $500 – $75 = $425.
Subtract the down payment to find the balance due.
$$\$425 - \$65 = \$360$$
Each installment is $\frac{1}{2}$ of $360.
$$\frac{\$360}{12} = \$30$$

2. **(D)** 2 gallons will cover $\frac{1}{4}$ acre.
4×2 gallons, or 8 gallons, will cover 1 acre.
10×8 gallons, or 80 gallons, will cover 10 acres.
Since 2 gallons cover $\frac{1}{4}$ acre, 2×2 gallons, or 4 gallons, cover $\frac{1}{2}$ acre.
80 gallons + 4 gallons, or 84 gallons, will cover $10\frac{1}{2}$ acres.

3. **(A)** The drawing and its enlargement will be similar. Therefore the lengths and widths will be in proportion.

$$\frac{\text{length of original}}{\text{length of enlargement}} = \frac{\text{width of original}}{\text{width of enlargement}}$$

$$\frac{18}{45} = \frac{12}{\text{width of enlargement } (X)}$$

Reduce $\frac{18}{45}$ by dividing numerator and denominator by 9.

$$\frac{2}{5} = \frac{12}{x}$$

To solve, cross-multiply the measurements.

$$2 \times x = 5 \times 12 = 60$$
$$x = \frac{60}{2}$$
$$x = 30$$

4. **(B)** Divide the number of acceptable products by the total number inspected. Then change your answer to a percent.

$$\frac{266}{280} = \frac{133}{140} = \frac{19}{20}$$
$$\frac{19}{20} = \frac{95}{100} = 0.95 = 95\%$$

5. **(D)** If 3 pounds of candy cost $4.80, then 1 pound costs $4.80 ÷ 3, or $1.60. There are 16 ounces in 1 pound.

1 ounce of the mix costs $\frac{\$1.60}{16} = \$0.10$

5 ounces cost $5 \times \$0.10 = \$0.50$

6. **(B)** The perimeter of a square is the sum of the lengths of all four sides. But the four sides of a square are all equal in length.

The length of one side = 13 feet, 8 inches ÷ 4

Change 1 foot to 12 inches so that 13 feet, 8 inches becomes 12 feet, 20 inches.

12 feet, 20 inches ÷ 4 = 3 feet, 5 inches

7. **(D)** If 20% of the unit are officers, then the percent of enlisted men is

$$100\% - 20\% = 80\%$$

To find the number of enlisted men, multiply the total number by 80%

$$360 \times 0.80 = 288.00$$
$$= 288 \text{ enlisted men}$$

8. **(D)** Her overtime is 10 hours – 8 hours regular work = 2 hours.

2 hours at "time and a half" is paid as $2 \times 1\frac{1}{2}$ hours, or $2 \times \frac{3}{2}$ hours, or $\frac{6}{2}$ hours, or 3 hours.

8 hours + 3 hours = 11 hours of pay. $11 \times \$8.50 = \$93.50$

9. **(A)** Find the relationship between each pair of numbers in the series. Thus,

$$\left(2\frac{1}{4};3\frac{3}{4}\right)2\frac{1}{4}+1\frac{1}{2}=3\frac{3}{4}$$

$$\left(3\frac{3}{4};3\frac{1}{4}\right)3\frac{3}{4}-2\frac{1}{2}=3\frac{1}{4}$$

$$\left(3\frac{1}{4};4\frac{3}{4}\right)3\frac{1}{4}+1\frac{1}{2}=4\frac{3}{4}$$

The pattern so far is:

$$+1\frac{1}{2},\ -1\frac{1}{2},\ +1\frac{1}{2}$$

To continue the series, subtract $\frac{1}{2}$ from the fourth member of the series.

$$4\frac{3}{4}-\frac{1}{2}=4\frac{1}{4}$$

10. **(A)** Find the amount collected for adult tickets.

$$265 \times \$4 = \$1,060$$

Out of the $1,200 in receipts, the remainder came from the sale of children's tickets.

$$\$140 \div \$2 = 70 \text{ tickets}$$

11. **(D)** If she budgets $\frac{1}{4}$ of her income for rent, she has $\frac{3}{4}$ of her income left.

$$\frac{4}{4}-\frac{1}{4}=\frac{3}{4}\text{ (remainder)}$$

She then budgets $\frac{2}{5}$ of this remainder for food.

$$\frac{2}{5}\times\frac{3}{4}=\frac{6}{20}=\frac{3}{10}\text{ (food)}$$

12. **(C)** The 3 who watched 2 hours each watched a total of 3 × 2 hours, or 6 hours. The 2 who watched 1 hour each watched a total of 2 × 1 hours, or 2 hours. 1 watched for 4 hours.
Add the numbers of hours watched.
6 + 2 + 4 = 12 hours (total time spent).
Add the number of people.
3 + 2 + 1 = 6 persons were in the group.
Divide the total time spent by the number of persons in the group to find the average number of hours one person watches.
12 hours ÷ 6 persons = 2 hours per person average.

13. **(D)** Multiply the cost per yard by the length of the material in yards.

3 feet = 1 yard, so 2 feet = $\frac{2}{3}$ yard.

3 yards, 2 feet = $3\frac{2}{3}$ yards.

$$\$9 \times 3\frac{2}{3} = \frac{9}{1} \times \frac{11}{3} = \$33$$

14. **(A)** Let x represent one of the 9 shares in which the profit must be divided. According to the ratio agreed on, the smaller partner's share is $4x$ and the larger partner's share is $5x$. Together, the share must add up to the \$63,000 profit. This can be written as an equation.

$$4x + 5x = 63,000$$

Solve by combining similar terms.

$9x = 63,000$

$x = 7,000$ (one share)

Multiply the value of 1 share by the number of shares the smaller partner is to get.

$$4x = 4 \times 7,000 = \$28,000$$

15. **(C)** The first courier will travel for 1 hour + 2 hours, or a total of 3 hours, before he is overtaken.

Travelling 30 m.p.h. for 3 hours will take the first courier 30×3 or 90 miles away.

The second courier must travel the 90 miles in 2 hours. Therefore, he must travel at a rate of $90 \div 2$ or 45 miles per hour.

16. **(B)** Find the discounted price paid by the merchant.

$\$60 \times 25\% = \$60 \times 0.25 = \$15$ (discount)

$\$60 - \$15 = \$45$ (price paid by the merchant)

Next find the merchant's selling price, based on an increase of 20% over the original wholesale price.

$\$60 \times 20\% = \$60 \times 0.20$ or $\$60 \times \frac{1}{5} = \$12$ (increase over wholesale price)

$\$60 + \$12 = \$72$ (merchant's selling price)

Finally, find the merchant's profit.

$\$72 - \$45 = \$27$

17. **(B)** To find the rate of speed when the distance and the time are known, divide the distance, x, by the time, y. x divided by y is expressed as $\frac{x}{y}$.

18. **(B)** Since the first 10 words cost \$1.50, the balance is left for the cost of the remaining words.

$$\$4.00 - \$1.50 = \$2.50$$

To find the number of words $2.50 will pay for at $0.05 per word, divide $2.50 by $0.05.

$$\$2.50 \div \$0.05 = 250 \div 5 \text{ (clearing decimals)}$$
$$250 \div 5 = 50 \text{ words}$$

50 words added to the first 10 words makes a total of 60 words.

19. **(D)** Since 1 inch represents 40 miles, divide 110 miles by 40 miles to find the number of inches required to represent it.

$$110 \div 40 = \frac{11}{40} = \frac{11}{4} = 2\frac{3}{4} \text{ inches}$$

20. **(A)** Multiply the purchase price of the home by the assessment rate to find the assessed value.

$$\$80,000 \times 75\% = \$80,000 \times \frac{3}{4} = \frac{80,000}{1} \times \frac{3}{4} = \frac{20,000}{1} \times \frac{3}{1} =$$

$60,000 (assessed value)

Find the number of hundreds in the assessed value.

$$60,000 \div 100 = 600 \text{ (hundreds)}$$

Multiply the number of hundreds by the tax rate.

$$600 \times \$4.83 = \$2,898.00 \text{ (tax)}$$

21. **(B)** Set up a proportion.

$$\frac{\text{recipe sugar}}{\text{sugar actually used}} = \frac{\text{recipe flour}}{\text{flour actually used}}$$

$$\frac{\frac{3}{4} \text{ cup}}{\frac{1}{4} \text{ cup}} = \frac{4\frac{1}{2} \text{ cups}}{x \text{ cups}} \text{ or } \frac{\frac{3}{4}}{\frac{1}{4}} = \frac{\frac{9}{2}}{x}$$

Simplify each side of the proportion.

$$\frac{3}{4} \div \frac{1}{4} = \frac{3}{4} \times \frac{4}{1} = \frac{3}{1}$$
$$\frac{9}{2} \div \frac{x}{1} = \frac{9}{2} \times \frac{1}{x} = \frac{9}{2x}$$

Solve the proportion by cross-multiplying.

$$6x = 9$$

Divide each side of the equation by 6 to find the value of x.

$$x = \frac{9}{6} = 1\frac{1}{2} \text{ cups of flour}$$

22. **(C)** Find the amount of the decline by subtracting.

$$1,200 - 1,044 = 156$$

To find the percent of decline, divide the amount of the decline by the original number of cars crossing the bridge.

$$156 \div 1{,}200 = \frac{156}{1{,}200} = \frac{13}{100} = 13\%$$

23. **(B)** First find the cost of one gallon. If 2 gallons cost $19.20, 1 gallon will cost $19.20 ÷ 2 or $9.60. There are 4 quarts in one gallon. Divide the cost of 1 gallon by 4 to find the cost of 1 quart.

$$\$9.60 \div 4 = \$2.40$$

24. **(D)** Find the distance he drove on each leg of the trip by multiplying the rate in miles per hour by the time in hours.

$$50 \times 3 = 150 \text{ miles}$$
$$55 \times 2 = 110 \text{ miles}$$

Add the two distances to get the total distance he traveled.

$$150 + 110 \text{ miles} = 260 \text{ miles}$$

Divide the total distance traveled by the number of miles per gallon of gas to get the amount of gas used.

$$260 \div 20 = 13 \text{ gallons}$$

25. **(D)** First find the income from the $5,000 invested at 8%.

$$\$5{,}000 \times 0.08 = \$400.00$$

Next find the income desired from the total investment of $15,000.

$$\$15{,}000 \times 0.09 = \$1{,}350.00$$

Subtract the income from the first investment to find out how much income she must get from the second.

$$\$1{,}350 - \$400 = \$950$$

Divide the income, $950, by the investment, $10,000, to find the rate of interest.

$$\$950 \div \$10{,}000 = \frac{950}{10{,}000} = \frac{95}{1{,}000} = .095 \text{ or } 9\frac{1}{2}\%$$

26. **(A)** Find the number of hours the generator operates.

From 9:15 A.M. to 3:15 P.M is 6 hours.

From 3:15 P.M. to 3:55 P.M. is 40 minutes (or $\frac{2}{3}$ of an hour).

6 hours + 40 minutes = $6\frac{2}{3}$ hours.

Divide the total time run by the time provided by one fuel tank filling (1 hour, 20 minutes, or $1\frac{1}{3}$ hours).

$$6\frac{2}{3} \div 1\frac{1}{3} = \frac{20}{3} \times \frac{3}{4} = 5 \text{ fillings}$$

27. **(B)** Find the total value of each kind of seed in the mixture.

10 pounds @ $1.20 per pound is worth 10 × $1.20, or $12.00.

8 pounds @ $3.00 per pound is worth 8 × $3.00, or $24.00.

Add the values of each kind to get the total value of the mixture.
$$\$12.00 + \$24.00 = \$36.00$$
Divide the total value of the mixture by the total number of pounds, 18, to get price per pound.
$$\$36.00 \div 18 = \$2.00 \text{ per pound}$$

28. **(A)** First multiply out the numerator.
$$\frac{0.02 \times 3}{0.001} = \frac{0.06}{0.001}$$
Clear the decimal in the divider by moving the decimal point in both numerator and denominator 3 places to the right.
$$\frac{0.06}{0.001} = \frac{60}{1} = 60$$

29. **(D)** Substitute the number values for the letters and then do the arithmetic operations.
$$1 + 5xy^2 - 3x^2y \qquad =$$
$$1 + (5 \times x \times y^2) - (3 \times x^2 \times y) =$$
$$1 + (5 \times 3 \times 2^2) - (3 \times 3^2 \times 2) =$$
$$1 + (5 \times 3 \times 3 \times 4) - (3 \times 9 \times 2) =$$
$$1 + 60 - 54 \qquad = 7$$

30. **(C)** Substitute the number values for P and R.
$$I = \sqrt{\frac{P}{R}}$$
$$I = \sqrt{\frac{48}{3}}$$
$$I = \sqrt{16}$$
The square root of 16 is the number that when multiplied by itself is 16; therefore $\sqrt{16} = 4$
$$I = 4$$

Word Knowledge—Subtest 3

Answer Key

1. **C**	6. **B**	11. **D**	16. **D**	21. **A**	26. **B**	31. **B**
2. **C**	7. **D**	12. **A**	17. **C**	22. **C**	27. **D**	32. **C**
3. **B**	8. **D**	13. **A**	18. **A**	23. **D**	28. **A**	33. **C**
4. **D**	9. **D**	14. **C**	19. **A**	24. **A**	29. **A**	34. **D**
5. **A**	10. **D**	15. **B**	20. **A**	25. **C**	30. **A**	35. **C**

Answer Explanations

1. **(C)** <u>Tell</u>, like *inform*, means to communicate knowledge or give information.
2. **(C)** <u>Crimson</u> is a vivid red or purplish red.
3. **(B)** <u>Caution</u> means forethought to avoid danger or harm; carefulness.
4. **(D)** <u>Intermittently</u> means starting and stopping, as in rain starting and stopping at irregular intervals.
5. **(A)** <u>Event</u>, like *occurrence*, means a happening or incident.
6. **(B)** <u>Fraud</u>, like *deception*, means the use of deceit.
7. **(D)** <u>Stop</u>, like *cease*, means to end.
8. **(D)** <u>Applause</u>, like *acclaim*, means enthusiastic approval.
9. **(D)** <u>Construct</u>, like *erect*, means to raise upright, as to erect or construct a building.
10. **(D)** <u>Enjoy</u>, like *relish*, means to take pleasure in.
11. **(D)** <u>Sufficient</u> means enough, adequate. Of the words given, sufficient most nearly means appropriate, as in a sufficient or appropriate amount.
12. **(A)** <u>Fortnight</u> means two weeks.
13. **(A)** A <u>defect</u>, like a *blemish*, is an imperfection, or fault.
14. **(C)** To <u>impose</u> or require means to make compulsory.
15. **(B)** <u>Scoff</u>, like *jeer*, means to mock or poke fun at.
16. **(D)** An assumed name is an <u>alias</u>.
17. **(C)** <u>Weaken</u>, like *impair*, means to worsen or to damage.
18. **(A)** <u>Itinerant</u> means traveling, as in an itinerant salesman.
19. **(A)** <u>Relinquish</u>, like *abandon*, means to give up possession.
20. **(A)** <u>Resolve</u> means to bring to a conclusion or end.
21. **(A)** <u>Plentiful</u>, like *ample*, means existing in great quantity.
22. **(C)** A <u>stench</u> is a foul odor; a stink.
23. **(D)** <u>Angrily silent</u>, like *sullen*, means resentful.
24. **(A)** <u>Rudiments</u> are fundamental skills or basic principles, like basic methods and procedures.
25. **(C)** To <u>conflict</u>, or clash, means to disagree or to be in opposition.
26. **(B)** <u>Camaraderie</u> means goodwill and rapport among friends.
27. **(D)** <u>Cursory</u>, like *superficial*, means hasty, not thorough.
28. **(A)** A <u>tapestry</u> is a fabric with multicolored woven designs.
29. **(A)** <u>Terse</u>, or pointed, as in a terse or pointed comment, means brief but expressing a great deal.
30. **(A)** A combination of ingredients, as in cookery, is a <u>concoction</u>.
31. **(B)** Shortness, or <u>brevity</u>, means briefness of duration.

32. **(C) Mercy**, like *clemency*, means leniency, especially toward an offender or enemy.
33. **(C) Disobedience**, like *insubordination*, means failure to recognize authority or to accept the authority of a superior.
34. **(D) Preferential** means having or obtaining an advantage, as in receiving special or preferential treatment.
35. **(C) Low spirits**, like *doldrums*, are marked by listlessness, inactivity, or depression.

Paragraph Comprehension—Subtest 4

Answer Key

1. **A**	6. **C**	11. **B**
2. **B**	7. **B**	12. **C**
3. **B**	8. **D**	13. **C**
4. **C**	9. **B**	14. **C**
5. **B**	10. **C**	15. **B**

Answer Explanations

1. **(A)** The main idea of this paragraph is given in the first sentence, which states that professional drivers have a low opinion of the average motorist.
2. **(B)** In this selection the word shuddered means shook.
3. **(B)** The paragraph clearly states that the Swedes and Finns (these two European peoples) were the first to use the log cabin.
4. **(C)** The tone or mood of this passage is one of contentment. The man is described at rest with a smile on his face.
5. **(B)** This paragraph points out the favorable or good points about apprentice training. It does not discuss any negative or bad points and it does not compare it to any other type of training.
6. **(C)** The paragraph states, "we never have enough closets no matter how many closets we have."
7. **(B)** A reactionary person looks to the past. The paragraph describes a liberal, using the key words liberated or free. The words "on the other hand" tell you that the description is about to shift from one way to another.
8. **(D)** You can infer from the passage that a conservation group wrote it. A lumber company or house-building company would more likely

want to cut the forest to use the lumber in its business. There is no reason to think that a religious group wrote the paragraph.

9. **(B)** The time for action suggests that the bridge should be built, but the paragraph makes it clear that official action—approval of bonds—must be taken first.

10. **(C)** The paragraph describes lightning as a "spark" and as a "release of energy."

11. **(B)** The paragraph clearly states that the morning rush hour starts two hours before 9 a.m.

12. **(C)** Acuity means sharpness. If you do not know the meaning of the word you can figure it out from the context. You can immediately eliminate A; you can eliminate D because pressure is referred to in the phrase "eye pressure." You must then choose between strength and sharpness and in terms of the subject of this passage—vision—sharpness is more accurate.

13. **(C)** More than one seed of wheat has to be tested to form a conclusion.

14. **(C)** The last sentence states that bread and cereal provide 40% of the daily needs of thiamine, one of the B vitamins.

15. **(B)** The second sentence states that most problems came from poor medical knowledge and lack of ways to fight disease.

Mathematics Knowledge—Subtest 5

Answer Key

1. **C**	6. **C**	11. **A**	16. **B**	21. **D**
2. **A**	7. **D**	12. **B**	17. **A**	22. **B**
3. **B**	8. **A**	13. **A**	18. **C**	23. **C**
4. **B**	9. **B**	14. **B**	19. **C**	24. **C**
5. **D**	10. **D**	15. **D**	20. **A**	25. **C**

Answer Explanations

1. **(C)** First isolate all terms containing x on one side of the equation and all terms not containing x on the other side. To do this, add x to both sides of the equation and also subtract 6 from both sides of the equation. Remember to change the sign of any term when it is moved from one side of the equation to the other.

$$2x + x + 6 - 6 = 12 - 6 - x + x$$
$$3x = 6$$

Divide each side of the equation by 3 to undo the multiplication of 3 by x.

$$\frac{3x}{3} = \frac{6}{3}$$

$$x = 2$$

2. **(A)** Write the binomial to be subtracted underneath the binomial from which it is to be subtracted, placing similar terms in the same columns.

From $\qquad 8x^2 - 7x$

Subtract $\quad -3x^2 + 2x$

Change the signs of the terms in the bottom row (the subtrahend) and combine the similar terms in each column.

$$8x^2 - 7x$$
$$\underline{3x^2 - 2x}$$
$$11x^2 - 9x$$

3. **(B)** Multiply $3x^2y$ by $2x^3y$ and also multiply -4 by $2x^3y$. To multiply $3x^3y$ by $2x^3y$, first multiply their numerical factors.

$$3 \times 2 = 6$$

To multiply powers of the same letter, add the exponents. Remember that y stands for y^1. Thus,

$$x^2 \times x^3 = x^5 \text{ and } y \times y = y^2.$$
$$2x^3y \times (3x^2y - 4) = 6x^5y^2 - 8x^3y$$

4. **(B)** Add the portions that each one does.

$$\frac{1}{3} + \frac{1}{5}$$

To add fractions, they must have a common denominator. The least common denominator for 3 and 5 is 15, the smallest number into which they both divide evenly. Change $\frac{1}{3}$ and $\frac{1}{5}$ to equivalent fractions having 15 as their denominator. Fractions with the same denominator may be added by adding their numerators.

$$\frac{5}{15} + \frac{3}{5} = \frac{8}{15}$$

5. **(D)** Subtract the length of the piece to be cut off.

5 feet, 3 inches

$\underline{- 3 \text{ feet, 9 inches}}$

Since we cannot subtract 9 inches from 3 inches, we borrow 1 foot from the 5 feet and convert it to 12 inches; thus 5 feet, 3 inches becomes 4 feet, 15 inches.

4 feet, 15 inches

$\underline{- 3 \text{ feet, } \quad 9 \text{ inches}}$

1 foot, 6 inches

6. **(C)** A hexagon is a polygon having 6 sides. If it has 6 sides, it must also have 6 angles. The sum of the 6 equal angles is 6 times the size of one of them.

$$6 \times 120° = 720°$$

7. **(D)** Set up the product like a multiplication example in arithmetic. Multiply each term of $(3a - 2)$ by a and write the results as the first line of partial products. Remember that the product of a positive number and a negative number is negative. Next multiply each term of $(3a - 2)$ by $+ 3$ and write the results as the second line of partial products. Add the partial products as you do in arithmetic to get the final answer.

$$
\begin{array}{r}
3a - 2 \\
\underline{a + 3} \\
3a^2 - 2a \\
\underline{+ 9a - 6} \\
3a^2 + 7a - 6
\end{array}
$$

8. **(A)** Substitute 3 for x in the given expression.

$$|x - 7| \text{ becomes } |3 - 7| \text{ or } |{-4}|$$

$|{-4}|$ stands for the absolute value of -4. The absolute value of a number is its value without regard to sign. Thus, $|{+4}|$ equals 4, and $|{-4}|$ also equals 4.

9. **(B)** To solve these equations for x, we must eliminate y. First multiply both sides of the first equation by 2.

$$2 \times (3x + y) = 2 \times 13$$
$$6x + 2y = 26$$

Adding the original second equation to the new form of the first equation will eliminate y.

$$
\begin{array}{r}
6x + 2y = 26 \\
\underline{x - 2y = 2} \\
7x = 28
\end{array}
$$

Divide both sides of the equation by 7 to undo the multiplication of x by 7.

$$\frac{7x}{7} = \frac{28}{7}$$
$$x = 4$$

10. **(D)** Convert all units of measure to inches.

In 1 yard, there are 36 inches, so in y yards there are y times as many, or $36y$. The total length of y yards and i inches, expressed in inches, is $36y + i$ inches.

There are 12 inches in 1 foot. To find the number of feet in $36y + i$ inches, divide $36y + i$ by 12.

$$(36y + i) \div 12 = \frac{36y + i}{12}$$

11. **(A)** The goal is to find an equation with F alone on one side and all other letters and numbers on the other side.

Begin by multiplying both sides of the formula by 9 to get rid of the fraction.

$$9 \times C = 9 \times \frac{5}{9}(F - 32)$$
$$9C = 5(F - 32)$$

Next remove the parentheses by multiplying each term inside them by 5.

$$9C = 5 \times F - 5 \times 32$$
$$9C = 5F - 160$$

To isolate the term containing F on one side of the equation, add 160 to both sides of the equation.

$$9C + 160 = 5F - 160 + 160$$
$$9C + 160 = 5F$$

To get an expression for F alone, divide both sides of the equation by 5.

$$\frac{9C + 160}{5} = \frac{5F}{5}$$

$$\frac{9}{5}C + 32 = F$$

The equation may be transposed to read

$$F = \frac{9}{5}C + 32.$$

12. **(B)** The path directly east forms a right angle with the path directly north. The distance from the starting point is measured on the third side (or hypotenuse) of the right triangle, which contains the paths to the east and to the north.

The Pythagorean Theorem states that in any right triangle, the square of the hypotenuse (c^2) equals the sum of the square of the other two sides, $a^2 + b^2$.

$$\text{Thus, } c^2 = a^2 + b^2$$
$$c^2 = 3^2 + 4^2$$

Perform the arithmetic operations.

$$c^2 = 9 + 16$$
$$c^2 = 25$$

To find c, take the square root of both sides of the equation. The square root of a number is another number which, when multiplied by itself, equals the original number. Thus, the square root of 25 is 5, and the square root of c^2 is c.

$$c = 5$$

13. **(A)** The line perpendicular to the base of the triangle makes a right angle with the base; a right angle contains 90°.

An equilateral triangle has 3 equal sides and 3 equal angles. Since the sum of all 3 angles of any triangle is 180°, each angle of an equilateral triangle is 180°/3 or 60°.

The 60° angle must be subtracted from the 90° angle to find the angle formed by the perpendicular and the other side of the triangle.

$$90° - 60° = 30°$$

14. **(B)** The inequality, $x - 5 \leq 5$, is a statement that x minus 6 is less than or equal to 5.

To solve this inequality, isolate x on one side of it by adding 6 to both sides.

$$x - 6 + 6 \leq 5 + 6$$
$$x \leq 11$$

The solution states that the inequality is true if x has any value less than or equal to 11. For example, suppose $x = 9$. Substitute 9 for x in the original inequality:

$$9 - 6 \leq 5 + 6$$
$$x \leq 11$$

The solution states that the inequality is true if x has any value less than or equal to 11. For example, suppose $x = 9$. Substitute 9 for x in the original inequality:

$$9 - 6 \leq 5$$
$$3 \leq 5, \text{ which is a true statement.}$$

15. **(D)** If the same fence fits around the rectangle and the square field, then their perimeters are equal. The perimeter of a rectangle is the sum of the lengths of its four sides.

$$P = 40 + 36 + 40 + 36$$
$$P = 152 \text{ feet}$$

The perimeter of a square is the sum of its four equal sides. Therefore, the length of one side is the perimeter divided by 4.

$$152 \div 4 = 38 \text{ feet}$$

16. **(B)** The volume of a rectangular box is equal to the length times the width times the height.
The volume of one individual-sized box = 3 × 2 × 4 = 24 cubic inches.
The volume of one family-sized box = 8 × 3 × 12 = 8 × 36 = 288 cubic inches.
Divide the volume of the larger box by the volume of the smaller box.
$$288 \div 24 = 12$$

17. **(A)** Rotation of a wheel as it rolls on the ground has the effect of "laying out" its circumference along the ground. One rotation will move the wheel along by a distance equal to the circumference. The circumference, C, of a circle is given by the formula C = 2 × Pi × R, where R is the radius, or by the formula C = Pi × D, where D is the diameter. If the first formula is used, R can be computed since the radius is one-half the diameter. However, it is easier in this case to use the second formula since we are given the diameter.
$$C = \frac{22}{7} \times 14 = \frac{22}{7} \times \frac{14}{1} = \frac{22}{1} \times \frac{2}{1} = 44 \text{ inches}$$

18. **(C)** The sine of an angle in a right triangle is the ratio of the length of the side opposite the angle to the length of the hypotenuse. If the unknown length is x, the ratio of x to the length of the hypotenuse must be the same as the ratio $\frac{3}{7}$.
$$\frac{x}{21} = \frac{3}{7}$$
To solve for x in this proportion, cross-multiply.
$$7 \times x = 3 \times 21$$
$$7x = 63$$
To undo the multiplication of 7 by x, divide both sides of the equation by 7.
$$\frac{7x}{7} = \frac{63}{7}$$

19. **(C)** $-x^4$ means $-(x)(x)(x)(x)$.
Substitute 0.1 for x.
$$-x^4 = -(0.1)(0.1)(0.1)(0.1)$$
To multiply (0.1)(0.1)(0.1)(0.1), remember that the number of decimal places in the product is the total of the number of decimal places in the numbers being multiplied together.
$$-x^4 = -0.0001$$

20. **(A)** Change 30% to a decimal and let x represent the total number of apartments, 30% of x is 108.

$$.30x = 108 \text{ or } .3x = 108$$

Clear the decimals by multiplying both sides of the equation by 10.

$$10 \times .3x = 10 \times 108$$
$$3x = 1080$$

Undo the multiplication of 3 by x by dividing both sides of the equation by 3.

$$\frac{3x}{3} = \frac{1080}{3}$$
$$x = 360$$

21. **(D)** Let x equal the score on the fourth test. The average is obtained by dividing the sum of the four marks by 4.

$$\frac{60 + 60 + 70 + x}{4} = 75$$

To remove the fraction, multiply both sides of the equation by 4.

$$4 \times \left(\frac{60 + 60 + 70 + x}{4} \right) = 4 \times 75$$
$$60 + 60 + 70 + x = 300$$
$$190 + x = 300$$

To isolate x on one side, subtract 190 from both sides of the equation.

$$190 - 190 + x = 300 - 190$$
$$x = 110$$

He would need 110% on the fourth test, which is impossible.

22. **(B)** First find the distance traveled.

Distance traveled is found by multiplying rate of speed by time.

3 hours $\times$ 40 miles per hour = 120 miles

2 hours $\times$ 50 miles per hour = 100 miles

The entire trip was 120 miles + 100 miles, or 220 miles.

The total time was 3 hours + 2 hours, or 5 hours.

The average rate of speed is obtained by dividing the total distance by the total time.

220 miles ÷ 5 hours = 44 miles per hour

23. **(C)** The radar is capable of covering a complete circle whose radius is 10 miles. First find the area of this circle, using the formula $A = \text{Pi} \times R^2$, where R is the radius.

$$A = 3.14 \times 10^2 = 3.14 \times 100 = 314 \text{ square miles}$$

There are 360° of rotation in the complete circle. If the radar is used to cover a portion of this, it covers 36/360 or 1/10 of the complete circle.

$$\frac{1}{10} \times 314 = 31.4 \text{ square miles}$$

24.   **(C)** To solve a quadratic equation like $x^2 + 2x = 15$, first move all terms to the same side of the equation so that they equal 0 on the other side.

$$x^2 + 2x - 15 = 0$$

Find the two binomial factors that would multiply to produce the polynomial on the left side. The factors of the first term, x^2, are x and x. Use them as the first term in each of the binomial factors.

$$(x \quad)(x \quad) = 0$$

Now find the two numbers that would multiply together to give 15. They could be 15 and 1 or 5 and 3. Remember that when multiplying the two binomials together, $+2x$ must result for the middle term. This suggests that $+5x$ and $-3x$ were added to give $+2x$. Therefore, $+5$ and -3 are the factors to choose for -15.

$$(x + 5)(x - 3) = 0$$

The equation is now in a form in which the product of two factors equals 0. This is possible if either one or both of the factors equals 0.

$$x + 5 = 0 \qquad\qquad x - 3 = 0$$
$$x = -5 \qquad\qquad x = 3$$

These results may be checked by substituting them in the original equation.

$$x^2 + 2x = 15 \qquad\qquad x^2 + 2x = 15$$
$$(-5)^2 + 2(-5) = 15 \qquad (3)^2 + 2(3) = 15$$
$$25 - 10 = 15 \qquad\qquad 9 + 6 = 15$$
$$15 = 15 \qquad\qquad 15 = 15$$

25. **(C)** First find the number of quarts of antifreeze in the original mixture.

$$.25 \times 12 \text{ or } \frac{1}{4} \times 12 = 3 \text{ quarts of antifreeze}$$

Let x equal the number of quarts of water to be added. The total mixture will now be $12 + x$ quarts. 20% of the new total mixture will be the 3 quarts of antifreeze still present in the mixture.

$$.20(12 + x) = 3 \text{ or } .2(12 + x) = 3$$

Remove the parentheses by multiplying each term inside by .2.

$$2.4 + .2x = 3$$

Clear decimals by multiplying each term in the equation by 10.

$$10 \times 2.4 + 10 \times .2x = 10 \times 3$$
$$24 + 2x = 30$$

Isolate the term containing x by subtracting 24 from both sides of the equation.

$$24 - 24 + 2x = 30 - 24$$
$$2x = 6$$

Undo the multiplication of 2 by x by dividing both sides of the equation by 2.

$$\frac{2x}{2} = \frac{6}{2}$$
$$x = 3$$

Electronics Information—Subtest 6

Answer Key

1. **A**	6. **A**	11. **C**	16. **B**
2. **B**	7. **D**	12. **B**	17. **A**
3. **C**	8. **B**	13. **C**	18. **B**
4. **B**	9. **D**	14. **D**	19. **B**
5. **B**	10. **B**	15. **C**	20. **B**

Answer Explanations

1. **(A)** The definition of current electricity is the flow of electrons. Static electricity is conceived of as standing still or collecting on surfaces.

2. **(B)** Conductors have free electrons that are easily moved along with the right kind of push or force. There are a number of ways to cause these electrons to progress along a conductor. Heat, light, magnetism, chemicals, pressure, and friction can cause the generation of an EMF useful in causing electrons to move along a conductor.

3. **(C)** Conventional current flow is said to be from + to –. This idea was originally used by Ben Franklin to explain the conduct of lightning. This conventional flow is still used today by electrical engineers and people working in physics.

4. **(B)** Electron flow can be demonstrated to flow from – to +. The action that takes place in a vacuum tube indicates that the + attracts the – electron to cause it to move from – to +.

5. **(B)** An insulator is a material that has tightly held electrons and very few, if any, free electrons. This means that it can be used to protect the conductor since the insulator will not allow free electrons from the conductor to knock loose any tightly held electrons of the insulator material.

6. **(A)** The unit of measure for resistance or opposition to current flow is the ohm. It was agreed on many years ago and has aided in making the electrical field progress so rapidly.

7. **(D)** The watt is the unit of power in electrical work. It is defined as the production of energy at the rate of one joule per second (per second is the basis for all electrical work).

8. **(B)** The Greek alphabet is used almost in its entirety in the electrical field to represent various quantities and effects. The Greek letter phi (ϕ) is familiar if you have been looking at three-phase power. It is used to represent the phases of electrical power.

9. **(D)** Total resistance of a parallel circuit can be found two ways: by using the reciprocal formula or by using the product of two resistors divided by the sum of the two resistors divided by the sum of the two and then using it again to obtain the final answer in the case of three in parallel. In this case the two 10-ohm resistors will reduce to an equivalent of 5 ohms. This leaves, then, two 5-ohm resistors in parallel, which reduce to 2.5 or half of the value of one.

10. **(B)** The symbols shown are for the resistor, the fuse, and the capacitor, as well as for a lamp or light bulb. The one for the fuse is shown as in B.

11. **(C)** The symbol for inductance is L. The symbol for an inductor is a loop as in a coil of wire.

12. **(B)** The formula for finding inductive reactance has to utilize the L in inductance and the fixed constant 2π, as well as taking into consideration the frequency of the power applied to the circuit.

13. **(C)** A microfarad is 1 million picofarads. Therefore, if you wish to convert microfarads to picofarads, you have to multiply by 1 million. That means the answer is C because 100 times 1 million is 100 million.

14. **(D)** Impedance is the total opposition to current flow in a circuit. It has its own symbol, Z.

15. **(C)** A cathode ray tube (CRT) is familiar to anyone who watches television or a computer screen.

16. **(B)** A junction diode has a larger surface area than a point-contact diode, therefore it can be used to handle larger currents at power-line frequencies.

17. **(A)** The SCR is a special type of rectifier. It is used in control circuits. The name SCR was a descriptive one given it by General Electric Company engineers and it caught on in the literature. Its correct name is not silicon-controlled rectifier but thyrister.

18. **(B)** On an FM receiver the AFC is automatic frequency control. It keeps the receiver from drifting from the station it is tuned to. This is done by having part of the signal fed back to the local oscillator to keep it operating on the correct frequency and not drifting.

19. **(B)** A receiver made to receive multiplex signals is usually designated as a stereo receiver, which means it can receive the two signals needed to produce the stereo effect. These signals are multiplexed, or one signal is impressed on another to get it from the transmitter to the receiver.

20. **(B)** The FM band covers 88 to 108. The AM band covers 550 to 1600 kilohertz.

Automotive & Shop Information—Subtest 7

Answer Key

1. **A**	6. **A**	11. **B**	16. **D**	21. **A**
2. **C**	7. **B**	12. **B**	17. **A**	22. **B**
3. **D**	8. **C**	13. **A**	18. **C**	23. **D**
4. **D**	9. **B**	14. **B**	19. **C**	24. **B**
5. **C**	10. **D**	15. **D**	20. **B**	25. **A**

Answer Explanations

1. **(A)** The universal joint allows the drive shaft to move up and down as the road surface changes. At least one, and in most instances two, are needed for rear-wheel drive cars and trucks.

2. **(C)** Much attention has been given to the pollutants emitted from today's cars. Nitrous oxides (NO_x) are of particular concern and the air pump and the catalytic converter have been added to reduce these emissions. Hydrocarbons, carbon monoxide, and the oxides of nitrogen are of concern since they can contaminate the air and kill trees, plants, and small animals, as well as damage the lungs of humans.

3. **(D)** The catalytic converter eliminates some pollutants and reduces other pollutants. It reaches high temperatures and needs to be shielded from the body of the car by a heat deflector. An air pump is used on most late model cars to add to the combustion that takes place inside the converter and helps to reduce the amount of NO_x emitted from the exhaust pipe.

4. **(D)** The differential is located in the rear of the car when it is a rear-wheel drive. It is located in front of the car on a front-wheel drive vehicle. It consists of two small bevel gears on the ends of the axle shafts

that are mounted in the differential frame. These bevel gears mesh with others to allow one wheel to turn faster than the other whenever the car makes a turn around a curve.

5. **(C)** The PCV valve is used to recirculate the fumes that would normally be exhausted to the atmosphere from the crankcase. By recirculating these fumes it is possible to cut down on the hydrocarbon contents of auto exhaust. This valve provides positive crankcase ventilation from the valve cover through the carburetor for recirculation.

6. **(A)** One of the ways to reduce the NO_x produced by the combustion of the internal combustion engine is to dilute the air/fuel mixture as it enters the combustion chamber.

7. **(B)** The number of teeth in a gear determines its speed when meshed with a second gear with similar teeth. The number of teeth in one gear is compared to the number of teeth in the one it meshes with. The number of teeth in the first gear as compared to the second is the gear ratio. If, for instance, one gear has 16 teeth and the one it meshes with has only 8, the gear ratio is 2:1 or 2 to 1. The gear with the greater number of teeth always turns slower and produces greater torque than the gear with the smaller number of teeth.

8. **(C)** The clutch is used to disconnect the engine from the wheels while the car is in neutral or when gears are being shifted.

9. **(B)** The first gear is used because of its ability to produce the starting torque needed to get the car moving from a standstill. The internal combustion engine is known as a fast engine. It must be revving up pretty fast to develop the torque needed to start the car rolling.

10. **(D)** The torque converter is located in the automatic transmission. It produces the torque needed to get the car started and to change speeds. Most torque converter transmissions also provide an intermediate and low gear range that can aid in braking the car when coming down steep hills and in hard pulling.

11. **(B)** Disc brakes use two pads to grasp the rotor that is attached to the wheel. The pads press against the rotor (disc) from both sides to make a faster and surer stop with little fading on hot days and with heavy braking.

12. **(B)** The transmission on front-wheel cars is located in the front engine compartment. It must be small enough to fit into the space allowed for the engine and the accessories. It took a few years to design a transmission to fit in front with the engine and leave space for the accessories needed to cause the engine to function properly.

13. **(A)** L_O or L on older automatic transmissions were the same as 1st gear in manual transmissions. In most recent cars the L has been replaced by a 1 to indicate 1st gear and 2 to represent 2nd gear instead of D_1, S, or L_2.

14. **(B)** Park (P) position on the automatic transmission gear selector indicator represents the position that locks up the transmission and prevents the wheels from rolling. The car is in neutral when placed in park and can be started only when in Park or Neutral.

15. **(D)** The internal combustion engine is best described as a high speed engine. We cannot run an internal combustion engine at slow speed and get enough torque to get the vehicle moving. A higher speed engine is needed to produce the torque. That is where the transmission plays an important role in allowing the engine to speed up and still not have a very fast moving drive shaft connected to the wheels. The transmission's gear ratio plays a role in producing the torque needed to get the car moving from a resting position.

16. **(D)** Buttering a concrete block means to put the mortar on it. This is usually done by taking the mortar from the hawk and applying it to the block's edges.

17. **(A)** Hardwood comes from deciduous trees such as the oak, maple, elm, and ash.

18. **(C)** Softwood comes from conifers, or trees with needles, usually called evergreens. Such trees are the pines, firs, and spruces.

19. **(C)** Sometimes logs are not cut into lumber immediately and must be kept from checking and splitting. This can be done by keeping them wet. At the sawmill the logs are kept floating in a pond until they are about ready to be used. This way they do not dry out too quickly and check or split.

20. **(B)** An auto repair collision worker uses a bumper hammer to take out some of the dents in a car's sheet metal. This hammer is ideally suited for the job.

21. **(A)** A groover is designed to cause the seams to become flattened and make a watertight seal.

22. **(B)** A squaring shear is used to cut sheet metal along a straight line. A bar folder is used to bend sheet metal, and a punch press makes holes in sheet metal. The slip roll is used to form the metal into round, cylindrical shapes.

23. **(D)** The tip of a soldering iron is tinned or coated with solder to make it more efficient in transferring the heat at the tip to the object being soldered. It also prevents copper oxide buildup on the tip.

24. **(B)** Punches are used in sheet metal for the same reason punches are used elsewhere—to punch holes.

25. **(A)** A squaring shear is used to cut sheet metal—usually keeping it square to one edge if properly aligned with the side of the unit. To shear means to cut.

Mechanical Comprehension—Subtest 8

Answer Key

1. **D**	6. **D**	11. **C**	16. **C**	21. **C**
2. **C**	7. **D**	12. **D**	17. **A**	22. **B**
3. **B**	8. **D**	13. **D**	18. **C**	23. **D**
4. **A**	9. **C**	14. **A**	19. **A**	24. **A**
5. **B**	10. **A**	15. **B**	20. **B**	25. **A**

Answer Explanations

1. **(D)** Force is something that can change the velocity of an object by making it start or stop, speed up, or slow down. This means that all the answers given are correct.

2. **(C)** Friction is used to stop a car. The brakes rub against the wheel drum or the disc to cause the car to stop. This rubbing is creating friction.

3. **(B)** Metric measurements are referred to as SI or international standards. The metric unit newton corresponds to our system unit of the pound.

4. **(A)** Gravity is the force that pulls things down whenever they are dropped. It is said that Isaac Newton discovered gravity while sitting under an apple tree and the obvious happened. Gravity is created by the mass of the earth. The pull of gravity is much less on the moon than on earth.

5. **(B)** When a rope or string or anything is stretched, it is in a state of tension until the tension is released.

6. **(D)** Friction causes drag, or the holding back of an object being pulled along a surface or running through the air. When there is drag or a retarding motion on an object in a liquid, it is referred to as viscous drag.

7. **(D)** Weight is not a fixed property of an object; it varies with location. Your weight is slightly less at the North Pole than it is at the equator. Your weight is much less on the moon than on earth. Everything weighs less where the acceleration due to gravity is smaller. Weight is directly proportional to the acceleration due to gravity.

8. **(D)** Buoyancy is the force that makes ships float and helium-filled balloons rise. This means that the force that acts in an upward direction on anything submerged in a liquid or a gas is called buoyancy.

9. **(C)** It is impossible to exert a force unless there is something there to push back. Forces exist in pairs. For every action, then, there is a reaction.

10. **(A)** Inasmuch as it is impossible to have a force acting unless in pairs, it means that these forces must be equal in magnitude and opposite in direction.

11. **(C)** An object in equilibrium may or may not be at rest. If two or more forces act, their effects may eliminate each other. When this condition of equilibrium is reached, there is no net force and the velocity does not change. Equilibrium is reached when the object is at rest or moving at a constant speed and in a straight line.

12. **(D)** The angle of the rope determines if the box is being pulled along the floor or being lifted from the floor. That means it can be both lifted and pulled along at any angle that is more than 0 degrees and less than 90 degrees.

13. **(D)** Simple machines are devices that make work easier. Some examples of simple machines are levers, hydraulic jacks, loading ramps, vises, and machines that spin—winches and gears. Door knobs, light switches, and manually operated pencil sharpeners are also simple machines.

14. **(A)** The effort times the effort distance is called the work *input*. The load times the load distance is called the work *output*.

15. **(B)** The load distance times the load produces the work output. This can be used as part of an equation to figure efficiency, or how efficiently a job is done.

16. **(C)** Efficiency is affected by friction. It is a ratio of how much effort went into a job compared to what was produced or outputted. Therefore, work input is more than the work output. Friction accounts for the loss in efficiency.

17. **(A)** In order to find out how well work was performed and how much effort was expended in getting the job done, the term *efficiency* is used to describe the ratio of work input to work output.

18. **(C)** By using a machine it is possible to multiply the amount of effort expended to get a job done. Mechanical advantage is the amount of magnification, or the ratio of load to effort.

19. **(A)** A ramp is a device commonly used to aid in lifting. The ramp is an inclined plane. The work output of an inclined plane is the work that

would have to be done to lift the load directly. The work input is the actual force exerted in pushing the load up the ramp times the length of the ramp. An ideal mechanical advantage of an inclined plane is equal to its length divided by its height.

20. **(B)** A screw is a simple device. It has been used for centuries as a means of lifting water out of wells and over the banks of irrigation canals. A screw consists of a single continuous spiral wrapped around a cylinder. The threads are cut into a rod in a spiral and make it possible to use the holding power of screw in fastening objects together.

21. **(C)** The distance between ridges on a screw is known as the pitch of its thread. Every time the screw makes one complete turn, the screw advances a distance equal to the pitch.

22. **(B)** The mechanical advantage of a screw (used in a vise) is equal to the length of the handle of the vise times 2π divided by the pitch of the thread. The vise is a high-friction device. It has to be, for it is the friction that keeps it from opening when you tighten it. A vise is a self-locking machine because its efficiency is considerably less than 50%.

23. **(D)** The principle of a winch is not much different from that of a lever. Since the crank and the shaft turn together, the torque exerted by the effort (the force on the handle) must be equal to the torque exerted by the load (the tension in the rope). The mechanical advantage then is the ratio of the radius of the crank to the radius of the shaft.

24. **(A)** In mechanical devices, gears are used to change torque. The ideal mechanical advantage of a gear is the ratio of the number of teeth in the load gear to the number of teeth in the effort gear.

25. **(A)** The English unit of power is foot-pound per second. It takes 550 foot-pounds to make 1 horsepower. The SI unit is the joule per second or watt. A horsepower is 746 watts. The rate at which work is done is called power. Power is work done per unit of time.

Assembling Objects—Subtest 9

Answer Key

1. **A**	5. **C**	9. **B**	13. **D**
2. **B**	6. **A**	10. **B**	14. **B**
3. **C**	7. **B**	11. **A**	15. **A**
4. **C**	8. **C**	12. **A**	16. **D**